THIS PRESENT KINGDOM

The Disruptive Message of the Sermon on the Mount

DONNA GAINES

MARGE LENOW

JEAN STOCKDALE

DAYNA STREET

ANGIE WILSON

This Present Kingdom: The Disruptive Message of the Sermon on the Mount

©2020 Bellevue Baptist Church

Cover and book design: Amanda Weaver
Editing: Dayna Street, Donita Barnwell, Melissa Bobo Hardee, Lauren Gooden, Paige Warren, Vera Sidhom

Unless otherwise indicated, Scripture taken from the NEW AMERICAN STANDARD BIBLE.® Copyright © 1960, 1962, 1963, 1968, 1971, 1973, 1975, 1977, 1995 by Lockman Foundation. Used by permission. www.Lockman.org

CONTENTS

—·———·—How to Use This Study—·———·—

This Present Kingdom: The Disruptive Message of the Sermon on the Mount is a ten-week, life transforming encounter with the most famous sermon ever preached. To the world around us, and at times to our own flesh, walking the way of the Sermon on the Mount is counter-cultural and counter-intuitive. Learning the ways of His Kingdom will require intentionality. But as you master the basics, as you begin to think and act like a citizen of the Kingdom, you will find it is worth every effort.

This study is designed to provide an opportunity for personal study throughout the week, leading up to a small group discussion and large group teaching time once a week. Each weekly session is divided into five daily homework assignments. Four days center on Bible study and personal application. On the fifth day, you will complete a Kingdom Exercise directed at practicing the spiritual disciplines. These exercises will equip you to live fully and freely in the Kingdom of God.

In your small group time each week, you will be able to connect with other women and build life-giving, sharpening relationships. As you meet together, be ready to share what God has shown you through His Word using the weekly studies as a guide. In the large group teaching time, you will be challenged by relevant, biblical instruction that will encourage you to stand firm on the truth of God's Word.

As you read and obey the message of the Sermon on the Mount, be ready for change. Expect transformation. Anticipate a different life, a life that is being increasingly set apart from the world. The King is marking you for His own and inviting you to step into a new way of living, a Jesus-shaped life. Life in *This Present Kingdom*.

THE SERMON ON THE MOUNT
— MATTHEW 5-7 —

5 When Jesus saw the crowds, He went up on the mountain; and after He sat down, His disciples came to Him. [2] He opened His mouth and *began* to teach them, saying,

[3] "Blessed are the poor in spirit, for theirs is the kingdom of Heaven.

[4] "Blessed are those who mourn, for they shall be comforted.

[5] "Blessed are the gentle, for they shall inherit the earth.

[6] "Blessed are those who hunger and thirst for righteousness, for they shall be satisfied.

[7] "Blessed are the merciful, for they shall receive mercy.

[8] "Blessed are the pure in heart, for they shall see God.

[9] "Blessed are the peacemakers, for they shall be called sons of God.

[10] "Blessed are those who have been persecuted for the sake of righteousness, for theirs is the kingdom of Heaven.

[11] "Blessed are you when *people* insult you and persecute you, and falsely say all kinds of evil against you because of Me. [12] Rejoice and be glad, for your reward in Heaven is great; for in the same way they persecuted the prophets who were before you.

[13] "You are the salt of the earth; but if the salt has become tasteless, how can it be made salty *again*? It is no longer good for anything, except to be thrown out and trampled under foot by men.

[14] "You are the light of the world. A city set on a hill cannot be hidden; [15] nor does *anyone* light a lamp and put it under a basket, but on the lampstand, and it gives light to all who are in the house. [16] Let your light shine before men in such a way that they may see your good works, and glorify your Father who is in Heaven.

[17] "Do not think that I came to abolish the Law or the Prophets; I did not come to abolish but to fulfill. [18] For truly I say to you, until Heaven and earth pass away, not the smallest letter or stroke shall pass from the Law until all is accomplished. [19] Whoever then annuls one of the least of these commandments, and teaches others *to do* the same, shall be called least in the Kingdom of Heaven; but whoever keeps and teaches *them*, he shall be called great in the Kingdom of Heaven.

20 "For I say to you that unless your righteousness surpasses *that* of the scribes and Pharisees, you will not enter the Kingdom of Heaven.

21 "You have heard that the ancients were told, 'YOU SHALL NOT COMMIT MURDER' and 'Whoever commits murder shall be liable to the court.' 22 But I say to you that everyone who is angry with his brother shall be guilty before the court; and whoever says to his brother, 'You good-for-nothing,' shall be guilty before the supreme court; and whoever says, 'You fool,' shall be guilty *enough to go* into the fiery hell. 23 Therefore if you are presenting your offering at the altar, and there remember that your brother has something against you, 24 leave your offering there before the altar and go; first be reconciled to your brother, and then come and present your offering. 25 Make friends quickly with your opponent at law while you are with him on the way, so that your opponent may not hand you over to the judge, and the judge to the officer, and you be thrown into prison. 26 Truly I say to you, you will not come out of there until you have paid up the last cent.

27 "You have heard that it was said, 'YOU SHALL NOT COMMIT ADULTERY'; 28 but I say to you that everyone who looks at a woman with lust for her has already committed adultery with her in his heart. 29 If your right eye makes you stumble, tear it out and throw it from you; for it is better for you to lose one of the parts of your body, than for your whole body to be thrown into hell. 30 If your right hand makes you stumble, cut it off and throw it from you; for it is better for you to lose one of the parts of your body, than for your whole body to go into hell.

31 "It was said, 'WHOEVER SENDS HIS WIFE AWAY, LET HIM GIVE HER A CERTIFICATE OF DIVORCE'; 32 but I say to you that everyone who divorces his wife, except for *the* reason of unchastity, makes her commit adultery; and whoever marries a divorced woman commits adultery.

33 "Again, you have heard that the ancients were told, 'YOU SHALL NOT MAKE FALSE VOWS, BUT SHALL FULFILL YOUR VOWS TO THE LORD.' 34 But I say to you, make no oath at all, either by Heaven, for it is the throne of God, 35 or by the earth, for it is the footstool of His feet, or by Jerusalem, for it is THE CITY OF THE GREAT KING. 36 Nor shall you make an oath by your head, for you cannot make one hair white or black. 37 But let your statement be, 'Yes, yes' *or* 'No, no'; anything beyond these is of evil.

38 "You have heard that it was said, 'AN EYE FOR AN EYE, AND A TOOTH FOR A TOOTH.' 39 But I say to you, do not resist an evil person; but whoever slaps you on your right cheek, turn the other to him also. 40 If anyone wants to sue you and take your shirt, let him have your coat also. 41 Whoever forces you to go one mile, go with him two. 42 Give to him who asks of you, and do not turn away from him who wants to borrow from you.

43 "You have heard that it was said, 'YOU SHALL LOVE YOUR NEIGHBOR and hate your enemy.' 44 But I say to you, love your enemies and pray for those who persecute you, 45 so that you may be sons

of your Father who is in Heaven; for He causes His sun to rise on *the* evil and *the* good, and sends rain on *the* righteous and *the* unrighteous. [46] For if you love those who love you, what reward do you have? Do not even the tax collectors do the same? [47] If you greet only your brothers, what more are you doing *than others*? Do not even the Gentiles do the same? [48] Therefore you are to be perfect, as your heavenly Father is perfect.

6 "Beware of practicing your righteousness before men to be noticed by them; otherwise you have no reward with your Father who is in Heaven.

[2] "So when you give to the poor, do not sound a trumpet before you, as the hypocrites do in the synagogues and in the streets, so that they may be honored by men. Truly I say to you, they have their reward in full. [3] But when you give to the poor, do not let your left hand know what your right hand is doing, [4] so that your giving will be in secret; and your Father who sees *what is done* in secret will reward you.

[5] "When you pray, you are not to be like the hypocrites; for they love to stand and pray in the synagogues and on the street corners so that they may be seen by men. Truly I say to you, they have their reward in full. [6] But you, when you pray, go into your inner room, close your door and pray to your Father who is in secret, and your Father who sees *what is done* in secret will reward you.

[7] "And when you are praying, do not use meaningless repetition as the Gentiles do, for they suppose that they will be heard for their many words. [8] So do not be like them; for your Father knows what you need before you ask Him.

[9] "Pray, then, in this way:

'Our Father who is in Heaven,
Hallowed be Your name.

[10] 'Your Kingdom come.
Your will be done, On earth as it is in Heaven.
[11] 'Give us this day our daily bread.
[12] 'And forgive us our debts, as we also have forgiven our debtors.
[13] 'And do not lead us into temptation, but deliver us from evil. [For Yours is the Kingdom and the power and the glory forever. Amen.']

[14] "For if you forgive others for their transgressions, your heavenly Father will also forgive you. [15] "But if you do not forgive others, then your Father will not forgive your transgressions.

[16] "Whenever you fast, do not put on a gloomy face as the hypocrites *do*, for they neglect their appearance so that they will be noticed by men when they are fasting. Truly I say to you, they have their reward in full. [17] But you, when you fast, anoint your head and wash your face [18] so that your

fasting will not be noticed by men, but by your Father who is in secret; and your Father who sees *what is done* in secret will reward you.

¹⁹ "Do not store up for yourselves treasures on earth, where moth and rust destroy, and where thieves break in and steal. ²⁰ But store up for yourselves treasures in Heaven, where neither moth nor rust destroys, and where thieves do not break in or steal; ²¹ for where your treasure is, there your heart will be also.

²² "The eye is the lamp of the body; so then if your eye is clear, your whole body will be full of light. ²³ But if your eye is bad, your whole body will be full of darkness. If then the light that is in you is darkness, how great is the darkness!

²⁴ "No one can serve two masters; for either he will hate the one and love the other, or he will be devoted to one and despise the other. You cannot serve God and wealth.

²⁵ "For this reason I say to you, do not be worried about your life, *as to* what you will eat or what you will drink; nor for your body, *as to* what you will put on. Is not life more than food, and the body more than clothing? ²⁶ Look at the birds of the air, that they do not sow, nor reap nor gather into barns, and *yet* your heavenly Father feeds them. Are you not worth much more than they? ²⁷ And who of you by being worried can add a *single* hour to his life? ²⁸ And why are you worried about clothing? Observe how the lilies of the field grow; they do not toil nor do they spin, ²⁹ yet I say to you that not even Solomon in all his glory clothed himself like one of these. ³⁰ But if God so clothes the grass of the field, which is *alive* today and tomorrow is thrown into the furnace, *will He* not much more *clothe* you? You of little faith! ³¹ Do not worry then, saying, 'What will we eat?' or 'What will we drink?' or 'What will we wear for clothing?' ³² For the Gentiles eagerly seek all these things; for your heavenly Father knows that you need all these things. ³³ But seek first His Kingdom and His righteousness, and all these things will be added to you.

³⁴ "So do not worry about tomorrow; for tomorrow will care for itself. Each day has enough trouble of its own.

7 "Do not judge so that you will not be judged. ² For in the way you judge, you will be judged; and by your standard of measure, it will be measured to you. ³ Why do you look at the speck that is in your brother's eye, but do not notice the log that is in your own eye? ⁴ Or how can you say to your brother, 'Let me take the speck out of your eye,' and behold, the log is in your own eye? ⁵ You hypocrite first take the log out of your own eye, and then you will see clearly to take the speck out of your brother's eye.

⁶ "Do not give what is holy to dogs, and do not throw your pearls before swine, or they will trample them under their feet, and turn and tear you to pieces.

⁷ "Ask, and it will be given to you; seek, and you will find; knock, and it will be opened to you. ⁸ For everyone who asks receives, and he who seeks finds, and to him who knocks it will be opened. ⁹ Or what man is there among you who, when his son asks for a loaf, will give him a stone? ¹⁰ Or if he asks for a fish, he will not give him a snake, will he? ¹¹ If you then, being evil, know how to give good gifts to your children, how much more will your Father who is in Heaven give what is good to those who ask Him!

¹² "In everything, therefore, treat people the same way you want them to treat you, for this is the Law and the Prophets.

¹³ "Enter through the narrow gate; for the gate is wide and the way is broad that leads to destruction, and there are many who enter through it. ¹⁴ For the gate is small and the way is narrow that leads to life, and there are few who find it.

¹⁵ "Beware of the false prophets, who come to you in sheep's clothing, but inwardly are ravenous wolves. ¹⁶ You will know them by their fruits. Grapes are not gathered from thorn *bushes* nor figs from thistles, are they? ¹⁷ So every good tree bears good fruit, but the bad tree bears bad fruit. ¹⁸ A good tree cannot produce bad fruit, nor can a bad tree produce good fruit. ¹⁹ Every tree that does not bear good fruit is cut down and thrown into the fire. ²⁰ So then, you will know them by their fruits.

²¹ "Not everyone who says to Me, 'Lord, Lord,' will enter the Kingdom of Heaven, but he who does the will of My Father who is in Heaven *will enter*. ²² Many will say to Me on that day, 'Lord, Lord, did we not prophesy in Your name, and in Your name cast out demons, and in Your name perform many miracles?' ²³ And then I will declare to them, 'I never knew you; DEPART FROM ME, YOU WHO PRACTICE LAWLESSNESS.'

²⁴ "Therefore everyone who hears these words of Mine and acts on them, may be compared to a wise man who built his house on the rock. ²⁵ And the rain fell, and the floods came, and the winds blew and slammed against that house; and *yet* it did not fall, for it had been founded on the rock. ²⁶ Everyone who hears these words of Mine and does not act on them, will be like a foolish man who built his house on the sand. ²⁷ The rain fell, and the floods came, and the winds blew and slammed against that house; and it fell—and great was its fall."

²⁸ When Jesus had finished these words, the crowds were amazed at His teaching; ²⁹ for He was teaching them as *one* having authority, and not as their scribes.

INTRODUCTION

*Jesus went throughout Galilee, teaching in their synagogues and
proclaiming the good news of the Kingdom…*
MATTHEW 4:23, NIV

*The whole point of Jesus' work was to bring Heaven to earth and join them together forever,
to bring God's future into the present and make it stick there.* [1]
~N. T. WRIGHT

God's Kingdom is the story that is told throughout Scripture, from the Garden of Eden in Genesis to the New Jerusalem in Revelation. And right in the middle of the story, God unveils His Kingdom in a new way, through His Son.

When Jesus steps onto the public stage around the age of thirty, His primary message is that God's eternal purpose, His rule and reign have arrived. And it is available for everyone. In Matthew's Gospel, the phrase Jesus uses to announce this good news is "Repent, for the Kingdom of Heaven is at hand" (Matthew 4:17, 10:7). The Greek word for "repent", *metanoia*, literally means "change your mind." [2] James Smith gives us an important insight:

> Most people think repent means "shape up"; thus they think Jesus' proclamation is a threat. But it is an invitation. The Kingdom of God (or Kingdom of Heaven) is an interactive life with God. Jesus is essentially saying, "Change the way you have been thinking—a life of intimacy and interaction with God is now in your midst." [3]

With Jesus, a door opens that can never again be shut. Access to the Kingdom of God has come.

In the Old Testament, the prophet Isaiah spoke of God's Kingdom as the time when the people of Israel would be rescued from their pagan oppressors, and God would usher in a new reign. A reign of justice and peace. At last, the world would be turned right-side up. It was a time the Jewish people had anticipated for centuries.

Jesus' proclamation about the Kingdom of God is not the first time His followers have heard someone use this language about a new Kingdom. Twice during His childhood, Jewish revolutionaries had led efforts to resist the taxation imposed by the Roman government. The rally cry of these insurgents was, "'There should be no king but God'…in other words, it's time for

God's Kingdom rather than these corrupt human ones." [4] Both rebellions were met with a brutal and crushing response from Rome.

Prior to Jesus' public ministry, His cousin, John the Baptist, announced that God's Kingdom was at hand (Matthew 3:2) and had been telling people to get ready for the One who was coming after him. For generations, the Jews had been awaiting the prophetic coming of their Messiah and King. [5] Because they have become so accustomed to the leadership of earthly kings, they have envisioned a king who will come as a revolutionary political ruler, a savior who will rescue them from their oppression. And with the coming of Jesus to the world, God's rescue plan has finally been put into effect, but it is not at all what the Jews expect.

As Jesus walks throughout Galilee healing and delivering people, God's Kingdom is visibly breaking into history. The news that this Man has the ability to heal has spread and people flock to Him to be healed and to witness the miracles He performs. In the midst of His escalating ministry, Jesus heads out into the wilderness beyond the Jordan River with the multitudes following Him. He finds a place on a mountainside and sits down in the customary posture of a rabbi. Surrounded by His disciples, He begins to teach them.

> **OBEDIENCE TO HIS MESSAGE WILL REQUIRE A DEMOLITION OF THE OLD STRUCTURE AND A CREATION OF THE NEW. IT WILL BE DISRUPTIVE.**

The message He delivers, the Sermon on the Mount, is radical. It is unlike anything those listening have heard before. Instead of inciting military rebellion, Jesus says it is time to show the world what God is really like, "not by fighting and violence but by loving one's enemies, turning the other cheek, going the second mile." [6] His message describes a radical reconstruction of the heart. And it will not be a casual shift; it will not happen by accident. Obedience to His message will require a demolition of the old structure and a creation of the new. It will be disruptive.

THE SERMON ON THE MOUNT

Along the western shore of the Sea of Galilee lies the town of Capernaum. This fishing village is located on an inlet known as the Cove of the Sower because it was the setting for the parable Jesus told about the farmer planting seeds in different types of soil. It is also what most believe is the setting for the Sermon on the Mount. At the top of the hill above the cove is the Church of the Beatitudes which marks the traditional site of the sermon.

Picture yourself in that setting. Imagine you are sitting there on the hillside two thousand years ago. Think about what it would have been like to be a part of the multitude that day listening to the most extraordinary Rabbi.

Biblical scholars have discovered that the area forms a natural amphitheater with excellent acoustical properties. In fact, the acoustics are so good that one researcher estimates that eight to ten thousand could have sat on the hillside and heard Jesus speak in His normal voice. [7]

The Sermon. As He speaks, the crowd is "amazed at His teaching" (Matthew 7:28). His teaching is different from other rabbis they have heard before. He is "teaching them as *one* having authority, and not as their scribes" (v. 29). He speaks with such great authority it is as if He knows the mind of God.

In just over 2200 words, Jesus delivers His comprehensive theology, making the Sermon on the Mount what many classify as the most profound section of the New Testament.

Kent Hughes expounds,

> Every phrase can bear exhaustive exposition and yet never be completely plumbed. Along with this, it is the most penetrating section of God's Word. Because the theme is entering the Kingdom of Heaven, it shows us exactly where we stand in relation to the Kingdom and eternal life (see 5:3; 7:21). As we expose ourselves to the X-rays of Christ's words, we see whether we truly are believers; and if believers, the degree of the authenticity of our lives. No other section of Scripture makes us face ourselves like the Sermon on the Mount. It is violent, but its violence can be our ongoing liberation! It is the antidote to the pretense and sham that plagues Christianity. [8]

As Jesus preaches His sermon, the shadow of the cross is looming. Those listening do not know what lies ahead, but Jesus does.

The Writer. To those living in Jesus' day, it would have been astonishing that Matthew was chosen to follow Christ. And even more so that he would leave his profession and say "yes" to Jesus' call. You see, Matthew was a tax collector, an occupation that was synonymous with being a licensed thief. Tax collectors, or publicans, as they were often called, were despised by their fellow Jews. They were considered to be turncoats because they collected money for the Roman government, a taxation system which allowed them to pad their pockets with any extra amount they could exhort from their fellow countrymen above the tax quota due in Rome.

But one day, something happens to Matthew. As he is sitting in his tax collector booth, Jesus approaches him and speaks the words, "Follow Me." His obedience is immediate. Leaving behind a life of prosperity, he joins the band of men known as Jesus' disciples.

We have the written text of the Sermon on the Mount because Matthew records the words for us. He writes them down because he is present on the mountainside that day to hear them. He is there because Jesus had called Him with the words, "Follow Me", and he had obeyed. And he records the sermon for others who will read it because they also have decided to follow the Preacher on the Mount.

The Audience. The Sermon on the Mount is a message primarily directed at the disciples of Jesus. As Matthew introduces the sermon in his account, it seems as if Jesus is trying to step away from the crowds to teach His disciples:

> When Jesus saw the crowds, He went up on the mountain; and after He sat down, His disciples came to Him. He opened His mouth and *began* to teach them… (Matthew 5:1-2).

But by the end of the sermon, it is not just the disciples who are listening to Jesus teach, crowds of people have also gathered to hear Him (Matthew 7:28-29). The two groups, the disciples and the crowd, are diametrically different.

The Crowd. The crowd that gathers on the hillside has a different, more self-serving agenda. They are there to be entertained. The crowd is more interested in what Jesus does than what He says. They have come from all over to see this Man who can heal the sick of their diseases and restore sight to the blind. These spectacle seekers are merely curious rather than being awestruck at the reality of the Kingdom Jesus is announcing.

The Disciples. Jesus does not say that the crowd is the salt of the earth and the light of the world. He reserves that distinction for His disciples who acknowledge that He is the Son of God and have already answered the call to follow Him, regardless of the cost. When they assemble on the mountainside, they come to sit at His feet, to learn from Him, and to worship Him. Sitting there, they are hanging on His every word. Jesus' message is meant for His disciples—the ones who were sitting with Him on the mountain over 2000 years ago and the ones who follow Him today.

THE MESSAGE WE HAVE MISSED

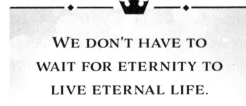

WE DON'T HAVE TO WAIT FOR ETERNITY TO LIVE ETERNAL LIFE.

It has been right in front of us. But we have missed it. For too long we have believed that the gospel message is solely about Jesus coming and dying to save us from our sins. Now, before you label me a heretic, that is a part of the good news. Part, but not all. James Smith challenges, "What is the point of this religion? To get us into Heaven? No, to get Heaven into us." [9] Think about that. What would our lives look like if we were living "on earth as it is in Heaven"? What would our words sound like? What would our actions look like?

Through Jesus, we are invited to enter a new way of living. And we don't have to wait until we get to Heaven to do so. To state it another way, we don't have to wait for eternity to live eternal life.

Dallas Willard explains,

> Jesus came among us to show and teach the life for which we were made. He came very gently, opened access to the governance of God with Him, and set afoot a conspiracy of freedom in truth among human beings. Having overcome death He remains among us. By relying on His Word and presence we are enabled to reintegrate the little realm that makes up our life into the infinite rule of God. And that is the eternal kind of life. Caught up in His active rule, our deeds become an element in God's eternal history. [10]

Eternal life is the Kingdom life. It is living a Jesus-shaped life, a life where every word and deed is under His influence. It is the life Jesus teaches in the Sermon on the Mount. It is the life He beckons us to step into when we answer His call to follow Him. Through Jesus, we are invited to enter into a new way of living, and to discover by following Him "that this new world is indeed a place of justice, spirituality, relationship, and beauty, and that we are not only to enjoy it as such, but to work at bringing it to birth on earth as in Heaven." [11] This is life in the Kingdom of God.

THE KINGDOM OF GOD

The terms, "Kingdom of God" and "Kingdom of Heaven", are used interchangeably in the Gospels. Matthew uses the term, "Kingdom of Heaven" because he directs his Gospel principally toward the Jews who avoid speaking the name of God out of reverence. The rest of the writers of the Gospels use the term "Kingdom of God" to communicate with their Greek audiences who would not have understood that "Heaven" meant "God". Throughout the Gospels, Jesus speaks of the Kingdom of God over a hundred times. It is His central message.

Most often when we think about the Kingdom of God, we think about it with the future in mind. We picture in our minds the time when Christ will return for the second time and rule over the nations. And yes, there is coming a time when the Kingdom of God will be fully consummated. But if the future Kingdom is the only aspect we consider, we will miss the present reality of the Kingdom of God. Writing about the present Kingdom, Smith says,

> It is here and is as real and powerful as it will ever be. Everything Jesus said about the Kingdom is true in our lives. Yes, one day it will be the governing power over the entire universe, but for now it is intended to be the governing power over you and me. [12]

God's Kingdom is where He is interactively present and where those who are simultaneously present respond to His will. Simply said, it is "God's reign". Consider Willard's definition of the Kingdom of God:

> God's own "Kingdom," or "rule," is the range of His effective will, where what He wants done is done. The person of God Himself and the action of His will are the organizing principles of His Kingdom, but everything that obeys those principles, whether by nature or by choice, is within His Kingdom. [13]

Although we *await* the future Kingdom of God, we do not have to *wait* for the Present Kingdom of God. Kingdom life is available to us within the ever-present rule of God. It is the life that consists of what we do together with God, "making us part of His life and Him a part of ours."[14]

Living in the Kingdom of God is learning how to live our lives the way Jesus would. As He lives in us, as we have experienced His saving, redeeming love, can we not but want to live any other way? A life where our every day is enmeshed with God's activity and under His rule.

THIS PRESENT KINGDOM

Thick clouds rolled over the English Channel on the morning of June 6, 1944, as the stage was set for the most significant event in Europe during World War II. That day more than 156,000 American, British, and Canadian troops stormed fifty miles of Normandy's fiercely defended beaches in northern France. The attack against Germany on D-Day marked a decisive turning point in the war and ensured the eventual destruction of the Axis powers in Europe. Although the war in Europe continued for another eleven months, the outcome was already determined. Finally, on May 8, 1945, V-E Day, the triumph set into motion on those beaches was realized when Germany signed an unconditional surrender.

This historical account provides spiritual perspective for us. Charles Colson writes,

> Christ's death and resurrection—the D-Day of human history—assure His ultimate victory. But we are still on the beaches. The enemy has not yet been vanquished, and the fighting is still ugly. Christ's invasion has assured the ultimate outcome, however—victory for God and His people at some future date. The second stage, which will take place when Christ returns, will complete God's rule over all the universe; His Kingdom will be visible without imperfection.[15]

Right now, we are living "on the beaches". Jesus has stormed the beaches of Satan's kingdom, signaling his defeat. The war has been won, yet the battle rages on. In the words of the great hymn,

> And though this world with devils filled should threaten to undo us.
> We will not fear, for God hath willed His truth to triumph through us.
> The Prince of Darkness grim, we tremble not for him.
> His rage we can endure, for lo, his doom is sure.
> One little word shall fell him.
>
> That word above all earthly pow'rs, no thanks to them, abideth.
> The Spirit and the gifts are ours through Him who with us sideth.
> Let goods and kindred go, this mortal life also.
> The body they may kill; God's truth abideth still.
> His Kingdom is forever![16]

Through Jesus, God's Kingdom was established on earth. It is forever. After Jesus died, rose again, and ascended into Heaven, He sent the Holy Spirit on the day of Pentecost and a new era began. This Present Kingdom. One day, when Jesus returns, His Kingdom will be clear to all. What we know by faith, will be made sight. But in the meantime, we do not have to wait for the future to arrive. We can live the way of the Kingdom now. This way of living, the Jesus-shaped, Spirit-led life, is the way that "anticipates, in the present, the full, rich, glad human existence which will one day be ours when God make all things new…It is about practicing in the present, the tunes we shall sing in God's new world." [17] This is the life that Jesus lived, the one He taught in the Sermon on the Mount. The life He wants us to live.

God's perfect Kingdom is coming, but His Present Kingdom is here. And it is within our reach.

Let His name be glorified and sanctified throughout the universe
which He created according to His purpose. May He bring about
the reign of His Kingdom in your lifetime, in your days,
and in the lifetime of all of the house of Israel, speedily and soon! [18]
~From the Kaddish, an ancient Jewish prayer

WEEK ONE
KINGDOM ATTITUDES - PART ONE
— • — • — MATTHEW 5:1-6 — • — • —

Blessed are those who hunger and thirst for
righteousness for they shall be satisfied.
MATTHEW 5:6

God cannot give us a happiness and peace apart from Himself,
because it is not there. There is no such thing. [1]
~C.S. LEWIS

For the first four chapters in the Gospel of Matthew, Jesus' words have been limited. Then in Matthew 5-7, Jesus delivers a powerful message that compactly sets forth the truth of the Kingdom He came to proclaim. As He opens His sermon, He begins with a series of conditional blessings that are traditionally referred to as The Beatitudes.

Each of the eight beatitudes begins with "blessed are" or "happy are". Happy and blessed. These are words with which we are all familiar – states of being that every living, breathing human longs for. The Greek word used for "blessed" in the Beatitudes here is *makarios*. James Bryan Smith offers insight into what these words, happiness and blessing, really mean in the original language.

> *Makarios* means something like 'truly well off' or 'those for whom everything is good.' *Blessed* is a religious word to many of us today and is associated with being pious. *Happy* refers to temporary condition based on externals; it denotes a more shallow state of being. Today, the most accurate translation of *makarios* might be 'well off'. [2]

As we begin our study into "the greatest sermon given by the greatest person who ever lived," [3] be reminded that the foundational truths given in the Sermon on the Mount are contradictory to the wisdom of the world. Just as Jesus' life and ministry mirrored the heart of the Father (as opposed to human reasoning), these life-giving words will do the same. The Sermon on the Mount gives us keen insight into Kingdom living, experiencing the Kingdom of God while living in the kingdom of the world.

The Kingdom attitudes we will study this week will help us in our relationship to God. What better place to begin...a necessary prerequisite to all the other beatitudes...than to realize our great need for Him.

Bow before Him for just a moment and offer yourself with these words, "Thy Kingdom come, Thy will be done in earth as it is in Heaven" (Matthew 6:10, KJV).

MATTHEW 5:1-3

Before we dive in, I want to share what I learned as I began studying this portion of Scripture. This was eye opening to my well-churched mind. I pray it will offer you a fresh perspective into the heart of the Father.

As I began looking deeply into these verses, I realized that Jesus' words are not a "prescription for how to get God to be happy with me." [4] His words are intended to teach us about the Kingdom of God and are meant for every human being on the planet.

As He begins to speak, Jesus is looking out over a crowd of "have-nots" in the Jewish community. They have been made to feel marginalized from God, riddled by cultural standards that have told them they are not good enough and are unworthy to receive blessing.

1. Read Matthew 21:31. What does Jesus say in this verse?

Smith comments on this verse, "How could Jesus say this? Because He is the Kingdom of God. He is a living, breathing, tangible, touchable, real-life expression and embodiment of the Kingdom. When He touches or dines with people, they have come into contact with the Kingdom." [5]

If Jesus willingly extends His hand to the poor, unlovely, broken, damaged, and most wretched of sinners, I am compelled to live in the same way. This is what the Beatitudes are – "words of hope and healing to those who have been marginalized." [6] No one is excluded from the happiness, joy and blessing that comes from following Christ. The only requirement is to choose Him and follow Him. And if you do, you will be *makarios*, truly well off.

Ask the Lord to give you fresh eyes and a tender heart as you read what may be very familiar verses. Ask Him to bring the Kingdom of God right into your daily life. Settle for nothing less than a life that mimics that of your Savior.

Read Matthew 5:1-3.

2. Write out verse 3. (Take a moment and look at other translations of this verse as well.)

3. How do you interpret "poor in spirit"?

In his book, *The Divine Conspiracy*, Dallas Willard writes, "The poor in spirit are blessed as a result of the Kingdom of God being available to them in their spiritual poverty. And so He (Jesus) said, 'Blessed are the spiritual zeros–the spiritually bankrupt, deprived and deficient, the spiritual beggars, those without a wisp of 'religion'–when the Kingdom of the Heavens comes upon them'" (parenthesis mine).[7]

I am confident that verse 3 came as a relief to the listeners of Jesus' day, and it should do the same for us. Do you ever find yourself feeling less spiritual than the next guy (or gal)? Do you doubt that God will move mightily in <u>your</u> life? Do you feel inadequate to discuss and explain certain portions of Scripture? Do you feel there is a "religious elite" from which you are excluded?

We have all experienced these types of thoughts and feelings to some degree at one time or another. Do I have some good news for you!

> Those poor in spirit are called 'blessed' by Jesus, not because they are in a meritorious condition, but because, precisely in spite of and in the midst of their ever so deplorable condition, the rule of the heavens has moved redemptively upon and through them by the grace of Christ.[8]

Once again, it is only because of Jesus Christ. There is nothing we can do to earn this indescribable gift of experiencing the Kingdom of God now, and then forevermore. Our part is to believe it, accept it, and then walk in a manner worthy of it. God has opened the windows of Heaven and made it available for all believers. Willard notes, "The religious system of His day left the multitudes out, but Jesus welcomed them all into His Kingdom. Anyone could come as well as any other. They still can. That is the gospel of the Beatitudes."[9]

WE HAVE NOTHING WITHOUT HIM.

In addition to realizing the availability of the Kingdom to all of us, we should also be aware of our condition apart from Christ. It is imperative for us to have an inward awareness that we have nothing without Him–we are poor, needy and completely dependent on Almighty God.

Warren Wiersbe writes, "This explains why 'blessed are the poor in spirit' is the first of the Beatitudes; for until we admit our need we can never receive what God has for us." [10]

4. Look up the following verses to see examples from Scripture of those who recognized their deep need for God.

Job 42:5-6

Isaiah 6:5

Luke 18:13

Romans 7:18

5. Are you desperate for God? Where do you lack in your dependence upon Him?

To be poor in spirit means knowing that in myself I am bankrupt, but in Christ I am rich. It means discovering the place God wants me to fill and filling it for His glory. [11]
~Warren Wiersbe

MATTHEW 5:4

Mourning. Just the sound as the word rolls off your lips puts a heaviness in your heart, doesn't it? As we noted yesterday, everyone desires happiness. And we can almost certainly say the opposite of sadness. No one wants to be sad. No one wants to mourn. However, sometimes mourning is just a part of life.

1. Write out the text of Matthew 5:4.

We will look at two perspectives regarding mourning in today's study. First, we will observe how it ties into yesterday's topic of being poor in spirit. These two subject matters can go hand in hand when we consider our position before Christ, our utter dependence on Him, and our condition apart from Him.

Mourning often comes as a result of deep conviction of the Holy Spirit over sin. Hopefully, when we experience this conviction, we respond with a contrite heart because we have sinned against a holy God. A riveting example of this in Scripture is David's sin with Bathsheba.

Read 1 Samuel 12:1-23 to be reminded of the rebuke David received from Nathan concerning his sin.

2. In your own words, recount how David mourns over his sin in Psalm 51.

When we encounter God in this manner, by way of repentance over sin, we experience the comfort Jesus speaks of in Matthew 5:4.

3. Read 2 Corinthians 7:10. What is the result of godly sorrow?

Wiersbe elaborates on the main thrust of this second beatitude with these words.

> Jesus is talking about repentance for sin, and that is the result of the supernatural working of God in your life. The person who is sincerely poor in spirit will mourn over himself and his sins, and through this mourning he will experience the comfort of God. [12]

Wiersbe goes on to distinguish between repentance, remorse, and regret by saying of repentance, "When my concern over my sin brings me to the place where I am willing to turn from it and obey God – when my concern affects my will as well as my mind and my heart – then I have experienced true repentance." [13]

Have you experienced the weight lifted when you respond to conviction over sin, the kind of comfort that can only come from God? That feeling of relief and freedom as a result of true repentance of mind, heart, and will. (Consider the prodigal son's repentance in Luke 15.) As we learned yesterday, Scripture tells us we are *makarios*, well off, when we experience comfort that comes as a result of mourning over sin.

4. Pause for a moment and ask the Lord to reveal any sin you may be harboring in your heart. Perhaps it is something you aren't even aware of. As He reveals it, open your Bible and use Psalm 51 to pour out your heart in repentance. Allow the comfort of the Savior to soak in and flood your soul. Journal your thoughts here.

The second way we will look at mourning is one we have all undoubtedly experienced: grief. Natural sorrow comes with the death of a child, parent, or spouse; a crumbling marriage; a diagnosis that promises a shortened life; a divided church; loneliness; isolation; financial debacle; and rejection. These are just a few of the things all of humanity faces at one time or another (either directly or indirectly) that cause our hearts to be stricken with overwhelming grief.

This second beatitude in Matthew 5 comes as a soothing balm to hearts that are grieving. "Jesus says an unblessable condition can be blessed." [14] What causes us to mourn can be turned into something good. Just as overwhelming as the grief can be, so can be the comfort of our Heavenly Father.

Referencing Luke 6:21, Willard says, "Luke refers to them as 'the weeping ones'…as they see the Kingdom in Jesus, enter it and learn to live in it, they find comfort and their tears turn to laughter. Yes, they are even better off than they were before their particular disaster." [15]

I recently read Elisabeth Elliot's book, *Suffering Is Never for Nothing*. As I consider what promised comfort for mourning looks like, I think of her words.

> Out of the deepest waters and the hottest fires have come the deepest things that I know about God. And I would add this, that the greatest gifts of my life have also entailed the greatest suffering. He can transform something terrible into something wonderful. Suffering is never for nothing. [16]

Remember that Jesus is communicating this message to a crowd of ordinary people, many of whom were rejected by the culture around them as outcasts. The Bible tells us that large crowds, or multitudes, followed to hear Jesus' teachings. So, I imagine, in groups this size, many were experiencing pain and hurt in various ways.

In the same way, many of you are undoubtedly experiencing pain and hurt, maybe even overwhelming grief.

Fall into the arms of Jesus and hear <u>His</u> words to you. "You're blessed when you feel you've lost what is most dear to you. Only then can you be embraced by the One most dear to you" (Matthew 5:4, MSG). Wiersbe encourages, "Sorrow plus Jesus Christ can bring a transforming experience of power into the life of the one who is mourning." [17]

5. Have you experienced the comfort of Jesus Christ during a time of deep sadness? (Consider sharing with your small group. Your testimony may offer hope to a hopeless heart.)

Every suffering can be blessed because it hollows out a place in us for God
and His comfort, which is infinite joy. [18]
~Peter Kreeft

MATTHEW 5:5

Meekness is the secret of possessing everything. [19]
~Warren Wiersbe

We live in a world that says meekness, or gentleness in spirit, is a sign of weakness. Our society worships power, so this admonishment from Jesus Christ is a stark contrast to what we are inundated with from the world, the enemy, and our human nature.

Wiersbe challenges the world's viewpoint, "Meekness is not weakness. Meekness is power under control." [20] The Bible is full of examples of bold, strong, and courageous people. Moses was anything but weak, yet God identified him as the meekest man, more humble than anyone on the face of the earth (Numbers 12:3). Jesus also said of Himself in Matthew 11:29 (KJV), "I am meek and lowly in heart." Jesus undeniably faced some of the most difficult and dangerous circumstances we can imagine, yet He remained gentle and humble as He served, ministered, and faced death on the cross.

Meekness has an opportunity to come into play (or not) when we face circumstances that anger us. As Christians, I believe this is one of the ways we can stand out most from the world.

1. Read these verses and record what they teach us about differing types of anger.

    Proverbs 16:32

    Proverbs 25:28

Wiersbe makes an enlightening comparison to fire. "When fire is under control, it is our servant and accomplishes great things for us; but when fire is out of control, it becomes our master, and the result is destruction. So it is with anger." [21]

When we think of meekness, we commonly refer to humility, which is an accurate correlation to make. One of my favorite examples of this is in the life of Joseph. His brothers sold him into slavery and he was later falsely accused of sexual assault by Potiphar's wife, which resulted in years of imprisonment. If Joseph had responded like many of us today, he may have looked forward to the day he could seek revenge for how unfair life had been. Perhaps he could later use his position of power to inflict the same pain and fear upon others as he had endured.

But as we see in Genesis 39 through 45, Joseph kept his power under control. He refused to be vengeful when given the opportunity. Joseph's reaction was not due to a lack of strength or a spineless character. The strength of character Joseph displayed is what Wiersbe says "reveals itself when I am right and when I have the power to hurt someone who is wrong." [22]

2. Using the text of Psalm 37 (NIV) provided, highlight the instructions which lead to a life of meekness found in verse 11. Place an asterisk (*) next to those with which you currently struggle.

[1]Do not fret because of those who are evil
or be envious of those who do wrong;
[2] for like the grass they will soon wither,
like green plants they will soon die away.

[3] Trust in the LORD and do good;
dwell in the land and enjoy safe pasture.
[4] Take delight in the LORD,
and he will give you the desires of your heart.

[5] Commit your way to the LORD;
trust in Him and He will do this:
[6] He will make your righteous reward shine like the dawn,
your vindication like the noonday sun.

[7] Be still before the LORD
and wait patiently for Him;
do not fret when people succeed in their ways,
when they carry out their wicked schemes.

[8] Refrain from anger and turn from wrath;
do not fret—it leads only to evil.
[9] For those who are evil will be destroyed,
but those who hope in the LORD will inherit the land.

[10] A little while, and the wicked will be no more;
though you look for them, they will not be found.
[11] But the meek will inherit the land
and enjoy peace and prosperity.

It is my prayer that you and I will allow the power of Almighty God to take our stubborn will, till up any hard ground, and plant the fruit of His Spirit in the area of meekness. The world in which we live can be dark, cold, and hard. We are bombarded with messages that say, "Look out for number one." "Do whatever you have to do to succeed." "Make her pay for what's been done to you." "You sure don't deserve that." Our attitudes and tempers can be easily ignited and flared, ready to explode at a moment's notice. This way is not the mind and heart of Jesus Christ.

3. Read Philippians 2:1-8. What characteristics of Jesus display meekness and humility?

4. Read 1 Peter 2:21-23. What actions of Jesus can we imitate to display meekness and humility?

I want to close today with a powerful thought on the blessing of inheritance as a result of obedience:

> You inherit something because somebody dies and leaves a bequest to you in his will. In this case, it is *we* who die—die to self—that we might grow in meekness; and as we grow in meekness, we share the rich inheritance that we have in Christ. [23]

> *You're blessed when you're content with just who you are—no more, no less.*
> *That's the moment you find yourselves proud owners of everything that can't be bought.*
> Matthew 5:5, MSG

It was fall of 2004. I walked into a Bible study at my church designed to minister to moms. I held my newborn baby boy of just a few months and sat toward the back of the chapel. I remember he had on a soft, white cotton onesie with "Thursday" stitched on the front alongside a cute forest animal. (Little did I know when I bought those, my sleep deprived brain would actually need help remembering the days of the week.)

I had been a Christian for many years, attended church my whole life, sang in choirs, attended youth camps…I did it all. But as I began listening to the rich truths of God's Word and how it was my responsibility to train up this little boy for the sake of the Kingdom, I realized I had much to learn, and a pivotal decision to make. I did not just need more head knowledge, but I needed an intimate relationship with my Savior, an uncompromised time of Bible intake and radical prayer, an authentic commitment to look more like Jesus, and a passionate intentionality to live it out before my son.

So, as the godly teacher shared with us the scripture she had prayed for herself as a young mother, I began to do the same. "Oh God, just as the deer longs for a drink of water, make my soul long for you in the same way." I prayed it day after day after day. (See Psalm 42:1.)

And God did it. He answered the cry of my heart. Please do not misunderstand me. It was not instantaneous, and I had a role to play. I had to choose to open the Bible and read it, to allow it to challenge and encourage me, to meditate upon its truths, and then to make a choice to obey. I had to choose to pray…even when I didn't feel like it. Especially, when I didn't feel like it. I was to be about the Father's business above all else. He had given me a built-in disciple with whom to share the truths of Scripture and then to live them out by the power of the Holy Spirit.

So, as I sit down to write today's study, my heart races. My eyes are filled with tears, and my mind is filled with reminders of what God has done in my life and in my heart. And if I could coerce every one of you to make the same choice, I would do it in a heartbeat. Because I know the truth of Matthew 5:6 which says, "Blessed are those who hunger and thirst for righteousness, for they shall be satisfied."

I can truly say I am satisfied. God held up His end of the deal, as He always does. I began to hunger and thirst for right living, for holiness, and He has been satisfying me ever since. I fall short daily, but I cannot imagine going back to a life without the desperate desire and need for Him. I <u>have</u> to have my time with Him each morning. I <u>have</u> to open my prayer box and pour out my praises and petitions to Him. I do not say this to boast. If I could have done it on my own, I would have, but I could not. It is because He is a faithful Promise Keeper and does what He says He will do. And when I face times of spiritual drought, He gently reminds me of what He's already taught me, and He lifts me up out of my pit and sets me back on solid ground. And again, I have to choose to follow.

Wiersbe makes this comparison, "Doctors tell us that we are what we eat. This principle is true not only of the body but also of the soul." [24] He continues, "The kind of appetite we have is an indication of the kind of heart we have." [25]

1. Take a moment to honestly evaluate your appetite for the things of God. What is your soul "eating" right now?

2. Has there been a time in your life that you hungered and thirsted for Him more than you do now? If so, what pulled you away?

3. Read Ecclesiastes 3:11. What does this verse teach us about humanity's thirst for God?

God, the Creator of all things, has placed eternity in our hearts. This means that we are designed with a "God-shaped hole" in our souls. Although He will not force us to choose Him, He has created us to want Him and to need Him. And then He goes on to tell us in Matthew 5 that if we hunger and thirst for Him, we will be satisfied. You will not pursue Him and find yourself empty. You will want more…but it will be more of Him.

The world promises fulfillment at every turn. Yet, we find ourselves empty and depleted when we do it our own way. We may experience a temporal satisfaction, but it will be just that–temporary. In John 6:35, Jesus says, "I am the bread of life; he who comes to Me will not hunger, and he who believes in Me will never thirst."

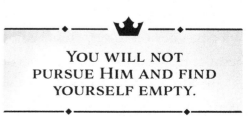

YOU WILL NOT PURSUE HIM AND FIND YOURSELF EMPTY.

4. According to John 4:34, what was Jesus' source of nourishment?

In Wiersbe's book, *Live Like a King*, he touches on holiness and happiness as he delves into this beatitude. He says to be filled, or satisfied, is "a hunger for holiness that fills the soul and satisfies the appetite of the inner man." [26] But so often, we settle for less than holiness. We allow the stench of sin to remain, minimizing it, justifying it, or refusing to see it as God sees it. We rob ourselves of this satisfying filling because we settle for lesser things.

I challenge you to look deep within the recesses of your heart. Is your deepest longing to know Jesus? To look more like Him each day? To pursue a life that is pure and blameless? Do you want Him so much that your heart aches to be with Him, to hear from Him?

5. Look up these verses and note what the Bible says about longing for more of Jesus.

Psalm 24:7-8

Psalm 143:6

Matthew 4:4

Philippians 3:7-11

Wiersbe goes on to say, "Jesus enjoyed life, even though life for Him was difficult. He was happy because He was holy." [27] He points out that the Pharisees, as religious as they were, were an unhappy people because they had a skewed view of holiness. Holiness for them was simply following a list of rules, not focusing on the inner man and being truly clean before the Lord. "If knowing God, enjoying God, and becoming like God is our highest desire, then the fulfilling of that desire will bring us the highest happiness." [28]

There is not a "fast pass" to holiness or happiness. Just like when I was a young mom sitting in the chapel gazing into the face of my newborn baby, we all have a choice to make. Will you satisfy your soul's appetite at the world's table or will you feast on the things of God? One will leave you constantly starving for more. One will fill you to overflowing, satisfying the depths of your heart in ways you cannot begin to imagine.

We are what we eat. "Blessed are they which do hunger and thirst after righteousness: for they shall be filled." [29]
~Warren Wiersbe

KINGDOM EXERCISE

Disciplines do not earn us favor with God or measure spiritual success.
They are exercises which equip us to live fully and freely in the present reality of God - and God
works with us, giving us grace as we learn and grow. [30]
~RICHARD J. FOSTER

THE DISCIPLINES OF SIMPLICITY AND WORSHIP

Simplicity: An inward reality that results in an outward lifestyle. [31]

Worship: Entering into the supra-natural experience of the *Shekainah*, or glory, of God. [32]

Simplicity and worship go hand-in-hand. I am writing this as our nation and world are dealing with an unprecedented virus called COVID-19. This has resulted in quarantine and isolation, thus interrupting life as we know it. We have been forced to simplify. We have all spent more time in our homes than usual, and have been cut off from our normal activities of church, sports, school, family gatherings, dinner with friends, etc. While some of this has been painful at times (frustrating at times, to be honest), it has also forced us to do less. For me, personally, this has led to a deeper place of worship. I have always enjoyed worshipping the Lord through music and prayer, but something about pulling away from the distractions of life has allowed me to "enter in" with fresh perspective.

A simpler way of doing life opens a pathway to worship in new ways.

As we look at simplicity, I want to focus on two areas. First, we will consider materialism and the desire to accumulate more "stuff". A second point of view will consider a conscious decision to prioritize differently and to appreciate what is often overlooked as mundane and ordinary. I believe a concerted effort to do both of these will result in a worshipful heart that declares, "With all my heart I will praise you, O Lord my God. I will give glory to your name forever" (Psalm 86:12, 13a, NLT).

I recognize this is not an exclusive statement for every reader of this book; however, for most of us, we have plenty. Most of us have a home, more clothes than we could ever wear in a season, and a pantry full of food. If you are like me, there are items in your closet and pantry that, if they went missing, you'd never know. We have a lot of stuff.

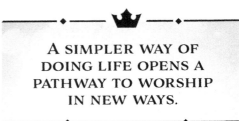

A SIMPLER WAY OF DOING LIFE OPENS A PATHWAY TO WORSHIP IN NEW WAYS.

Not only do we *have* a lot of stuff, but we *do* a lot of stuff. Bible study, grocery shopping, carpooling, sports, errands, working out, visiting grandchildren, caring for aging parents, leading and organizing school events, hanging out with friends, and the list goes on and on. None of these are bad. In fact, most of them are good, and even necessary. We, and the ones we love, benefit when we do them. But too often, these things (along with all the others you can think of right now) dominate our time and energy, draining us physically, emotionally, and spiritually. Could we be missing out on a life of simplicity that leads to a heart of worship as we take time to pause and consider our magnificent God?

If your material possessions or activities and commitments are depleting your heart and mind in a way that pulls you away from the heart of God, I encourage you to evaluate where you can implement change.

In Psalm 46:10 (NIV), God tells us, "Be still and know that I am God." If we are cluttering our lives with wealth, possessions, and bulging calendars, we are not able to obey this scripture.

THE EXERCISE

This week's activity will be two-fold.

First, for one week, look for an item per day in your home that you can pass along to someone else. No matter how big or small, get rid of something that physically fills your space. Donate clothes, take canned goods to a food pantry, give gently used books to a school, clean out toys and find a needy family, or donate to your church nursery. And do not replace those items with something else.

Second, simplify your heart and mind. Rather than launching into your day full speed ahead, stop and look out your window at the flowers and trees. Watch the early morning sun as it peeks through the window. Sit outside for a moment and listen to the birds singing. Let something go and appreciate what God has given you. During this time of quarantine, I have made a point to stop and just look at the faces of my boys. I am getting extra time with them that I, otherwise, would not have had. My oldest will be leaving home in less than three years. I've stopped to sit with him more than usual, just to have a conversation or shoot basketball with him. Enjoy the simple, yet abundant, blessings the Lord has lavished upon you. Clear your schedule for a day. Set the to-do list aside. (That's a big one if you're a lover of lists like me!)

As you remove items from your home (simplifying your material things) and remove clutter from your heart and mind (simplifying your inner woman), I pray the result is a full heart. A heart overflowing with gratitude for all God has blessed you with will result in worship!

In his book, *The Life You've Always Wanted*, John Ortberg says, "Hurry is the great enemy of spiritual life in our day. Hurry can destroy our souls. Hurry can keep us from living well. Hurry is not just a disordered schedule. Hurry is a disordered heart." [33]

REFLECTION QUESTIONS

1. What did you get rid of materially?

2. How did you clear (and simplify) your schedule?

3. What struggles did you face as you did both of these?

4. How did you enter into worship as a result of simplifying?

5. In what ways did God speak or bring about change to your heart?

6. How would you describe this exercise of simplifying and worshipping?

WEEK TWO
KINGDOM ATTITUDES – PART TWO
——•——•—— MATTHEW 5:7-12 ——•——•——

Blessed are the pure in heart, for they shall see God.
MATTHEW 5:8

*The Sermon on the Mount is a statement of the life we will live when
the Holy Spirit is having His way with us.* [1]
~OSWALD CHAMBERS

A changed heart produces a transformed life. This is the message at the core of the Sermon on the Mount. This discourse is directed to those who have been regenerated by the Holy Spirit. No natural man can keep the tenants of this text. Only those who are indwelt and empowered by the Holy Spirit of God can step into the Kingdom living detailed in the message Jesus delivers. The life Jesus is calling His people to transcends religious ritual and routine; it requires His supernatural enabling which begins with a heart change. Having received His divine nature, we begin to manifest His divine attributes as we engage in Kingdom living.

John MacArthur summarizes The Beatitudes:

> The first four beatitudes deal entirely with inner principles, principles of the heart and mind. They are concerned with the way we see ourselves before God. The last four are outward manifestations of those attitudes. Those who in poverty of spirit recognize their need of mercy are led to show mercy to others (v. 7). Those who mourn over their sin are led to purity of heart (v. 8). Those who are meek always seek to make peace (v. 9). And those who hunger and thirst for righteousness are never unwilling to pay the price of being persecuted for righteousness' sake (v. 10). [2]

Salvation is a free gift. Free to us, that is. God bankrupted Heaven in order to redeem us when He gave us His Son. God "caused the iniquity of us all to fall on Him" (Isaiah 53:6). "He made Him who knew no sin to be sin on our behalf, so that we might become the righteousness of God in Him" (2 Corinthians 5:21). Peter writes, "He Himself bore our sins in His body on the cross, so that we might die to sin and live to righteousness; for by His wounds you were healed" (1 Peter 2:24). Our sin cost, but God loved the world so much "that He gave His only begotten Son" (John 3:16) to redeem us, and more surprisingly—to redeem one like me.

I did not grow up going to church. In fact, before I came to faith in Jesus, I had only been inside a church a total of 10 or 15 times. As young marrieds, living outside a personal relationship with Christ, my husband and I began to attend Bellevue Baptist Church at the invitation of my in-laws. Our attendance was sporadic at first, but then became more frequent. There, we were exposed to the powerful and passionate preaching of Dr. Adrian Rogers. Within a short time, the Holy Spirit began to do His work and the Word of God did its work. Within a few months, we both individually prayed and invited Jesus to be our Lord and Savior. Praise God, "He rescued us from the domain of darkness, and transferred us to the Kingdom of His beloved Son, in whom we have redemption, the forgiveness of sins" (Colossians 1:13-14). Hallelujah! What a Savior!

We glory in His free gift of salvation. "For by grace you have been saved through faith; and that not of yourselves, it is the gift of God; not as a result of works, so that no one may boast" (Ephesians 2:8-9). May we not fail to remember that the free gift of salvation carries with it great responsibility. "For we are His workmanship, created in Christ Jesus for good works, which God prepared beforehand so that we would walk in them" (Ephesians 2:10). Good works should naturally follow our conversion experience. They are the birthmark of a genuine conversion and should be the natural overflow of a life surrendered to Christ. Christ died for us. Can we not live for Him?

In the Sermon on the Mount, Jesus introduces a radically different way of living, a manner of life that would set the child of God apart from those who belong to the world. Peter called us, "a chosen race, a royal priesthood, a holy nation, a people for God's own possession, so that [we] may proclaim the excellencies of Him who has called [us] out of darkness into His marvelous light; for [we] once where not a people, but now [we] are the people of God; [we] had not received mercy, but now [we] have received mercy" (1 Peter 2:9-10). As we "grow in the grace and knowledge of our Lord and Savior Jesus Christ" (2 Peter 3:18), the Kingdom attitudes dictated by Jesus in The Beatitudes become the sweet aroma of His presence in us.

MATTHEW 5:7

The Roman world into which Jesus entered did not admire mercy. In fact, it was viewed as the supreme sign of weakness, something to be abhorred and avoided. The Romans glorified brute strength, courage, strict justice, firm discipline, and above all, absolute power.

MacArthur describes the culture of the Roman world:

> During much of Roman history, a father had the right of *patria opitestas*, of deciding whether or not his newborn child would live or die. As the infant was held up for him to see, the father would turn his thumb up if he wanted the child to live, down if he wanted it to die. If his thumb turned down the child was immediately drowned. Citizens had the same life-or-death power over slaves. At any time and for any reason they could kill and bury a slave, with no fear of arrest or reprisal. Husbands could even have their wives put to death on the least provocation. [3]

It is into this world that Jesus brings the disruptive message embodied in the Sermon on the Mount.

Read Matthew 5:7.

1. What words come to mind when you think of someone who is merciful?

2. What is the opposite of being merciful?

The fifth beatitude does not teach that mercy *to* men automatically evokes a response of mercy *from* men. Neither Scripture nor experience bears out that idea. What it teaches is that God will show mercy to those who have been merciful to others. Demonstrating mercy reveals the Kingdom of God here on earth. As with the previous beatitudes, God gives the divine blessings to those who obey His divine standards.

GOD GIVES THE DIVINE BLESSINGS TO THOSE WHO OBEY HIS DIVINE STANDARDS.

God's mercy gives us access to His forgiveness and withholds the judgment our sin deserves. God's grace is manifested in the salvation of sinners and the bestowal of blessings.

Dr. Adrian Rogers explains, "Justice is God giving us what we deserve; mercy is God not giving us what we deserve; and grace is God giving us what we don't deserve." [4] Praise God!

God is just and merciful. The justice of God requires that sin cannot be overlooked and must be punished. When we recognize we are a sinner in need of a Savior, we cry out for mercy. God, having sent His Son to be "the propitiation for our sins" (1 John 2:2), deals with us on the basis of His mercy. In this way, He is both "just and the justifier of the one who has faith in Jesus" (Romans 3:26). We experience God's mercy when we trust Jesus Christ as Lord and Savior. "But God, being rich in mercy, because of His great love with which He loved us, even when we were dead in our transgressions, made us alive together with Christ (by grace you have been saved), and raised us up with Him, and seated us with Him in the heavenly places in Christ Jesus" (Ephesians 2:4-6).

Because we have received mercy from God the Father, we are to extend mercy to others. William Hendriksen describes mercy as "love for those in misery and a forgiving spirit toward the sinner. It embraces both the kindly feeling and the kindly act." [5] Mercy engages in showing compassion. Its character is demonstrated by feeding the hungry, extending help to the needy, giving love to the unlovable, comforting the grieving, offering companionship to the lonely, and extending forgiveness to the offender. Nothing moves us to be merciful like the radical realization that we have received God's mercy despite the terrible sin debt we had accrued. Demonstrating mercy gives solid evidence of a genuine conversion springing forth from a grateful soul.

We cannot claim to have repented of our sins and been saved if we are unmerciful to the sins of others or unmoved by their needs. At the end of the age, the Lord will separate the lost from the saved. The unbelievers will be to His left, and His followers will be put on His right.

3. Read Matthew 25:34-40. What acts will characterize believers?

Grace and mercy are gifts from the Lord. They are similar but have a slight difference. John MacArthur explains the difference between grace and mercy:

> Grace and mercy have the closest possible relationship; yet they are different. Mercy and its related terms all have to do with pain, misery, and distress—with the consequences of sin. Whether because of our individual sins or because of the sinful world in which we live, all of our problems, in the last analysis, are sin problems. It is with those problems that mercy gives help. Grace, on the other hand, deals with sin itself. Mercy deals with the symptoms, grace with the cause. Mercy offers relief from punishment; grace offers pardon for the crime. Mercy eliminates the pain; grace cures the disease. [6]

Christ is the supreme example of mercy. Hebrews 2:17 says, "Therefore, He had to be made like His brethren in all things, so that He might become a merciful and faithful high priest in things pertaining to God, to make propitiation for the sins of the people." When we bestow mercy as His earthly ambassadors, we pierce the heavenlies and bring His Kingdom from Heaven to earth.

In The Parable of the Good Samaritan, Jesus illustrates how mercy is demonstrated.

4. Read Luke 10:30-37. What are the circumstances that caused the Jewish man to be injured?

5. What do the priest and the Levite do?

6. What does the Samaritan do for the injured man?

The Samaritans were a mixed race who were unilaterally despised by the Jews. The Jews who had been left behind after the Assyrian captivity in 722 B.C. intermarried with the pagan inhabitants of the land, producing the race known as the Samaritans. In showing compassion, the Samaritan stepped over centuries-old barriers. He demonstrated Kingdom living as he showed mercy through his actions.

What a precious parable, rich with meaning and overflowing with mercy! Consider these insights which can be drawn from this story. The priests were the religious people of that day, performing all the rituals and sacrifices. The priest in the parable pictures ritualism, religious activity with lots of show but little substance. The Levites were the keepers of the Law. The Levite represents rules, demanding strict adherence to external regulations. Religion cannot save us. Rules cannot save us. Salvation is only available through a personal relationship with Jesus Christ.

In the parable, Jesus is pictured by the Samaritan. He was "despised and rejected of men" (Isaiah 53:3, NIV). The Samaritan bandaged the wounds of the injured traveler and poured oil and wine on them. The oil represents the Holy Spirit, our Comforter who "heals the brokenhearted and binds up their wounds" (Psalm 147:3). The wine pictures the blood of Jesus, poured out as a sacrifice for sin. The compassionate Samaritan laid the injured man on his donkey, took him to a place of healing and rest, and spent the night tending to his injuries. In the morning, the Samaritan instructed the innkeeper to care for the wounded traveler, promising to pay the expenses incurred on the return trip. What a picture of salvation! "Blessed be the God and Father of our Lord Jesus Christ, who according to His great mercy has caused us to be born again to a living hope through the resurrection of Jesus Christ from the dead" (1 Peter 1:3). On the cross, as an atoning sacrifice for sin, Jesus paid the price for sin. Grace and mercy were (and continue to be) extended to us.

7. In Matthew 18:21-35, Jesus tells another parable that pictures God's mercy in relation to forgiving others. Read this passage. What is Jesus teaching through this parable?

Since we have received God's mercy, it is our "reasonable service" (Romans 12:1, KJV) to be merciful to others. If we should foolishly withhold mercy where God has clearly instructed us to dispense it, the Lord will chasten us in order to bring us to repentance (Hebrews 12:5-11).

Being the happy recipients of God's mercy, we should endeavor to share His mercy with others. In doing so, we put His Kingdom attitudes on full display!

A changed heart produces a transformed life.

Read Matthew 5:8.

1. What do you think "pure in heart" means?

Those who are pure in heart manifest outward behaviors that indicate the inward transformation of their heart. They operate under the control of the Holy Spirit, a life reserved for those who are indwelt by Christ. This life far surpasses the ritualistic cleansing practiced fervently by the religious rulers of Jesus' day. In Matthew 23:27-28, Jesus confronts the Pharisees about their obsession with external, ceremonial purity, which belied an unchanged heart to the casual observer, "Woe to you, scribes and Pharisees, hypocrites! For you are like whitewashed tombs which on the outside appear beautiful, but inside they are full of dead men's bones and all uncleanness. So you, too, outwardly appear righteous to men, but inwardly you are full of hypocrisy and lawlessness."

In *The Good and Beautiful Life*, James Bryan Smith writes:

> Jesus is teaching about the difference between inner and outer righteousness, and on becoming a new kind of person in the Kingdom of God. Jesus is most concerned with the heart, particularly with developing a good heart…In the Kingdom of God we are being transformed into a new kind of person, based on our new identity as "one indwelt by Christ." [7]

The goal of the Christian life is to see God. Obviously, we know we will see God when we are gathered to Him in eternity, but we desire more now. We want to see God and experience His presence in the grind of daily living. We want to, we need to see God in the midst of our circle of life, turning the mundane into the miraculous. To see Him in everyday events. To see Him at work in our lives. To see Him in the midst of our circumstances. To see Him working in our family life, church life, workplace, and among our friends. Imanuel Christian makes this observation, "If we see God, that will open up the treasure trove of all the blessings, not only for eternity, but also for life here and now. And the key to open that treasure trove is a pure heart!" [8]

Pure hearts. John MacArthur states, "Pure translates *katharos*, a form of the word from which we get catharsis." [9] It basically means to be cleansed. The word also has the idea of being unmixed or unadulterated. It was used for grain that was separated from the chaff or for metal that had been smelted until all the impurities were removed. The word *heart* is used to designate the control center of the inner person consisting of the mind, will, and emotions. When Jesus puts the two words together, He is referring to those who have a single-minded devotion to God and are committed to walking in integrity. Blessed are those with pure motives from the overflow of a pure heart.

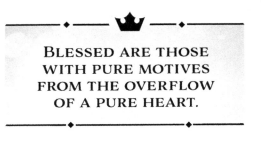

BLESSED ARE THOSE WITH PURE MOTIVES FROM THE OVERFLOW OF A PURE HEART.

Purity of heart is not something that can be manufactured or manipulated, rather it is granted by God through a personal relationship with Christ. In his commentary on the Gospel of Matthew, John MacArthur writes, "When God imputes His righteousness to us He imputes His purity to us." [10] As David prays, "Create in me a clean heart, O God, and renew a steadfast spirit within me" (Psalm 51:10).

2. Read Psalm 24:1-4. Who may come before the Lord?

3. What is bestowed upon those who walk before the Lord in integrity?

Remaining single-minded has always presented a problem for God's people. We desire to serve the Lord, but the pull of the world, the flesh, and the devil often overpower us. James 1:8 says, "A double-minded man [is] unstable in all his ways." As Jesus will say later on in His sermon, "No one can serve two masters; for either he will hate the one and love the other, or he will be devoted to one and despise the other. You cannot serve God and wealth" (Matthew 6:24). James echoes, "Do you not know that friendship with the world is hostility toward God? Therefore whoever wishes to be a friend of the world makes himself an enemy of God" (James 4:4).

God desires a clean heart and the transformed life it produces. Israel wanted a king "like all the nations" (1 Samuel 8:5). God called Saul and "changed his heart" (1 Samuel 10:9). Saul started his reign well, but he began to disobey, and God rejected him. Samuel said to Saul, "Your kingdom shall not endure. The Lord has sought out for Himself a man after His own heart" (1 Samuel 13:14). God then sent Samuel to anoint a new king.

Read 1 Samuel 16:1-13 and answer these questions.

4. What did the Lord tell Samuel as the oldest son Eliab stood in front of him?

5. Seven sons were paraded before Samuel, but God did not accept any of them. What was Jesse's reaction when Samuel asked if there were more children?

6. What happened when David appeared before Samuel?

David was a man after God's own heart. Evidence of this is seen throughout the Psalms. "I will give thanks to the Lord with all my heart" (Psalm 9:1). "Let the words of my mouth and the meditation of my heart be acceptable in Your sight" (Psalm 19:14). David had a pure heart that was stayed on the Lord.

Some years back, a friend, actually someone we counted as a dear friend, took up an offense against my husband. My husband was unaware of any rift in the relationship. Unbeknownst to us, this person began to spread vicious lies about my husband rather than coming to discuss the perceived trespass. When my husband became aware of the rumors, he went to our friend in an attitude of contrition and humility, in hopes of discovering the problem and repairing the breach. Our friend assured my husband he was mistaken, and there was no unresolved issue between them. We assumed all was well and considered the friendship restored. Rumors continued to swirl, gaining momentum, and becoming more malicious. Two more times my husband contacted this friend, only to be reassured he was not the source of the innuendoes and that there was nothing unsettled between them.

In time, it was revealed our friend was indeed the source. Several attempts toward reconciliation were made. Each one was rebuffed and in time the friendship dissolved and ended on unhappy terms. The grief of being wounded by *friendly fire*, that is being betrayed by a friend, made the wound doubly painful. Psalm 41:9 says, "Even my close friend in whom I trusted, who ate my bread, has lifted up his heel against me." My husband was devastated over the lost friendship and the lies which continued to circulate. As I prayed for him, I found solace in God's Word. Psalm 15 was of particular comfort, and I prayed it on his behalf for many months. This Psalm speaks of a man with a pure heart. Despite the fact that his friend had disparaged his reputation and spread lies about his character, I knew the truth about who he was, a man of godly character. In time, God brought healing to our troubled hearts, although the path to wholeness was a long and circuitous route.

7. Read Psalm 15:1-5. This psalm remains a favorite of mine, and I still pray it over my husband. It beautifully describes a follower of Christ. Who may dwell in the presence of the Lord?

The Bible cautions us to "watch over [our] heart with all diligence" (Proverbs 4:23). Sin is a heart issue. Imanuel Christian puts it this way, "The heart of the matter is the matter of the heart." [11] In Matthew 15:19-20, Jesus said, "For out of the heart come evil thoughts, murders, adulteries, fornications, thefts, false witness, slanders. These are the things which defile the man." When we received Christ as Lord and Savior, our personal sin debt was paid in full. However, we continue to commit sins of commission (doing what we should not) and of omission (not doing what we should). We must continually come to the Lord to ask for forgiveness. "If we confess our sins, He is faithful and righteous to forgive us our sins and to cleanse us from all unrighteousness" (1 John 1:9). In this way, we maintain a pure heart.

8. In what areas do you struggle to maintain a pure heart?

"Blessed are the pure in heart, for they shall see God" (Matthew 5:8). During our pilgrim's sojourn, we see the Lord through the eye of faith while we eagerly anticipate that time when faith will become sight. "For now we see in a mirror dimly, but then face to face; now I know in part, but then I will know fully just as I also have been fully known" (1 Corinthians 13:12).

Ceremony and tradition were the core values of the Pharisee's teaching. Jesus said, "This people honors Me with their lips, but their heart is far away from Me. But in vain do they worship Me, teaching as doctrines the precepts of men" (Matthew 15:8-9). In total contrast to their outward religious rituals and superficial belief system, Jesus speaks of the innermost part of a person being in right relationship with God. Writing about the difference in tradition and what Jesus is teaching, Smith writes, "The Beatitudes countered the rabbinic teaching of Jesus' day. Jesus used words and phrases and expressions similar to well-known rabbinic quotations, but in each case he turned them upside down." [12] His radical words disrupted the status quo, pitting Him against the Jewish leaders and ushering in a new way of living, one which invades the world with the Kingdom of God.

MATTHEW 5:9

Read Matthew 5:9.

1. Look up the word *peacemaker* in a dictionary and write the definition.

In this seventh beatitude, Jesus uses a compound word that is not found anywhere else in the New Testament when He speaks of peacemakers. The Greek word for *peace* has the idea of quietness and harmony. Rick Ezell comments on the second part of the compound word, "The word *make* in the term "peacemakers" comes from the Greek verb that means "to do" or "to make." It is a word bursting with energy. It mandates action and initiative." [13] Joined together, the word *peacemaker* describes one who actively pursues peace. Every believer is expected to be a peacemaker in the church and in the community at large.

Peace is not the same as appeasement. It is not the absence of conflict or war. Dr. Rogers coined a working definition of the word peace:

Peace is a right relationship with God that leads to a right relationship with self and guides us in a right relationship with other people. That's what peace is. It is a sense of wellbeing. And literally, peace is the result and fruit of righteousness. [14]

Righteousness and peace are irrevocably linked. Psalm 85:10 says, "Lovingkindness and truth have met together; righteousness and peace have kissed each other." Those outside a personal relationship with Christ do not know the Prince of Peace. Therefore, they cannot experience His peace.

MacArthur notes how God has woven the thread of peace throughout the Bible, from Genesis to Revelation:

Scripture contains four hundred direct references to peace, and many more indirect ones. The Bible opens with peace in the Garden of Eden and closes with peace in eternity. The spiritual history of mankind can be charted based on the theme of peace. Although the peace on earth in the garden was interrupted when man sinned, at the cross Jesus Christ made peace a reality again, and He becomes the peace of all who place their faith in Him. Peace can now reign in the hearts of those who are His. Someday He will come as Prince of Peace and establish a worldwide Kingdom of peace, which will eventuate in ultimate peace, the eternal age of peace. [15]

Sin is the enemy of peace. Sin separates men from God and causes disharmony and enmity with Him. "'There is no peace for the wicked,' says the Lord" (Isaiah 48:22). Cut off from peace with God, every relationship is marred by unrest, conflict, and war. The resulting turmoil is exploited by Satan and his spiritual forces to wreak havoc on every level. At this present time, the enemy of peace rules the world, and "the whole world lies in the power of the evil one" (1 John 5:19).

2. Read Ephesians 2:1-3. How are those outside a personal relationship with Christ characterized?

Christ is God's remedy for man's ruin. He became the mediator between God and man (1 Timothy 2:5), the only way whereby sinful man can be reconciled with Holy God. Paul writes, "For it was the Father's good pleasure for all the fullness to dwell in Him, and through Him to reconcile all things to Himself, having made peace through the blood of His cross" (Colossians 1:19-20).

Warren Wiersbe adds great insight:

> Our God is the God of peace, and our Savior is the Prince of Peace. The Holy Spirit is the Spirit of peace, for it is He who applies and supplies the peace of God in our lives. "But the fruit of the Spirit is love, joy, peace" (Galatians 5:22). The source of peace is God; there is no other source. If you and I are going to be peacemakers, we must know God and draw upon His supply of grace. [16]

Peacemaking is divine work, being rooted in God who is the Author of peace and reconciliation. As those who are "called sons [and daughters] of God" (Matthew 5:9), we are to be engaged in introducing those outside a personal relationship to Christ to our King.

3. Read 2 Corinthians 5:17-20. How does Paul describe believers?

4. What is our assignment?

5. What are some ways we actively engage in being His ambassadors?

God has chosen us to be vessels through whom He works to draw unbelievers to the saving knowledge of Christ. The work of salvation is ultimately dependent on His Word and His Spirit, but He desires to use us as His representatives to a lost and dying world.

6. Read Matthew 10:34-39. These verses seem to contradict the seventh beatitude. What does Jesus say?

John Stott sheds light on this passage that seems a bit confusing at first glance:

> And what He meant by this was that conflict would be the inevitable result of His coming, even in one's own family, and that, if we are to be worthy of Him, we must love Him best and put Him first, above even our nearest and dearest relative (Matthew 10:37). It is clear beyond question throughout the teaching of Jesus and His apostles, however, that we should never ourselves seek conflict or be responsible for it. On the contrary, we are called to peace (1 Corinthians 7:15), we are actively to 'pursue' peace (1 Peter 3:11), we are to 'strive for peace with all men' (Hebrews 12:14), and so far as it depends on us, we are to 'live peaceably with all' (Romans 12:18). [17]

Truth divides. Truth reveals. When believers adhere to God's holy standard of righteousness in the midst of a world which loves wickedness, there is the potential for conflict. When we live by Kingdom principles, there are times when we will be at odds with this world, but we can be encouraged by Jesus' words, "Take courage; I have overcome the world" (John 16:33).

MATTHEW 5:10-11

Read Matthew 5:10-11.

1. Write a paraphrase of the eighth beatitude.

2. Imagine that you are hearing the final beatitude for the first time. What thoughts would probably have gone across your mind?

The tone of The Beatitudes takes an abrupt turn when Jesus changes the subject from peacemaking to persecution. Up until this point, blessedness is the result of godly character development and yields a great reward. Now Jesus approaches the subject of persecution for His name's sake.

The word *persecution* in the Greek language means "to put to flight, drive away" or "to pursue." [18] Paul writes in 2 Timothy 3:12, "Indeed, all who desire to live godly in Christ Jesus will be persecuted." The unbelieving world system is set against God and His Christ.

In an article published in *Christianity Today,* Sunday Bobai Agang writes on present-day persecution, "Jesus wants our idea of suffering and pain to be transformed to such an extent that we begin to see it as a positive way of life. Our view of happiness as the absence of suffering, sorrow, and pain must give way to Christ's perspective." [19] Rather than being astonished at the world's reaction to the gospel and its hatred of God's people, we are to expect it. Our faith is demonstrated when we courageously remain faithful for righteousness' sake amid opposition.

Persecution for Christ's sake is a token of genuineness, a certificate of Christian authenticity. It is the result of Kingdom living, which entails pursuing righteousness for the name of Christ. We are called "to be blameless and innocent, children of God above reproach in the midst of a crooked and perverse generation, among whom you appear as lights in the world, holding fast the word of life" (Philippians 2:15-16). When the practical outworking of our faith matures to the point that we are intentionally endeavoring to live according to Kingdom principles, those who do not share the reality of relationship we have will begin to take notice and persecution will result.

The unbelieving world's reaction to the disruptive message of the gospel can range from mild irritation to full-blown aggression. Jesus said, "You will be hated by all because of My name" (Matthew 10:22). What should we do when reviled because of Jesus? As Jesus goes on to say, "Rejoice and be glad, for your reward in Heaven is great; for in the same way they persecuted the prophets who were before you" (Matthew 5:12). Let's take a look at God's first prophet.

3. Abel is the first one to forfeit his life because of persecution. Read the account of Cain and Abel in Genesis 4:1-11. What is God's response to Abel's offering?

4. Why does God reject Cain's offering?

5. Cain becomes angry with the Lord and with his brother. What does the Lord say to Cain?

Cain failed in his offering to God and violated the biblical principle of blood atonement. In an attempt to win God's favor by his own good works, "Cain brought an offering to the Lord of the fruit of the ground" (Genesis 4:3). We can only come to God on the basis of blood atonement. Hebrews 9:22 says, "Without shedding of blood there is no forgiveness." God instituted the sacrificial system when He "made garments of skin for Adam and his wife, and clothed them" (Genesis 3:21). He killed an innocent animal to make a covering for their sin, an act of grace that prefigured Calvary. We can be assured that Adam and Eve had taught their sons about sin, judgment, imputed righteousness, and blood atonement. Cain chose the way of good works; Abel offered a blood sacrifice, pointing forward to the atoning sacrifice of the Lamb of God.

God called Cain to repentance. Cain was guilty of self-righteousness, as evidenced by his offering which was produced by the sweat of his brow and the works of his hands. He was guilty of self-indulgence, as evidenced by his misdirected anger. But Cain would not repent. In anger, he rose up and killed his brother. Jesus referred to Abel as a prophet who was killed for his faith (Luke 11:49-51). "By faith Abel offered to God a better sacrifice than Cain, through which he obtained the testimony that he was righteous" (Hebrews 11:4).

6. Read 1 John 3:11-13. How are the brothers described?

Cain

Abel

Abel was the first martyr. Many others have followed him. Our faith in Jesus Christ does not protect us from suffering or pain. On the contrary, Scripture assures us that persecution is part and parcel of the Christian life. Persecution puts us in good company. The Old Testament prophets suffered for the cause of Christ. The early church knew little else. The apostles were beaten and threatened by the Sanhedrin. Yet, the Bible says, "they went on their way from the presence of the Council, rejoicing that they had been considered worthy to suffer shame for His name" (Acts 5:41). The distinction of being despised and rejected, slandered and persecuted, is as much a benchmark of Christian discipleship as are the other Kingdom attitudes taught in the Sermon on the Mount. Agang goes on to say,

> Our natural instinct is to avoid pain, yet when Jesus foretold His crucifixion, He linked His suffering directly to our discipleship: "The Son of Man must suffer many things…and He must be killed and on the third day be raised to life…Whoever wants to be My disciple must deny themselves and take up their cross daily and follow Me" (Luke 9:22-23). [20]

Jesus said, "If the world hates you, you know that it has hated Me before it hated you. If you were of the world, the world would love its own; but because you are not of the world, but I chose you out of the world, because of this the world hates you" (John 15:18-19). While we are not currently experiencing widespread persecution for our faith in the United States, we are aware many of our brothers and sisters in Christ are living under horrible threats because of their faith. The 2020 World Watch List from Open Doors reports staggering statistics of Christian persecution, "Around the world, more than 260 million Christians live in places where they experience high levels of persecution, just for following Jesus. That's 1 in 8 believers, worldwide." [21]

God's Kingdom ways are so radically different than the ways the world extols. Stott describes this topsy-turvy manner of living,

God exalts the humble and abases the proud, calls the first last and the last first, ascribes greatness to the servant, sends the rich away empty-handed and declares the meek to be His heirs. The culture of the world and the counter-culture of Christ are at loggerheads with each other. In brief, Jesus congratulates those whom the world most pities, and calls the world's rejects "blessed." [22]

As we give attention to The Beatitudes and adopt the manner of life described in the Sermon on the Mount, we find ourselves at increasing odds with the world but at peace with the Savior. Our lives begin to mirror our Lord, and we leave His imprint on our sphere of influence.

Stott summarizes The Beatitudes:

The Beatitudes paint a comprehensive portrait of a Christian disciple. We see him first alone on his knees before God, acknowledging his spiritual poverty and mourning over it. This makes him meek or gentle in all his relationships, since honesty compels him to allow others to think of him what before God he confesses to be. Yet he is far from acquiescing to his sinfulness, for he hungers and thirsts after righteousness, longing to grow in grace and in goodness.

We see him next with others, out in the human community. His relationship with God does not cause him to withdraw from society, nor is he insulated from the world's pain. On the contrary, he is in the thick of it, showing mercy to those battered by adversity and sin. He is transparently sincere in all his dealings and seeks to play a constructive role as a peacemaker. Yet he is not thanked for his efforts, but rather opposed, slandered, insulted and persecuted on account of the righteousness for which he stands and the Christ with whom he is identified.

Such is the man or women who is 'blessed', that is, who has the approval of God and finds self-fulfilment as a human being. [23]

The Beatitudes present to us, as Christ followers, a new standard of living. Not one governed by rules and ritual; that's legalism. And not one that boasts that grace allows us to live anyway we choose; that's license. Jesus presents to us a way of living based on His Word and enabled by His Spirit; that's liberty.

KINGDOM EXERCISE

After walking with the Lord for nearly 40 years and being a serious student of the Word for the majority of that time, I can truly say, much to my amazement, "The more I learn, the less I know!" God's Word is inexhaustible. Concerning the Word of God, Dr. Rogers said,

> It's so majestically deep that scholars could swim and never touch the bottom. Yet so wonderfully shallow that a little child could come and get a drink of water without fear of drowning. That is God's precious, holy Word. The Word of God. Know it. Believe it. It is True. [24]

Psalm 19:7 says, "The law of the Lord is perfect, restoring the soul; the testimony of the Lord is sure, making wise the simple." In pain, the Word is our comfort. In joy, the Word is our songbook. In crisis, the Word is our peace. In confusion, the Word is our clarity. In life, the Word is our guide.

Using powerful imagery and poetic phrases, Billy Sunday, a powerful evangelist and revivalist of the early 1900s, penned this soaring treatise in honor of the Word of God and tucked it into his Bible:

> Twenty-nine years ago, with the Holy Spirit as my Guide, I entered at the portico of Genesis, walked down the corridor of the Old Testament art galleries, with pictures of Noah, Abraham, Moses, Joseph, Isaac, Jacob, and David hung on the wall. I passed into the music room of the Psalms where the Spirit sweeps the keyboard of nature until it seems that every reed and pipe in God's great organ responds to the harp of David, the sweet singer of Israel.

> I entered the chamber of Ecclesiastes, where the voice of the preacher is heard, and into the conservatory of Sharon and the lily of the valley where sweet spices filled and perfumed my life.

> I entered the business office of Proverbs and on into the observatory of the prophets where I saw telescopes of various sizes pointing to far off events, concentrating on the bright and morning Star which was to rise above the moonlit hills of Judea for our salvation and redemption.

> I entered the audience room of the King of Kings, catching a vision written by Matthew, Mark, Luke, and John. Thence into the correspondence room with Paul, Peter, James, and John writing their Epistles.

I stepped into the throne room of Revelation where tower the glittering peaks, where sits the King of Kings upon His throne of glory with the hearing of nations in His hand, and I cried out:

> All hail the power of Jesus' name!
>
> Let angels prostrate fall;
>
> Bring forth the royal diadem
>
> And crown Him Lord of all. [25]

For the Christian, the Word of God is our external control while the indwelling Spirit of God is our internal control. Careful attention to the study of the Word is a necessary component for living the abundant life Christ has promised. Obedience to the Word and dependence on the Spirit are required as well. Otherwise we are guilty of operating in the energy of the flesh, conforming our behavior to external rules by sheer willpower, and not operating in the supernatural realm of the Holy Spirit. Such living is sure to bring frustration and disillusionment.

THE DISCIPLINE OF GUIDANCE

The secret to spiritual maturity is abiding in Jesus. Jesus said, "Abide in Me, and I in you. As the branch cannot bear fruit of itself unless it abides in the Vine, so neither can you unless you abide in Me. I am the vine, you are the branches; he who abides in Me and I in him, he bears much fruit, for apart from Me you can do nothing" (John 15:4-5).

John Phillips shares this insight regarding the unique relationship between the Vine and the branches:

> This illustration depicts the need for the believer individually and for the local church to be linked with Christ, and for Christ to express His life through them. The Lord uses the word *abide* to convey the idea of remaining close to one another, in intimate connection. The believer takes up his abode in Christ; Christ takes up His abode in the believer. The life of Christ becomes the life of the believer, supplying grace and power for living the "Christ life" on earth. The life of the believer becomes the life through which the Lord expresses His life today in a world of time and sense. [26]

Beginning the day reading the Word and praying allows us to walk through the day with a God-consciousness. Our minds are renewed by the Word. Our spirits become pliable as our wills become surrendered. We tune our hearts to the still small voice of the Holy Spirit. The end result of abiding in the True Vine is fruitfulness.

Abiding in Christ requires careful attention to the study of the Word. As the branch draws sustenance from the vine, God's Word begins to flow through us. His truth becomes interwoven into our innermost being. Our heart becomes sensitive. Our will becomes surrendered. Our spirit becomes serene.

THE EXERCISE

This activity is designed to help you fine tune your time with the Lord in order to increase your sensitivity to His guidance throughout the day.

Set aside one hour to spend in the Word and prayer this week for the purpose of seeking God's guidance in a particular area(s). Talk with God as a friend talks to a friend. Read His Word as guidance and instruction directed to you.

REFLECTION QUESTIONS

1. In what area(s) did you seek the Lord for guidance?

2. How did God speak to you through His Word?

3. How will you follow God's guidance and direction?

FOR THE CHRISTIAN, THE WORD OF GOD IS OUR EXTERNAL CONTROL WHILE THE INDWELLING SPIRIT OF GOD IS OUR INTERNAL CONTROL.

Our continual exposure to the Word of God focuses our thoughts on the Lord, making us sensitive to His guidance. Obedience to the Word and dependence on the Spirit produces spiritual growth and fruitfulness which result in Kingdom living and blessings untold!

WEEK THREE
KINGDOM DWELLERS
MATTHEW 5:13-20

*Let your light shine before men in such a way that they may see your good
works, and glorify your Father who is in Heaven.*
MATTHEW 5:16

*Jesus' good news then, was that the Kingdom of God had come, and
that He, Jesus, was its herald and expounder to men. More than that,
in some special, mysterious way, He was the Kingdom.* [1]
~MALCOLM MUGGERIDGE

When Jesus came to earth, He came to announce the Kingdom of God. Where is this Kingdom? It is present wherever what God wants done is done. Completely. Totally. Without reserve. All around us. Now. The Kingdom of God is the reign of God.

As followers of Christ, we are to be Kingdom Dwellers. The next section in the Sermon on the Mount, Matthew 5:13-20, gives us a picture of the impact our lives are to have on this fallen world as we embrace the values of the Kingdom of God. What is our function as Kingdom Dwellers? In a word, influence. We are God's only witnesses on the earth. Remember the adage, "You may be the only Bible some person may read"? If someone is reading your life, would it point directly to Him?

REMEMBER THE ADAGE, "YOU MAY BE THE ONLY BIBLE SOME PERSON MAY READ"? IF SOMEONE IS READING YOUR LIFE, WOULD IT POINT DIRECTLY TO HIM?

The Beatitudes portray the inner character of those who belong to the Kingdom of God. These eight norms of the Kingdom are not just reserved for interactions with fellow believers. To the contrary, where these attitudes exist, their accompanying activity is always visible. We are to live them out everywhere we go. Kent Hughes notes that The Beatitudes "are powerfully social and outward when put to work. That is why Christ crowns them with two brilliant and searching metaphors (salt and light) that tell us how those who live The Beatitudes must relate to the world." [2] Today we will look at the first of the two metaphors, salt.

Read Matthew 5:13.

Salt is a preservative. It not only purifies, but it also adds flavor. In the Roman world, salt was a valued commodity. In fact, Roman soldiers were paid with salt rations and would rebel if their salt allowances were reduced. As a result, salt was synonymous with wages. The English word, "salary", is derived from the Latin word for salt, "salarium", a reminder of the value of salt during the time Jesus lived. [3]

As Jesus employs the metaphor of salt, He is pointing out the penetrating power of the gospel in the life of a believer, giving His disciples motivation to live the salty life of The Beatitudes. Live this way so that others can taste it. Our lives are to have a distinct flavor; we must be diligent to keep the purity of the gospel from being tainted or compromised by the world. When we compromise the Word of God, we become salt that has lost its flavor and consequently lose the ability to preserve and penetrate culture. When that happens, as the old saying goes, "We are not worth our salt!" We are good for nothing!

As disciples of Christ, we are new creations with a new citizenship. We are now primarily citizens of Heaven and are to live as Christ's ambassadors on earth. In the Sermon on the Mount, Jesus tells us how to live as salt in a place that is not our true home. One commentary provides this insight:

> Jesus is apparently thinking of the function of salt as a preservative, as the enemy of decay, and as giving taste to food. What is good in society His followers keep wholesome. What is corrupt they oppose; they penetrate society for good and act as a kind of moral antiseptic. [4]

1. Take a few moments and think back to the quarantine during COVID-19.

   a. What did you use to purify or cleanse your hands and surfaces that might have been contaminated by the virus?

   b. How careful were you? To what lengths did you go to prevent contamination by the virus?

Now consider how diligent we should be to not be contaminated by sin. When Jesus is talking about salt losing its saltiness, He is referring to impurities being added to the salt that contaminate it and render it useless.

2. What impurities contaminate and dilute our faith, making us impotent and useless for the Kingdom?

As Jesus is speaking to the crowd on the hillside, He is aware of the corruption that exists in their world and knows that "salt" is the only way to halt the rampant moral disintegration. D.A. Carson explains, "In the first metaphor Jesus likens His disciples to salt. Implicitly He is saying that apart from His disciples the world turns ever more rotten: Christians have the effect of delaying moral and spiritual putrefactions." [5]

3. Be honest about the things in your life that pull you away from the gospel and its priority in your life. Write down the one you struggle with the most.

Just like tasteless salt, Christians "who fail to arrest corruption become worthless as agents of change and redemption. Christianity may make its peace with the world and avoid persecution, but it is thereby rendered impotent to fulfill its divinely ordained role. It will thus ultimately be rejected even by those with whom it has sought compromise." [6]

So often, the things that vie for our attention and tempt us to compromise are the things we say to ourselves that are influenced by the world, our flesh, and the devil. Rachel Jankovic makes this truthful observation:

> The world distracts us (I am too busy…Life is too crazy…When I finish watching this…When I am done with shopping online…). The flesh is weak (I forgot…I don't like when I am behind on the reading, so I'll wait until the new year to start again…I don't feel like it…It sounds like so much work…). And the devil accuses (You are the worst Christian…How long has it been since you really read the Bible?…I can't believe you…Everyone else does this, what is wrong with you?…). [7]

4. If we do not stay on the alert, any of us can fall prey to these temptations. Do you find yourself most susceptible to the voice of the world, your flesh, or the devil?

It is so easy for us to be swayed and discouraged. I have found that in my life, the only way I can keep my focus on Christ and the things of His Kingdom is to read the Bible daily and spend time listening to Him. My consumption of His Word through reading, meditating, and memorizing renews my mind.

Feeding on God's Word also enables us to stand firm. Peer pressure and a desire to be accepted can cause us to compromise. We have all been there.

5. When we seek to fit in with the culture, how do we compromise our witness to a watching world?

Seeking to fit in, to be liked, to be anything other than a whole-hearted lover of God, will leave us empty, unsatisfied, and often times derailed in our faith. When we hear about the demise of a Christian, or the deconstruction of someone's faith, it is always because they have begun to worship themselves instead of God. One seemingly small compromise can be the very lie of self-worship that leads you into a dark pit of unbelief.

Does following Christ seem too hard? Does dying to the flesh seem too radical? Not if you want what Christ has to offer. Not if you want your life to count for eternity. "When we love the Good News, we will willingly endure the hard words. When we discard the hard words to protect our feelings, we find that we have also discarded the Good News." [8]

My prayer for us, fellow Kingdom Dweller, is that we would be salty salt. That our presence in this world would cause others to thirst after the Fountain of Living Water. As one man has said, "You are either being corrupted by the world, or you are salting it." [9] There is no in between.

Just as the world needs salt because it is corrupt, it needs light because it is dark. In this second metaphor, Jesus calls us, the Kingdom Dwellers, to be light. John MacArthur expounds on the need for both salt and light in the world:

> Whereas salt is hidden, light is obvious. Salt works secretly, while light works openly. Salt works from within, light from without. Salt is more the indirect influence of the gospel, while light is more its direct communication. Salt works primarily through our living, while light works primarily through what we teach and preach. Salt is largely negative. It can retard corruption, but it cannot change corruption into incorruption. Light is more positive. It not only reveals what is wrong and false but helps produce what is righteous and true. [10]

Read Matthew 5:14-16.

1. What does Jesus mean when He calls His followers "the light of the world"?

In a world of darkness, Christ followers are those who have been transferred from darkness into light. We are to reflect the light we have found in Jesus and radiate God's light in a world that is engulfed by darkness. Dallas Willard provides insightful commentary:

> Speaking to these common people, "the multitudes," who through Him had found blessing in the Kingdom, Jesus tells them it is they, not the "best and brightest" on the human scale, who are to make life on earth manageable as they live from the Kingdom (Matthew 5:13–16). God gives them "light"—truth, love, and power—that they might be the light for their surroundings. He makes them "salt," to cleanse, preserve, and flavor the times through which they live.

> These "little" people, without any of the character or qualifications humans insist are necessary, are the only ones who can actually make the world work. It is how things are among them that determines the character of every age and place. And God gives them a certain radiance, as one lights a lamp to shed its brilliance over everyone in the house. Just so, Jesus says to those He has touched, "Let your light glow around people in such a way that, seeing your good works, they will exalt your Father in the Heavens" (Matthew 5:16). [11]

The character of our age, as Willard puts it, is not determined by the sins of the majority. It is "how things are among [us, the Kingdom Dwellers] that determines the character of every age and place." [12]

Light must be visible in order to illuminate. By definition, darkness is "the partial or total absence of light." [13] If the world is dark, it is not because the darkness increased. It is because there are fewer lights, or the light has gone into hiding.

Think about what happened when Christ, the Light of the World, hung on the cross. From noon until 3:00 p.m., "darkness fell upon the land" (Matthew 27:45). What blocked the light? Our sin! The sins of the world were placed upon Christ. At the moment Jesus cried out, "It is finished", the veil was torn from top to bottom in the Temple, and the power of sin and darkness was broken forever (Matthew 27:51-53). This is the Good News!

As followers of Christ whose sins are forgiven and who have His Spirit living within us, we are now the light of the world. So, how are we to shine in a world of darkness so that hearts are open to hear the Good News and glorify God?

Ours is not a call to retreat, but to shine.

2. What causes us to hide our light?

One of the main fleshly responses that causes us to hide is fear:

- Fear of rejection by our neighbors, coworkers, friends
- Fear of being misunderstood
- Fear of insults and slander
- Fear of persecution

Remember what Jesus has just said about persecution in Matthew 5:11-12?

Persecution will happen. It's "when", not "if".

We don't seek persecution. We seek the Lord. We seek to walk in the light.

Why do those who "love darkness" (John 3:19) often persecute those who walk in the light? Because the light of Christ exposes their sinful deeds. But just as there were men and women drawn to the light of Christ, there will be those drawn to Christ's light in us.

3. After calling His followers the "light of the world," what does Jesus say about attempts to hide His light?

Could it be that the basket over the lamp is sin? That the things masking His light in us are our own fleshly impulses and our refusal to believe?

We have two choices — to hide or to shine. Will we build bunkers or will we become beacons? A bunker is a reinforced underground shelter, typically for use in wartime. Are we hiding in our bunkers, concealing the light of the gospel? Or are we willing to give our lives away, just as Christ did and beckon others to Him by His light shining through us? That is exactly what a beacon does. It is a "guiding or warning signal, as a light or fire, especially one in an elevated position." [14]

Do you see the difference? Jesus said we are the "light of the world." That means we are to live lives that serve as a guide for others on the path to eternity.

4. Review the contrasting mindsets below and evaluate yourself by your responses during the past 6 months.

BUNKERS	BEACONS
Scarcity mindset	Abundance mindset
The Kingdom of God awaits. 1. We wait passively for Jesus to return and rescue us from the darkness. 2. We forget that the Kingdom is right now, not just eternal.	The Kingdom of God is available today. 1. "The eternal life that begins with confidence in Jesus is a life in His present Kingdom, now on earth and available to all. So the message of and about Him is specifically a gospel for our life now, not just for dying. It is about living now as His apprentice in Kingdom living, not just as a consumer of His merits." [15]
"Us versus Them" Mentality 1. We worry so much about being contaminated by the world that we share our light only with those who think like us - in our Christian spaces.	"Us with Them" Mentality 1. We are called to Immanuel living, God with us right where we are. 2. "For God did not send His Son into the world to condemn the world, but in order that the world might be saved through Him" (John 3:17, ESV).
Hide We have found our home; now we must protect it.	Shine We have found our home, and we are lighting the way so that others can join us.

For which Kingdom are you living? Are you trying to protect your life here or are you focusing on your life in Christ and what lies before us? Don't be short-sighted. Live to light the path for yourself and others. Just as the lampstand in the Temple lit the area just in front of it, God will give us enough light for each new day. God has woven these Kingdom principles throughout Scripture and within our hearts.

The Kingdom is here and not yet. While we wait, we remember:

1. Darkness cannot overcome the light – "In Him was life, and the life was the Light of men. The Light shines in the darkness, and the darkness did not comprehend it" (John 1:4-5).

2. We have the armor of light, no bunker needed – "The night is almost gone, and the day is near. Therefore, let us lay aside the deeds of darkness and put on the armor of light" (Romans 13:12).

Do you have a Kingdom mindset? If not, what needs to change?

5. Read Philippians 2:14-16a. Write out your own paraphrase of these verses.

Do you see how closely linked gratitude, goodness, light, and life are? Our good works are to shine before men and bring glory to God. That means we do not do good works for personal recognition but to reflect on our Father.

6. What "good works" are you involved in that bring praise to the Father?

7. As lights in the world, we are to shine on all those around us. How are you currently sharing the light of the gospel?

MATTHEW 5:14-16

Begin today by reading Matthew 5:14-16 once again.

As we saw yesterday, the purpose of light is to dispel darkness. Jesus has called us to be light. How do we shine? Our good works cause the light to shine. But those good works are not to bring attention to us, they are to glorify the Father. If what we do does not point to the Father, there is something amiss with the way our light is shining.

The Kingdom is the visible expression of God's goodness in our world. God's light and life flow through love. His love is the light.

When Jesus is asked by a lawyer what the greatest command is, He replies: "You shall love the Lord your God with all your heart, and with all your soul, and with all your strength, and with all our mind; and your neighbor as yourself" (Luke 10:27).

We shine when we love God. And when we love our neighbor. Let's consider both of these.

First, how do we love God?

Jesus makes it clear. We are to love the Lord with our all! Is Christ your all? Are you able to join with Paul and say, "For to me, to live is Christ and to die is gain" (Philippians 1:21)?

How would you fill in this blank? For me to live is_____. You will know how to fill in that blank by what occupies your thoughts and by how you spend your time and money.

1. Reflect over the last year of your life and then truthfully fill in the blank. For me to live is_____.

Loving the Lord with our whole being leads to a radical reconstruction of the heart. C.S. Lewis writes about loving God with everything we are from God's perspective:

> Give me all of you!!! I don't want so much of your time, so much of your talents and money, and so much of your work. I want YOU!!! ALL OF YOU!! I have not come to torment or frustrate the natural man or woman, but to KILL IT! No half measures will do. I don't want to only prune a branch here and a branch there; rather I want the whole tree out! Hand it over to Me, the whole outfit, all of your desires, all of your wants and wishes and dreams. Turn them ALL over to Me, give yourself to Me, and I will make of you a new self – in My image. Give Me yourself and in exchange I will give you Myself. My will, shall become your will. My heart shall become your heart. [16]

Moses longed to see God's glory. God granted his request (Exodus 33:18-19) and allowed all of His "goodness" to pass before Him. After spending 40 days and 40 nights experiencing the unveiled glory of God, he came down from the mountain glowing. God's goodness is His glory. When His goodness is manifest in our lives it will cause us to shine in such a way that others will notice.

God's goodness changes us from the inside out. As you surrender to His great love, His love will begin to flow through you. John 3:16 tells us "For God so loved the world that He gave." We are never more loving or more like God than when we are giving. Are you beginning to get the picture? Loving, giving, serving, and gratitude are all a reflection of God's goodness. Just as Moses reflected His glory from being in His manifest presence, we too will shine with the goodness (glory) of God as we reflect Him to a darkened world.

As Paul writes, "for you were formerly darkness, but now you are Light in the Lord; walk as children of Light (for the fruit of the Light *consists* in all goodness and righteousness and truth)" (Ephesians 5:8-9). The fruit of Light is the character of Christ reflected in our lives. That is what being a disciple is all about – being like Christ.

And like Moses, all those who have been in God's Presence shine!

A second way we shine is by loving our neighbor. How do we love our neighbor? As Luke 10:27 tells us, we love them the way we love ourselves. If you do not love yourself, you will not be able to truly love your neighbor, no matter how hard you try.

Dear friend, it is time to accept yourself as God created you for His purposes. If I could, I would look you right in the eye as I cup your precious face and declare over you all that God says about you! You were created in the very image of God, and He delights in you. In fact, He sings over you! You have infinite worth and purpose. Every spiritual blessing is yours in Christ. And all of the promises of God are for you! Start being grateful and celebrating Him!

That doesn't mean that we don't have work to do. When we look intently into the perfect law of God (James 1:22-27), we begin to see ourselves as we really are. God reveals those things that are darkening His image in us and preventing us from experiencing all that Christ died to purchase for us. And our flesh will put up a fight – against giving up old ways of thinking: protecting, comparing, judging…in the place of thanksgiving, giving, and celebrating.

Listen to the sound of the contrasting words in the previous paragraph. Who would choose the ways of the flesh over the ways of the Spirit? And yet, we do just that when we choose to coddle our flesh instead of crucifying it (Galatians 2:20). It sounds just like the descriptions of Wisdom and Folly in the Book of Proverbs. Who in their right mind chooses the path that leads to death? Sinners, that is who. Those who have not had their spiritual eyes and ears opened to all that God has prepared for those who love Him!

Only after loving the Lord with your whole being, and accepting and loving yourself, will you be able to really love your neighbor.

2. What kinds of things do you do for yourself?

These are the very things you are to do for your neighbor. Did you know…

> …that those who perform five acts of giving over six weeks are happier than those who don't, that when you give, you get reduced stress hormone levels, lowered blood pressure, and increased endorphins, and that acts of kindness reduce anxiety and strengthen the immune system? Five random acts of kindness in a week can increase happiness for up to three months later. [17]

Loving God and loving your neighbor are good for your health!

Who is our neighbor? Who are we to love as we love ourselves? The lawyer Jesus is talking to in Luke 10 has this question too. Jesus responds with the Parable of the Good Samaritan that we looked at in our study last week.

Look back at Luke 10:30-37.

3. What moves the heart of the Samaritan? (v. 33)

4. Look up the word "compassion" in a concordance. Biblestudytools.com and biblehub.com are two free online concordances you can use. Are you amazed by how many entries there are? In the NASB, there are 131! Write out two Old Testament verses about God showing compassion and two New Testament verses about Jesus showing compassion.

The Samaritan demonstrates love with both compassion and generosity.

5. Read 2 Corinthians 9:6-8. Make a list of the superlatives Paul uses in describing what the Lord will provide for those who are generous.

The Samaritan demonstrates love to someone who was ignored by others, even religious leaders.

If we walk in the flesh, we can easily begin to feel superior over those who are poor, uneducated, or disabled in any way. Think back to The Beatitudes. Who does Jesus say is blessed?

6. Read Matthew 9:35-36. What does Jesus feel for the people He spends time with?

Isaiah 58:7-9 in *The Message* reads,

> What I'm interested in seeing you do is: sharing your food with the hungry, inviting the homeless poor into your homes, putting clothes on the shivering ill-clad, being available to your own families. Do this and the lights will turn on, and your lives will turn around at once. Your righteousness will pave your way. The God of glory will secure your passage. Then when you pray, God will answer. You'll call out for help and I'll say, "Here I am."

7. In this Old Testament passage, what acts of love cause the lights to turn on?

These good deeds will be noticed by God. They are evidence of a heart like His. This is what He values and what He promises to bless.

You don't have to be wealthy to be generous with your time, talents, creativity, and material goods. It can be something as simple as sending an encouraging note or giving a blessing with spoken word. We DO NOT live from a scarcity mindset – we live from abundance (John 10:10b). Remember, Kingdom Dwellers, we do not hide in bunkers; we are beacons!

On the Mount of Transfiguration, when His glory is revealed, Jesus is gleaming (Matthew 17:2)! We know that He is the Light of the World. Could it be that His light in us would shine brighter the more we give?

Near the end of her book *The Broken Way*, Ann Voskamp issues a two-word challenge: "live given".[18] Most of us begin our day with a plan. But when interruptions crop up, we find ourselves feeling inconvenienced. Rather than loving, it is easy to find ourselves resenting. And if we are not careful, we can begin to feel like people are "taking" from us. Too often, we "live taken" instead of "given".

8. Journal your thoughts about the power of living "given".

MATTHEW 5:17-20

As Jesus begins the Sermon on the Mount, He opens with The Beatitudes, describing the inner character of righteousness that will permeate those who are members of the Kingdom of Heaven. He follows that description with two metaphors, salt and light, explaining the way this inner righteousness will impact the world. Then in verses 17-20, Jesus summarizes the radical righteousness of the Kingdom.

Read Matthew 5:17-20.

After presenting The Beatitudes and the two metaphors, Jesus addresses those in His audience who thought He was advocating an overthrow of Old Testament Law. He gives a disclaimer which establishes His relationship to the Law. He came to fulfill the Law and the prophets. He is very clear that not one stroke of a letter will pass away without being fulfilled.

1. Make a list of some of the Old Testament Law and prophecies that Christ fulfilled. (Need one to get you started? Read Isaiah 9:2-7.)

KINGDOM LIVING IS FOCUSED ON WALKING WITH JESUS MOMENT BY MOMENT, LISTENING, AND THEN DOING WHAT HE WOULD DO IN LOVE IF HE WERE LIVING IN OUR CIRCUMSTANCE.

In verses 19-20, Jesus explains how believers are to relate to the Old Testament. He asks His listeners to picture the scribes and the Pharisees, the spiritual teachers and leaders of their day. And He says you'll have to do better than that to enter the Kingdom.

What?

Kingdom living is only possible with Jesus. On our own, we turn the Kingdom into a rigid set of "dos" and "don'ts". We focus on external compliance instead of the internal transformation that characterizes Kingdom citizens.

Kingdom living does not focus on sin management or behavior modification. Kingdom living is focused on walking with Jesus moment by moment, listening, and then doing what He would do in love if He were living in our circumstance. Such a way of life is only possible through surrender. If we are totally honest, checklists are much easier.

Jesus is about to turn their thinking inside out and upside down. He tells the crowd gathered before Him that they are the blessed ones. It is not reserved for the ones they have in mind as He speaks – the religious of the day. He says, "I am here to bring the Kingdom to you. You are the ones who bring the Kingdom to the culture that you live in. It is not a political kingdom or all those things you have in mind. It is the Kingdom of God come to earth."

Let's bring this part of His message forward into the present. To us. As we really grasp what He is saying, His message is as disruptive for us today as it was for the original crowd on the hillside. Willard writes, "We cannot behave 'on the spot' as He (Jesus) did and taught if in the rest of our time we live as everybody else does." [19] Romans 8:4 tells us that this is why the Holy Spirit has been given to us, "so that the requirement of the Law might be fulfilled in us, who do not walk according to the flesh but according to the Spirit."

2. How can you respond in the Spirit and not react in the flesh?

In Matthew 5:19, we see that we are not to loosen God's Word or add to it. We are simply to obey it and teach it – "So if you ignore the least commandment and teach others to do the same, you will be called the least in the Kingdom of Heaven. But anyone who obeys God's laws and teaches them will be called great in the Kingdom of Heaven."

3. What is an example of a way that we have loosened God's Word in our day?

4. What is an example of a way we have added to God's Word?

Legalism is just as deadly as liberalism. Both are rampant in our day. If you don't believe me, check out some of the social media wars between various groups of "Christians". All while a lost world looks and then turns away.

Jesus says, "But I warn you—unless your righteousness is better than the righteousness of the teachers of religious law and the Pharisees, you will never enter the Kingdom of Heaven!" (Matthew 5:20, NLT). As the crowd hangs on His every Word, a greater righteousness than the scribes and Pharisees would have seemed impossible. As we will see next week, Christ is going to take them to the heart of the matter – their own hearts.

Would you pause for a moment and reflect back over what we have studied for the last four days? Ask the Lord to open your eyes to any area of your life where your heart has been led astray. Any area where you have been deceived or have compromised the Word of God. Pray as you reflect. His Holy Spirit is your teacher. He will guide you, and He will reveal Himself and your heart as you seek Him.

Now repent of any area of compromise. Ask Him to give you eyes to see and ears to hear as we seek to live in His Kingdom here on earth.

KINGDOM EXERCISE

As Kingdom Dwellers, we are salt and light and should impact culture as we allow the Spirit of God to guide us and use us to light the darkness and prevent decay.

Reflect back on Isaiah 58:7-9 from Day Three. The scripture that corresponds to Isaiah 58 in the New Testament is Matthew 25:31-46.

Are you serving the least of these?

THE DISCIPLINE OF SERVICE

When Jesus exploded into the world, He came to serve, not to be served. He didn't just flip the established pecking order of the day; He abolished it (Matthew 20:25-28). Remember when He washed the feet of His disciples? He picked up His towel and voluntarily took on the lowest of duties. He set an example for us to follow. But to be clear, service is not about us. It is not an act we do to feel better about ourselves. It is not an occasion to pat ourselves on the back. Service is not about human effort. It is a discipline that requires us to go beyond ourselves.

True service flows from our relationship with God.

"For God so loved the world that He gave His only begotten Son that whoever believes in Him should not perish but have everlasting life" (John 3:16). God gave the greatest gift ever given, that we might be like Him. To be like Him is to be a giver.

If we choose to "live given", we will "be the gift." I am convinced that as we grow in our love for Christ and He becomes preeminent in our lives, we will love our neighbor. We will desire to serve and will not be satisfied with the status quo. It is then that we get in on what Paul wrote about to the Corinthians, "always having all sufficiency in everything, you may have an abundance for every good deed" (2 Corinthians 9:8).

We will sow generously and reap generously – what we reap is never for us to hoard, but to give away. Do you see it? Is the Lord opening your eyes? His love is the light! Donald Whitney writes, "There is no better fuel for service that burns longer and provides more energy than love." [20]

It is as we love our neighbors that we will serve our neighbors. Then our "light will shine before men in such a way that they will see our good works and glorify our Father who is in Heaven" (Matthew 5:16).

THE EXERCISE

This week, purposely engage in loving your neighbor by serving them as defined in Isaiah 58 and Matthew 25. It can be anything from a small act of love to a full day of service. The only requirement is that you in some way care for the needs of others.

REFLECTION QUESTIONS

1. How did you serve this week?

2. Describe the way you felt as you served.

Service produces within us the virtue of humility. There is nothing that disciplines the desires of the flesh the way service does. When we serve, we die to our flesh. And when we crucify the flesh, we crucify our pride and arrogance. This is Kingdom living.

3. What are some ways that serving others helps us die to our flesh?

4. What did you learn by serving someone this week?

Would you engage in a lifestyle of service by praying daily, "Lord Jesus, as it would please You, bring me someone today whom I can serve"?

WEEK FOUR
KINGDOM DISORIENTATION – PART ONE
——•—•—— MATTHEW 5:21-30 ——•—•——

You have heard that the ancients were told...But I say to you...
MATTHEW 5:21-22

The eternal life...is a life in His Present Kingdom,
now on earth and available to all...it is about living now
as His apprentice in Kingdom living. [1]
~DALLAS WILLARD

Several years ago, my husband accepted a call to a new church, a move that meant that we would be relocating to a different state. Knowing that it could possibly take a few months for our home to sell, the church graciously offered to pay the rent on a home for us. Because all of this happened pretty quickly, and I was wrapping up my own job responsibilities before we moved, we did not have time to make a trip to scout out a rental home. So we were pleased and excited when someone from the church called to say that a church member had the perfect rental home for us. The description of the home sounded like it would be a wonderful place for our family in our transition. Over the phone, we made arrangements to rent it.

When the day arrived, we loaded all of the belongings we could possibly fit into our two vehicles, being careful to leave enough room to squeeze in our two boys, one slightly temperamental dog, and a beta fish. When we pulled out of the driveway from what had been our home for six years, we could hardly contain our excitement about our future. The closer we got to our new home, the more our anticipation grew.

As we pulled up to what was about to be our new home, it looked just like the description we had been given. Red brick with white shutters and a welcoming front porch. Although it might not have exactly been my dream home, it would certainly be a good place for us to land for a while. The couple who owned the rental home were out of town, so they left the house key with a neighbor. My husband and our youngest son, Matthew, went to retrieve the key. In short order, Matthew, who was eight at the time, ran back with the key in his hand and asked if he could be the one to open the door to our new home. With a beta fish in one hand and a drugged dog (this pup suffered from motion sickness, so car trips were always difficult) in the other hand, I nodded, and up the stairs he bounded. Almost simultaneously, he inserted the key, pushed open the door, and darted inside. Immediately, he bolted back out, doubled over, and said, "I'm going to be sick!"

While I went to see what was wrong with him, his dad and his older brother went to check out the house for themselves. Their exit from the house was almost as fast. Jonathan, in his typical matter of fact manner pronounced, "Mom, something is dead in there." I am sure the look on my face registered some combination of shock, alarm, and denial. When I asked my husband if something was really dead inside the house, he replied, "Well, it smells like it." I thought to myself, "It can't be that bad." Bravely, I stuck my head inside the front door and to my dismay, it was that bad!

Apparently, between the time the people who owned the house had last been inside and the time we arrived, something had crawled up into the attic and died. And since it was August, the air was infused with the stench of death. We called an exterminator, confident that he could find the root of the issue. And he did, but then he delivered staggering news. It was unlikely that the smell would go away. Apparently, the combination of heat and putrid smell had permanently stained the air inside the house.

To this day, when I think about the exterminator's words, I am reminded of Jesus' condemnation of the scribes and Pharisees:

> Woe to you, scribes and Pharisees, hypocrites! For you are like whitewashed tombs which on the outside appear beautiful, but inside they are full of dead men's bones and all uncleanness. So you, too, outwardly appear righteous to men, but inwardly you are full of hypocrisy and lawlessness (Matthew 23:27-28).

Jesus' critique of these Jewish leaders in Matthew 23 provides an expanded commentary on His startling words we looked at last week, "For I say to you that unless your righteousness surpasses that of the scribes and Pharisees, you will not enter the Kingdom of Heaven" (Matthew 5:20). As we continue our study, we will see that statement is the linchpin for the rest of Jesus' message in the Sermon on the Mount. As you will recall from last week, the "righteousness" Jesus is talking about is an internal rightness, a heart righteousness, a juxtaposition from the eternal appearances that were lauded by the religious leaders of Jesus' day.

The beauty of the Kingdom life that Jesus is teaching in His sermon is that we can become different from the inside out. And that is the exact solution the exterminator advised for our rental house. The cure for our rancid air problem was to replace the old air with completely new air, a process that took a couple of days, but in the end, the air in our house was transformed into clean, pure air. Air that smelled like life instead of death.

A word of caution here. As we progress in our understanding of Kingdom living in the present, we need to be careful not to truncate its meaning to a substitution of one set of activities for another. As as reminder, living in the Kingdom is not behavior modification. It is not an addition to our salvation. Rather, it is the whole point of the gospel. As James Smith challenges, "And what is the point of this religion? To get us into Heaven? No, to get Heaven into us." [2] Just like the air in our rental house, Kingdom living requires a total transformation. Out with the old and in with the new.

In Matthew 5:21-30, Jesus will expose the distance between external appearances and internal transformation. And He will do so by revealing the hypocrisy of attempting to cover up a putrid heart with outward obedience to the law.

MATTHEW 5:21-22

The invitation of the Sermon on the Mount is to step into the Kingdom and live there. It is an invitation that we must choose to accept. Every single day.

The blessed and good Kingdom life in the present will be ours as we determine to live in the Kingdom as Jesus did. And we do that by learning from Him, by becoming His students. Dallas Willard explains that the first step is "to be His disciple, and constantly to be learning from Him how to live my life in the Kingdom of God now—my real life, the one I am actually living." [3]

Over the next two weeks, we will see that Jesus makes six comparisons between external performance and internal obedience. In each case, He calls His followers to commit ourselves not just to obeying the external requirements of the law, but also to allowing the Kingdom to govern our thoughts, our motives, and our attitudes. Today, we begin with the first of these six contrasts as Jesus teaches us about anger.

Read Matthew 5:21-22.

As Jesus' rookie disciples sat there on the hillside 2000 years ago, they had no idea what He was going to say next. They had been prepared for an orientation on this new way of life to which they had been called, perhaps looking forward to getting a better handle on the job responsibilities that went along with being a part of His inner circle. But as they listened closely, trying to grasp and assimilate exactly what Jesus was saying, it became clear that His message was more of a disorientation than an orientation. While they were still trying to wrap their minds around a righteousness that exceeded the most upright human example they could imagine, Jesus gives the first example that demonstrates the need for surpassing righteousness.

1. Read Exodus 20:13. According to Matthew 5:21, does what the Pharisees have been teaching line up with the law of Moses?

If the Pharisees were passionate about anything, it was in their desire to outwardly obey God's law. Over time, they had developed an oral tradition, "the tradition of the elders," [4] to help prevent pious Jews from breaking one of the Ten Commandments. This oral tradition, which even added a few extra rules, had actually become a law unto itself and had taken precedence over the true Law in the Word of God.

They correctly repeated God's prohibition of murder given in the Law to Moses, but then reduced it by their traditions to only being liable to the judgment of the court if you actually physically murdered someone. When Jesus says, "You have heard that the ancients were told," He is about to expose this legalistic emphasis solely rooted in external behavior. It is not that what they were teaching was wrong. The issue is that these religious leaders cared very little about whether they were doing what God wanted; they only cared that they <u>appeared</u> to do exactly what God told them to do. And there is a big difference.

2. If not committing murder was the standard for righteousness, how much would you feel your need for a Savior?

3. How does expanding the standard for righteousness to the category of anger change how you feel about your need for a Savior?

The Pharisees were willing to condemn sins that could be seen and measured by men, sins like murder. However, anger can be lurking inside someone who appears to be at peace, and it can be hidden from everyone. Everyone, that is, except God.

In Matthew 5:21, Jesus enlarges the boundary of murder so that it includes all kinds of anger.

4. In what ways are murder and anger similar?

When Jesus links murder and anger, He connects them at the level of the heart, where they share the same root of selfishness. We have an unmet need. We want something, and we aren't getting it. And so we take action. Some people use guns, others use words. Both weapons can be lethal.

I can hear some of you asking: Didn't Jesus get angry over sin and injustice? Can't I be "angry and sin not" (Ephesians 4:26a)? The answer to both questions is yes. But that is not the anger Jesus is talking about in the Sermon on the Mount. Jesus is talking about issues of the heart that will either preserve or destroy human relationships.

5. Look at the list below and circle the forms of anger that are most familiar to you personally. Feel free to list other forms as they come to mind.

yelling	criticism	cynicism
withdrawal	depression	sarcasm
defensiveness	moodiness	blame

6. Look up the following warnings about anger and summarize them:

Proverbs 29:22

2 Corinthians 12:20

Ephesians 4:31

James 1:20

Jesus isn't through exposing the fatal consequences of anger. He proceeds to reveal three levels of anger that spiral downward in their devaluation of the person we are angry with.

7. Read Matthew 5:22 and fill in the blanks in the table. (The first one is done for you.)

Levels of Anger	Definition	Matthew 5:22 Wording
Anger	A strong feeling of being upset or annoyed in response to an unmet need or blocked goal.	"is angry with his brother"
Contempt		
Malice		

Let's take a moment and look at the two "name calling" words Jesus used in verse 22. What makes both words wrong is that they are directed toward the sinner rather than the sin. The first word, *Raca*, is translated "You good for nothing" [5] in the NASB. It is a word used to express arrogant contempt. As bad as that is, the next word, "You fool," the Greek word *moros*, is much worse. W.E. Vines says that the word *Raca* "scorns a man's mind and calls him stupid; *moros* scorns his heart and his character; hence the Lord's more severe condemnation." [6]

Ed Welch provides a challenging commentary on Matthew 5:21-22:

> Have you ever thought someone was an idiot—the rude cashier at the store, the person who kept you on hold for twenty minutes, the neighbor who promised to help but didn't? Jesus is putting casual name-calling within those same murderous boundaries. Someone interfered with your interests, so you judge them to be a fool. You might keep your critical comments to yourself, or you might roll your eyes rather than make an obscene gesture, but it doesn't matter. Welcome to the band of murderers. Why is Jesus so hard-hitting on this? Anger destroys. Jesus wants life for us all. And we can't turn toward life until we see the murderer who lurks within. Try this identity today: murderer. [7]

8. Read Galatians 5:16-17. Apply Paul's words about walking in the Spirit versus walking according to the desire of the flesh to anger.

TO CHOOSE ANGER OVER LOVE IN OUR RELATIONSHIPS IS TO CHOOSE TO LIVE ACCORDING TO OUR OWN LIMITED RESOURCES IN NEGLECT OF GOD AND HIS RESOURCES.

To choose anger over love in our relationships is to choose to live according to our own limited resources in neglect of God and His resources. Spend a few minutes in prayer asking God to reveal any areas related to anger that He wants to evict from your heart. Ask God to help you to deal with your anger, to enable you to forgive others who have wronged you, and to be able to cultivate peace and love in your relationships with others.

The Sermon shows us what life should look like for a heart that has been melted and transformed by the gospel of grace, while also making clear the true nature of God's standards of righteousness—high standards which mean that our right standing with God is ultimately dependent on the grace of the One who tells us of them. [8]
~ Frank Theilman

MATTHEW 5:23-24

There is a part of your life that people see, and then there is a part of your life that God sees. It is vital that we remember which audience is the most important. We may hate someone in the privacy of our thoughts and think no one else knows. But here is the truth. Our thoughts echo louder in Heaven than our words do on earth. And our relationships with others impact our relationship with God. Not being angry lays the foundation for the contrast Jesus is making between a Kingdom heart and the traditional religious teaching of external rightness. With the transitional word, "Therefore" (v. 23), He draws practical application from the sixth commandment and gives two illustrations that capture what it looks like to love others with a Kingdom heart. We will look at the first one today.

Read Matthew 5:23-24.

1. Summarize what Jesus says about broken relationships.

On the Day of Atonement, the Jews were required to go to the temple to present an animal sacrifice as an offering for their sins. The sacrifice was intended to be the cure that would restore the relationship with God that sin had fractured. It was one of the holiest moments in the life of the religious faithful. When the worshiper would come to the court of the priests, he would lay his hands on the animal as if to transfer his sin to it and then present the animal as an offering to the priest on his behalf. So this scene of "presenting your offering at the altar" was familiar to those sitting on the hillside listening to Him.

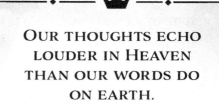

OUR THOUGHTS ECHO LOUDER IN HEAVEN THAN OUR WORDS DO ON EARTH.

On this side of Calvary, no longer do we have to go to a temple and offer gifts on an altar. Jesus did away with that ritual through His once-and-for-all sacrifice of Himself. Now it is God's people who are being built up as a holy temple and the dwelling place of God (Ephesians 2:19-22; 1 Peter 2:4-5). What Jesus is really talking about here is the New Testament pattern of worship that was foreshadowed in the Old Testament. This is not a sermon point about altars and gifts; it is about our relationships with each other. It is about loving our neighbor, whom we are to love as God loves.

In Matthew 5:21-22, Jesus was talking about your anger and your heart. But now, in verses 23-24, He has flipped the anger issue.

2. In the scenario Jesus gives, who is the one who is angry?

3. Whose responsibility is it to make things right?

The phrase "your brother has something against you" means that even if we do not hold something against him, we should do everything in our power to restore the relationship. Max Lucado writes,

> As far as I know, this is the only time God tells you to slip out of church early. Apparently, He'd rather have you give your olive branch than your tithe. If you are worshiping and remember that your mom is hacked-off at you for forgetting her birthday, then get off the pew and find a phone. Maybe she'll forgive you; maybe she won't. But at least you can return to your pew with a clean conscience. [9]

In addition, the phrase does not require actual wrongdoing on our part. Even if the break in a relationship is based in perception rather than fact, we are to do everything in our power to close that breach.

4. How does Jesus say a broken relationship with someone will impact our ability to worship God?

Jesus is clear. Reconciliation is more important than the external duties of worship. Our worship means nothing to God if we are not seeking to walk in peace with each other. John MacArthur writes, "True worship is not enhanced by better music, better prayers, better architecture, or even better preaching. True worship is enhanced by better relationships between those who come to worship." [10]

External conformity is not enough. Attending church, singing in the choir, and giving will never produce a clear conscience. If we are at odds with others because of something we have done and are unwilling to do anything about it, showing up for church is simply an exercise in hypocritical futility.

Those sitting on the mountain would have been stunned as they heard Jesus say that reconciliation is more important than religion. Jesus isn't interested in empty religion. He wants to bring us to terms with what is in our hearts. Dallas Willard poses the following:

> Just think of what the quality of life and character must be in a person who would routinely interrupt sacred rituals to pursue reconciliation with a fellow human being. What kind of thought life, what feeling tones and moods, what habits of body and mind, what kinds of deliberations and choices would you find in such a person? When you answer these questions, you will have a vision of the true "rightness beyond" that is at home in God's Kingdom of power and love. [11]

But what if someone refuses our attempts to make things right? Obviously, we cannot change another person's heart. We are responsible to pursue reconciliation; we are not responsible to make the reconciliation happen.

5. Read Romans 12:18. As much as it depends upon you, what are you to do?

Sometimes in spite of all that we do, the other person does not want to make peace. Do everything you can to make peace. And then, just determine to love. Certainly, it would be great if the person forgave you. But you don't need their forgiveness to love them. Your ability to love doesn't come from them. Your power to love comes from God. Outcomes cannot be controlled, but our contributions toward reconciliation can be.

Ask yourself the following:

1. Do you have a relationship that needs reconciliation?
2. Does your heart honestly long for reconciliation?
3. What have you done to try to make peace with the person?
4. Is there anything more that you can do?

5. Read John 17:21. What is Jesus' prayer request to the Father regarding us?

Unity is so important to Jesus that it is one of the last things He prays about before He goes to Calvary. Is it that vital to you?

As you wrap up today's study, spend some time in prayer. Ask God to help you move beyond "the righteousness of the scribes and Pharisees" in your relationships with others. If you have a strained or broken relationship, ask God to show you how to make reconciliation. If you have honestly and in humility done all you can to reconcile with someone, and they have rejected your efforts, lay that relationship at the feet of Jesus and leave it there.

One last thought on Matthew 5:23-24 from Oswald Chambers:

> The test Jesus gives is not the truth of our manner but the temper of our mind. Many of us are wonderfully truthful in manner but our temper of mind is rotten in God's sight. The thing Jesus alters is the temper of mind. [12]

Our internal condition far outweighs our external action. Remember, our thoughts echo louder in Heaven than our words do on earth.

Charles Dickens' novella, *A Christmas Carol*, has the most joy-filled ending of any of his literary works. Ebenezer Scrooge awakens with his life changed after nighttime visits from the Ghosts of Christmas Past, Present, and Future. His last visit from the faceless, voiceless, Ghost of Christmas Future, foretells his own death as well as the death of Tiny Tim and prompts Scrooge to plea, "Assure me that I yet may change these shadows you have shown me, by an altered life!" [13] When he opens his eyes, the first thing he sees is his bedpost, which jolts him with the realization that he is still in the present:

> Yes! and the bedpost was his own. The bed was his own, the room was his own. Best and happiest of all, the Time before him was his own, to make amends in! [14]

And as you remember from this much-loved Christmas story, that is exactly what Scrooge does. And it brings him so much joy!

To "make amends" means that we do whatever it takes on our part to mend or restore the relationship. In Matthew 5:23-24, the question of actual wrongdoing was left unanswered. Simply, if you remembered somebody had something against you, it was your duty to try to reconcile so that your worship would not be hindered. In Matthew 5:25-26, the focus is on the one who is guilty.

In this second illustration that exemplifies loving with a Kingdom heart, Jesus uses the scenario in which we would have an adversary in the legal system. In today's terminology, it would probably mean that someone is suing us with cause.

Read Matthew 5:25-26.

In these verses, Jesus poses a situation in which a person owes money to another and has not repaid the debt. Jesus encourages this person to come to an agreement with their legal opponent, the one to whom something is owed.

1. What is the goal of a settlement outside of court?

2. Why should the person try to resolve the issue before it lands in court?

Under the Roman legal system, a debtor could seek an "out of court" settlement up until the time the two parties arrived in court. However, once in court, the matter was totally in the hands of the judge and could no longer be settled by a private agreement between the two parties involved. If the judge ruled against an individual in debtor court, that person was thrown into prison and remained there until the entire debt could be repaid.

Jesus uses this illustration to stress the urgency of seeking reconciliation. Without it, things can escalate out of control and damage us as well as our influence. What Jesus is teaching is a Kingdom lifestyle lesson. Reconciliation, mercy, and forgiveness are to be part of our everyday life.

3. Debts are not just limited to finances. What are other examples of "debts" we may have that need to be settled?

4. Read Psalm 51:4. Who is all sin ultimately against?

With that realization, is there any possible reason for not seeking reconciliation quickly? When we approach an adversary with a Kingdom heart to make amends, we need to be sure that our love for them leads the way. Dallas Willard writes,

> By truly loving our adversary, we stand within the reality of God's Kingdom and resources, and it is very likely we will draw our adversary into it also. Things are really different there, and a resolution manifesting the divine presence becomes possible. See what will happen. Venture on the Kingdom. [15]

If we do not approach our "adversary" in genuine love, it will be evident and it is unlikely that our attempt at reconciliation will be successful.

5. Read Ephesians 4:2; 1 Peter 4:8; and John 15:12. Describe the kind of love with which we should approach someone we have offended.

Now, what if the shoe is on the other foot? What if you are the person who has been offended and someone is asking you to forgive them?

6. Read the following verses that speak to our responsibility when someone asks for forgiveness. Make notes as you read.

Colossians 3:12-13

Mark 11:25

Luke 6:37

At times forgiving someone is like picking up an eraser and immediately wiping the offense away. Done. Over. Forgiven. Forgotten. Just like when my toddler grandson does something wrong and then says, "I'm sorry". But at other times, it is not that easy.

1. **If someone sins against us and then asks forgiveness, it doesn't mean we shouldn't talk about that sin and how it hurt us.** Sin is destructive. It can take time to get to the place where we can restore the relationship. Biblical counseling from a third party may be needed.

2. **Forgiveness doesn't mean there should not be consequences.** Certain sins have legal ramifications. Others result in different repercussions. If your child is deliberately disobedient and asks forgiveness, you are to forgive. But that doesn't mean that he or she escapes the consequences of the disobedient act.

3. **Forgiveness doesn't mean we must immediately trust the person.** Sin shatters trust. Once a trust has been violated, it can take time to earn trust back.

Forgiving others is a choice we make. When we choose to resume a relationship after a violation, we do so in and through the power of God. We can't forgive in our own strength. At times, you may need to seek the counsel of a mature Christian or a biblical counselor to help you walk through the issue. Do not hesitate to seek help. Today.

Like Ebenezer Scrooge, if we are still breathing, we are in the present. All of the resources of Heaven are available to us to make responsible decisions in love, to seek forgiveness, and to forgive. As Willard says, we do so "with assurance that how things turn out for us does not really matter that much because, in any case, we are in the Kingdom of the heavens. In that Kingdom, nothing that can happen to us that is 'the end of the world.'" [16]

Have you ever wondered why the Ghost of Christmas Future never spoke to Scrooge? It was because the future is not yet written, and no words can be ascribed to what has not yet become. This is the beauty of living in *This Present Kingdom*. We enter it through surrender and trust, and with a willingness for Jesus to shape our hearts and character. Your future begins with what happens in your heart today.

MATTHEW 5:27-30

On September 3, 1989, Varig, a Brazilian airline, had a flight scheduled from São Paolo to Belém with six stopovers. When the plane landed in Marabá, the sixth stopover before they reached Belém, the co-pilot got out to conduct the external inspection of the Boeing 737 while the pilot consulted the flight plan and set the navigation system. The pilot, who had just returned from vacation, was unaware that the airline had just changed their flight plan notations from four digits to three and had eliminated the use of a decimal point. The flight plan read 0270 which the pilot interpreted as 270 degrees, but the intended meaning was 027.0 degrees. When the co-pilot got in the plane, instead of following the protocol to check his own flight plan, he just set his indicator to match that of the pilot. So when the plane took off, they were headed nowhere close to their intended destination.

When the pilot believed he was close to Belém, he requested clearance for descent and received it. As he began his descent, he thought it odd that he did not recognize the geographic characteristics of the Belém area. He even asked the controller if the city was without electricity. At the time, the Belém airport had no radar, and so the controller informed the pilot that their flight was the only one in its airspace and gave landing clearance. After the plane's system showed they should have already arrived at Belém, the pilot decided to execute a 180-degree turn and try to locate the airport visually. He saw a river that he believed to be the Amazon. The river was actually the Xingu, which runs south-north, while the Amazon runs west-east. By this time, the flight was thirty minutes past its arrival time.

The co-pilot began to examine the flight path and recognized the initial mistake the pilot had made in his calculations. The pilot then decided to contact the Marabá airport again to get on the right path. However, Marabá shared radio frequency with another airport and the pilot mistakenly reached the wrong one, an airport located almost 800 miles south. By this time, the plane was dangerously low on fuel and they decided to head for Carajás Airport, which would have been the correct decision if he had actually connected with Marabá. Lost in the air and almost out of fuel, it became apparent that the plane would have to attempt a landing in the rain forest. Once the plane exhausted its fuel supply, it crashed into the forest, killing 13 of the 54 onboard and leaving another 34 injured. [17]

All because of a decimal point. One error that set off a chain of events which ended in death. Likewise, one sinful choice is all it takes to get us off course from where God wants us to be.

As we continue to examine the rightness of the Kingdom heart, we see that Jesus is cutting to the core of what a life looks like apart from His Kingdom reign. Murder comes from the heart filled with anger. Anger is what sets off the chain of events that leads to death. And the issue we are looking at today follows the same path of destruction.

Read Matthew 5:27-28.

1. From what Old Testament verse would the disciples and the crowd have learned that it is wrong to commit adultery?

Adultery is generally defined as sex between two people who are not married to each other and at least one of them is married to someone else. The difference in our day and Jesus' day is that adultery then was applied almost exclusively to women. A man, even if he was married, could have sex with other women. A woman could only have sex with her husband. If a woman was found guilty of adultery, it warranted her execution. In Matthew 5:27-30, Jesus is speaking directly to men, but the application is to both men and women.

2. What is the new standard regarding adultery that Jesus is teaching? (v. 28)

Jesus is teaching about the difference between internal and external righteousness and on becoming the kind of person who will be at home in the Kingdom of God.

Just as uncontrolled desire is what escalates anger to murder, uncontrolled desire is what escalates a lustful look to adultery. To be clear, Jesus is not saying that temptation to lust is the same as adultery. James Smith explains,

> The word that is used for lust in this passage is *epithumia*. This word had a very specific meaning. It does not refer to ordinary sexual attraction but to intentionally objectifying another person for one's own gratification...*Epithumia* is not referring to the first look but to the second. The first look may be simple attraction, but the second look is leering. Lust does not value the person but mere body parts. *Epithumia* goes beyond mere sexual attraction. It intentionally cultivates sexual desire for the sake of the feeling itself. It is the opposite of love. Love looks into the eyes; *epithumia* steals glances below them. Love values the other as a person; *epithumia* degrades the other. We must make a clear distinction between attraction and objectification, between feeling sexual desire and *epithumia*. When we fail to make the distinction, we adopt the first false narrative and think that sexual attraction is evil in itself. [18]

Temptation begins with suggestion. A choice is then made to reject the suggestion or linger there and take pleasure in it. Adultery begins with a look that is not brought under control. The lingering look that takes pleasure is what Jesus is talking about.

Are you thinking to yourself this is only a problem that men have? What does *epithumia* look like for women? Whereas for men the object of *epithumia* is a body, for women the object of *epithumia* can be a persona, an image. I remember one time receiving a phone call from a woman who told me, weeping, that she had fallen in love with a man other than her husband. As she began to unfold her story, to my surprise, the object of her affection was a man on a soap opera that she watched every day. She had developed a fantasy relationship with a man she had never met. With make-up, lighting, and scripted lines, the man appeared to be everything her husband was not. And she fell for him. I have heard similar stories from women regarding characters from romance novels.

Here is the bottom line. Women long to feel special and be valued. In the Kingdom of God, those are needs that are met as we set our hearts on Him. But when we venture outside of His Kingdom, we will look for other ways to meet those needs.

And that can lead to lust of the eyes. Increasingly, women struggle with Internet pornography. In fact, one-third of all internet porn users are women. [19]

3. Read Job 31:1. What covenant did Job make?

Kay Arthur notes, "Job was fully aware of the weakness of his flesh, of the ability of a man's heart to be enticed by a woman. So he was determined to flee lust by making a covenant with his eyes; he would not permit them to gaze on what would entice him and consume his righteousness." [20] (p. 183) Job knew well that his heart would follow his eyes. He makes this clear in Job 31:7-9: "If my step has turned from the way, or my heart followed my eyes...If my heart has been enticed by a woman..." Job was able to control his heart because he was able to control his eyes.

4. Read Galatians 5:19-21. How seriously does God take adultery?

Note that Paul says that those who "practice" these sins will not inherit the Kingdom of God, not that those who "commit" these things. The emphasis is on the habitual practice that reveals the inner condition of the heart.

5. Take a moment and consider society's view of lust and adultery. How easy is it for the culture of the day to seep into the hearts and minds of believers?

Immorality has become commonplace in America. On television, in the news, on the Internet, and sadly, in the church.

Read Matthew 5:29-30.

6. Is Jesus literally asking us to gouge out our eye or cut off our hand?

Jesus is using hyperbole to communicate that we should take drastic actions in order to follow Him, the King of the Kingdom. The issue is not our hand or our eye. The problem is in our heart. And when we are not walking in close union with God and His Kingdom, a void opens up. And like every void, it is the nature of it to be filled. Smith explains, "I want to feel something, to be caught up in something, and when I am disconnected from God and His Kingdom, one of the more thrilling alternatives is *epithumia*." [21] When we allow ourselves to be enticed by the temporal, we will stray from the spiritual. Every time. But when we live with God in His glorious Kingdom, our desires, every need we have, will be fulfilled.

7. Think back to the Brazilian airplane crash that began with one wrong act. Job set specific measures into place in his life to keep him from committing adultery in his heart. What are some examples of boundaries you have established (or need to establish) in your life to keep you from venturing down a destructive path?

Dear friend, listen well to my words; tune your ears to my voice.
Keep my message in plain view at all times.
Concentrate! Learn it by heart!
Those who discover these words live, really live;
Body and soul, they're bursting with health.
Keep vigilant watch over your heart; that's where life starts.
Don't talk out of both sides of your mouth;
Avoid careless banter, white lies, and gossip.
Keep your eyes straight ahead; ignore all sideshow distractions.
Watch your step, and the road will stretch out smooth before you.
Look neither right nor left; leave evil in the dust.
PROVERBS 4:20-27 (MSG)

KINGDOM EXERCISE

We live in a noisy world. A world that is almost always connected by wireless Internet, 5G, and Bluetooth. A world with the advanced technology of cell phones, Wi-Fi, satellite television (and 24/7 news), cars with hotspots, smart refrigerators, video doorbells, Bluetooth headphones, and toothbrushes that use wireless technology to help you have a better smile. A world with a permanent "on" button.

But did you know that it is not that way every place in the United States? Tucked away from the world in a quiet spot surrounded by the Allegheny Mountains, the town of Green Bank, West Virginia is referred to as "America's Quiet Zone" because Wi-Fi is banned and cellphone signals are non-existent. This near radio silence is required by the town's most prominent resident, the Green Bank Observatory, which opened in 1958 as the United States' first national astronomy observatory. It is one of the most vital research facilities in the field of radio astronomy and home to the world's largest steerable radio telescope, the Robert C. Byrd Green Bank Telescope, which demands electromagnetic silence to do its important research.

So in Green Bank, landline phones are still the norm. You can still find phone booths along the rural roads. Paper maps are common. In this small town, the residents are less distracted by the dominating technology that frames 21st century American life.

A recent article in the New York Times observes, "At a time when nearly 60 percent of American teens say they have been bullied or harassed online, and studies have found links between social media use and teen mental health problems, the digital limitations around Green Bank have created a unique kind of modern childhood, providing a glimpse into what it means to grow up without the constant buzz of texting and social media." [22] The young people growing up in Green Bank actually know what it means to experience "quiet". They pursue real-life connections, spend lots of time outdoors, check out books to read from the public library, and spend less time online when they do happen to use dial up internet connections.

In Green Bank, families gather around the dinner table and talk. They maintain eye contact. They go on adventures together. They hang out in their family rooms, playing games and putting puzzles together. It is almost like time has been stopped…by the silence.

THE DISCIPLINE OF SILENCE AND SOLITUDE

If you are like me (and I suspect most of you are), you read about life in Green Bank and there is a yearning deep within to return to a simpler and more silent time. Too often, our lives feel like overpacked suitcases bursting at the seams. We are occupied with much and pre-occupied with even more. We crave stimulus like it is junk food. And oddly, it seems the more we do, the less fulfilled we are.

Our souls long to be set free from the web of noise that fills the space around us. They desire renewal and rest. More importantly, they need to "be still and know" that He is God, (Psalm 46:10, KJV)—to hear from Him, and to be in His presence. To be set free to become who He wants us to be.

The prophet Elijah found himself in a similar situation. The noise of the world had gotten to him. He was on the run and at the end of his rope. An angel of the Lord appeared to him and gave him instructions that would lead him to a life-changing encounter with God. He obediently made a forty-day journey to a cave, and when he arrived, the Lord asked:

> "What are you doing here, Elijah?" Elijah replied, "I have zealously served the Lord God Almighty. But the people of Israel have broken their covenant with you, torn down your altars, and killed every one of your prophets. I am the only one left, and now they are trying to kill me, too."

> "Go out and stand before me on the mountain," the Lord told him. And as Elijah stood there, the Lord passed by, and a mighty windstorm hit the mountain. It was such a terrible blast that the rocks were torn loose, but the Lord was not in the wind. After the wind there was an earthquake, but the Lord was not in the earthquake. And after the earthquake there was a fire, but the Lord was not in the fire. And after the fire there was the sound of a gentle whisper. When Elijah heard it, he wrapped his face in his cloak and went out and stood at the entrance of the cave (1 Kings 19:9b-13, NLT).

Elijah did not encounter God in the mighty windstorm, or in the earthquake, or even in the fire. He met God in permeating silence where the whisper of the Almighty could be heard.

While we may not be able to up and move to Green Bank, West Virginia or to turn back the hands of time five or six decades, we can, like Elijah, learn to practice the spiritual discipline of silence and solitude that will create space in our souls and lives for God to do His Kingdom work within us. When His Kingdom reigns within, it manifests itself without. Anti-Kingdom behaviors (i.e. anger, contempt, malice, lust) will dissipate. If we are to live the Kingdom life that God desires of us in the present, we must be able to hear His voice speaking to us. And we learn to recognize His voice in silence and solitude.

THE EXERCISE

Spend one hour in silence and solitude.

Find a quiet place. Perhaps you can go for a walk on a nature trail or find a place to sit beside a lake. Even a secluded chair in a room in your house with the door shut will work. Turn off your phone. Silence every piece of technology you own. Spend sixty minutes in silence. Do nothing. No activity. No noise. Just the presence of God.

But first, a word of caution. Solitude is not just a synonym for privacy. It is not merely a time to recharge our batteries with the end goal of being more productive. Henri Nouwen describes how our time in silence and solitude will feel:

> Solitude is not a private therapeutic place. Rather, it is the place of conversion, the place where the old self dies and the new self is born, the place where the emergence of the new man and the new woman occurs.
>
> In solitude I get rid of my scaffolding: no friends to talk with, no telephone calls to make, no meetings to attend, no music to entertain, no books to distract, just me — naked, vulnerable, weak, sinful, deprived, broken — nothing. It is this nothingness that I have to face in my solitude, a nothingness so dreadful that everything in me wants to run to my friends, my work, and my distractions so that I can forget my nothingness and make myself believe that I am worth something. But that is not all. As soon as I decide to stay in my solitude, confusing ideas, disturbing images, wild fantasies, and weird associations jump about in my mind like monkeys in a banana tree. Anger and greed begin to show their ugly faces. I give long, hostile speeches to my enemies and dream lustful dreams in which I am wealthy, influential, and very attractive — or poor, ugly, and in need of immediate consolation. Thus I try again to run from the dark abyss of my nothingness and restore my false self in all its vainglory.
>
> The task is to persevere in my solitude, to stay in my cell until all my seductive visitors get tired of pounding on my door and leave me alone. [23]

When you push through the initial challenge of silence and solitude, you will realize the refreshment of God's peace that "surpasses all comprehension will guard your hearts and your minds in Christ Jesus" (Philippians 4:7). But you will also discover what happens when we center our lives upon Him. His purifying presence in our lives will make us more like Him. And in becoming like Him, we will learn to love like He loves, and we will bring Him into our relationships with others.

Reflection Questions

1. Where did you spend your hour of silence and solitude?

2. What kinds of distractions did you encounter?

3. How did you re-center your focus on the Lord?

4. In what ways did God speak to you?

5. What one word best describes your hour of silence and solitude?

All of man's problems stem from his inability to sit quietly in a room alone. [24]
~Blaise Pascal

WEEK FIVE
KINGDOM DISORIENTATION – PART TWO
—•——•—— MATTHEW 5:31-48 ——•——•—

Therefore you are to be perfect, as your heavenly Father is perfect.
MATTHEW 5:48

*The command "Be ye perfect" is not idealistic gas. Nor is it a command
to do the impossible. He is going to make us into creatures
that can obey that command.* [1]
~C. S. LEWIS

Imagine yourself transported to the hillside, the site of the Sermon on the Mount, as we resume our study of the biblical narrative. Picture in your mind's eye Jesus seated in the posture of a rabbi teacher, His face animated with an intensity of truth and love gleaming in His eyes. The crowd that has gathered to listen is no doubt mesmerized. I envision the religious hierarchy scattered throughout and hovering around the fringes while seeking to ensnare Jesus with an accusation of heresy. The message that Jesus is proclaiming, however, is countercultural not only to the firmly established Jewish culture of the day, but also to human nature. The Jewish people do indeed long for the promised Messiah, but their portrait of Him is of a warrior king who would deliver them from the tyranny of the Roman Empire. Yet, Jesus exhorts them to love their enemies.

Following their return to their homeland from captivity, Judaism transitioned from a temple-focused, priest-taught religion to one that included synagogues where teacher-rabbis also taught the law.

> This resulted in new and different forms of interpretation and the birth of traditions, often additional laws, which supposedly expanded and clarified the written Torah. During the NT period these additional laws were taught and passed on both orally and in written form (note the frequent mention of "scribes" in the NT). Many people regarded these rabbinic traditions as having divine origin, equal to the laws in the written Scriptures, but Jesus pronounced them "the tradition of men" (Mark 7:1-23, esp. v. 8). [2]

Several sects developed among the religious leaders, such as the Pharisees, Sadducees, Zealots, and the Essenes, seeking power and influence among the ordinary people and the ruling class. "Most people in the land of Israel belonged to none of these groups, being too busy earning a living and caring for their families." [3] And it is against this backdrop that Jesus teaches His powerful message about Kingdom living. His teaching is so divergent from mankind's natural response and the religious teaching of the day that it must have seemed other-worldly, and indeed it was—it was heavenly in origin.

MATTHEW 5:31-32

Today we pick up our study of the Sermon on the Mount in the middle of Jesus' discourse on Kingdom living. Last week, we saw Jesus use the phrases, "You have heard" and "But I say to you" to contrast the current acceptable interpretation of Jewish law with the higher standard of Kingdom living. The topic for today is divorce, which was a natural progression from the previous discussion of lust and adultery. The two verses in this passage are by no means an exhaustive study of the topic so we will pull in additional references.

1. Read Matthew 5:31-32. What does verse 31 say is necessary to get a divorce?

2. What does Jesus say constitutes grounds for divorce, and what is the consequence of not adhering to that stipulation?

A detailed account of an encounter Jesus has with some Pharisees concerning divorce is found in Matthew 19:3-9. Their discussion is very timely since divorce was rampant in the Jewish culture of the day, and two schools of thought were held by followers of two leading rabbis.

3. Examine Matthew 19:3-9. What is the Pharisees' purpose in coming to Jesus?

4. What question do they ask Jesus?

The Pharisees are convinced they have caught Jesus in a snare since the two prominent first century rabbis embraced totally different positions on divorce. Rabbi Shammai supported a conservative view based on Deuteronomy 24:1, while Rabbi Hillel maintained that a man could divorce his wife for practically anything, even for something as trivial as burning his dinner. Regardless of Jesus' stand, the Pharisees imagine He will offend many.

5. Consider Deuteronomy 24:1. What offense did Moses give as a reason for divorce?

6. Describe Jesus' response to the Pharisees, and why is His comment significant? (Matthew 19:4-6)

Rather than answer the question, Jesus guides the discussion all the way back to the Creation and God's original, divine plan for marriage. One man and one woman for life. Theologian John Stott penned, "The Pharisees were preoccupied with the grounds for divorce; Jesus was concerned with the institution of marriage." [4]

7. Based on the verses Jesus quoted from Genesis (vv. 1:27, 2:24), why would a divorced woman who remarries be guilty of adultery? (Matthew 5:32, 19:4-6, 9)

Whether divorced for some sexual impurity, a minor infraction, or simply because her husband desired another, a woman's life was absolutely ruined when her husband handed her the certificate of divorce, while the man rarely suffered any harm. Dallas Willard outlines her heart-breaking prospects:

> For the woman, however, there were only three realistic possibilities in Jesus' day. She might find a place in the home of a generous relative, but usually on grudging terms and as little more than a servant. She might find a man who would marry her, but always as "damaged goods" and sustained in a degraded relationship. Or she might, finally, make a place in the community as a prostitute. [5]

The Pharisees were not convinced of the gravity of divorce in a culture that took it lightly and responded with what they conceived would be a strong rebuttal. "Why then did Moses command to give her a certificate of divorce and send her away?" (Matthew 19:7)

8. What did Jesus state was the root cause for divorce?

John Stott points out, "The Pharisees called Moses' provision for divorce a command; Jesus called it a concession to the hardness of human hearts." [6]

A hard heart—truly the root of all our rebellion against God. It might happen gradually, little by little, taking us almost by surprise. Or it may march in like storm troopers for an instantaneous takeover. The symptoms of a hard heart are easily recognizable—days filled to the brim so there is no time to read the Word and no desire to pray. Other people or things making claims on our allegiance—not too different from the idols that enticed the children of Israel. Their plight is recorded in the book of Ezekiel. After continued rebellion against God, Judah was exiled in Babylon. But their merciful God had their redemption in mind. "Then I will sprinkle clean water on you, and you will be clean; I will cleanse you from all your filthiness and from all your idols. Moreover, I will give you a new heart and put a new spirit within you; and I will remove your heart of stone from your flesh and give you a heart of flesh" (Ezekiel 36:25-26).

Take a moment for a heart inventory. Is there any area where your heart has become hard and cold toward God? Anything you are unwilling to relinquish to Him? If so, take a moment, and, in repentance, ask the Lord Jesus to remove your heart of stone and replace it with a heart of flesh. He is a faithful Deliverer, having stepped out of Heaven to provide salvation for any who will trust in Him. Kneel your heart before Him.

MATTHEW 5:33-37

Words—I love words. Long words, obscure words, impressive words that send me scurrying to the dictionary. I have been known to spend an inordinate amount of time in a thesaurus investigating synonyms in a quest to discover the perfect word to communicate exactly what I desire to say. I am fond of compound-complex sentences with a multiplicity of words. Why use one word when you can savor three? However, words can be formidable when you plummet in over your head as I did when I attempted to read my son's dissertation. As I told him what I had absorbed so far, he teasingly remarked, "I see you have made it through the introduction."

Words are important. Words are how we reveal ourselves to the world, how we share our thoughts and feelings, and, yes, how we deceive and lie. Words are birthed in the heart, so a pure heart, greatly valued by God, is needed for Kingdom living rather than the hard heart which we contemplated in yesterday's lesson. The Scripture reminds us, "The tongue of the righteous is as choice silver, the heart of the wicked is worth little" (Proverbs 10:20). The battle between truth and deception has raged since Satan declared to Eve, "You surely will not die" (Genesis 3:4), and Cain raised to God, "Am I my brother's keeper?" (Genesis 4:9).

> **WORDS ARE HOW WE REVEAL OURSELVES TO THE WORLD, HOW WE SHARE OUR THOUGHTS AND FEELINGS, AND, YES, HOW WE DECEIVE AND LIE.**

The passage we are studying today concerns an issue that was very prevalent in Jesus' day—oaths or swearing. The use of oaths preceded even the Old Testament Law when Jehovah God swore by Himself to confirm a promise to Abraham. The Law included much to say about oaths.

1. Review these background verses on oaths and record their instructions.

Exodus 20:7

Leviticus 19:12

Numbers 30:2

Deuteronomy 23:21

What was once used as a means to enhance a commitment by utilizing God's name has now morphed into something entirely different in an effort to find a loophole to eliminate the need to fulfill a vow. "In ancient times, there was a commentary called the *Mishnah*. A whole section was given to oaths, including which were binding and which were not. You would have thought that an oath was an oath! But this is the way legalistic people get around the Law—by looking for those loopholes." [7] Against this backdrop of deceit perpetuated by the religious leaders in the Jewish culture of His day, Jesus proposes a better way. Take time now to read Matthew 5:33-37 in preparation for our study.

2. Record Jesus' comments after these phrases He has repetitively used in the sermon. (vv. 33-34a)

You have heard:

But I say to you:

James Smith clarifies Jesus' subject, "Jesus is dealing with the issue of 'swearing,' which does not refer to cussing or using profane language, but to making a verbal promise that what is said is true, such as taking an oath." [8]

3. List the four things Jesus mentions being used to avoid being held responsible for an oath and relate His reasoning behind His statements. (vv. 34-36)

4. What simple instruction does Jesus conclude with? (v. 37)

Despite Jesus' clear instructions in this passage concerning swearing, people, even Christians, attempt to manipulate others by referencing God. "They are declaring some promise or purpose of some point of information or knowledge dear to them. They want their hearers to accept what they say and do what they want. So they say, 'By God!' or 'God knows!' to lend weight to their words and presence." [9]

5. Name some expressions that you hear today that take the form of swearing.

Others employ the tactics of substituting another focal point other than God such as "I swear on my mother's grave." The *Commentary Critical and Explanatory of the Whole Bible* notes, "The practice of going beyond Yes and No in affirmations and denials—as if our word for it were not enough, and we expected others to question it—springs from the vicious root of untruthfulness which is only aggravated by the very effort to clear ourselves of the suspicion of it." [10]

6. What final admonition does Jesus impart at the end of verse 37?

In our passage today, Jesus urges us to let our "yes" be "yes" and our "no", "no". No oath is needed for one who walks with Kingdom principles. When we feel the need to convince others of our truth-telling, it is usually because we have a tendency or temptation to lie. "Too much talk leads to sin. Be sensible and keep your mouth shut" (Proverbs 10:19, NLT). Humans might tend to categorize lies, i.e., white lies, but God scorns all lying. "The Lord detests lying lips, but He delights in those who tell the truth" (Proverbs 12:22, NLT).

7. Why do you think most people lie?

Smith shares this insight, "These are two of the main reasons why we lie: we think we need to (1) in order to get what we want, or (2) to avoid something we don't want." [11] Contemplate the child looking straight into his mother's eyes and, despite the telltale ring of proof around his mouth, declaring, "No, I didn't eat the candy." Lying comes naturally to our sinful nature, even to our little ones, but has no place in Kingdom living. Smith continues:

> As He has been doing, Jesus continues to address the heart, the inner person, the place from which all things flow. The standard of righteousness in Jesus' day was clear: You can tell lies and not be liable (until you get caught), but if you lie "under oath" you are guilty. Jesus as always, is aiming for something higher, for a new kind of person with a new kind of character. He is saying, "Under oath or not, those who live in the Kingdom can and should tell the truth." [12]

8. Are you a person of your word? Do you keep your commitments? Do others often doubt your truthfulness? Search your heart before you answer.

9. Keep a journal in this space of any lies you have told this week. Ponder your motivation. Seek forgiveness. Incorporate this verse in your prayer: "Remove from me the way of lying. And grant me Your law graciously" (Psalm 119:29, NKJV).

Do not lie to one another, since you laid aside the old self and its evil practices.
Colossians 3:9

Our unadorned word should be enough, "yes" or "no".
And when a monosyllable will do, why waste our breath by adding to it. [13]
~John Stott

Walk in truth and integrity, my friend.

MATTHEW 5:38-42

As we continue in our study of the Sermon on the Mount, we arrive at another thought-provoking passage as Jesus challenges us to live according to a higher standard—the way of the Kingdom. Again Jesus uses the phrases that we have encountered earlier in the chapter, "You have heard" and "But I say to you," to alert us to be on the lookout for a new way of living. This passage defies the very foundation of human nature and behavior. Now that your curiosity is awakened, let's dive in.

Read Matthew 5:38-42.

Jesus commences by quoting, "You have heard that it was said, 'An eye for an eye and a tooth for a tooth.'" (Matthew 5:38) from the Old Testament Law. Actually this phrase is known as the *Lex Talionis* and first appeared in the Code of Hammurabi, a Babylonian ruler from 2285 to 2242 B.C. Often called the Law of Retaliation, this concept might seem harsh, but truly was merciful since the tendency to seek revenge often resulted in a much more costly price, such as death. And this concept became a part of the judicial law of Israel.

1. Review Leviticus 24:19-20 from the Old Testament Law, and record what it says concerning retribution.

While clearly each person was to be held accountable under the Law, generally it was used to make an estimate of financial responsibility to the person wronged. Rarely was it ever used literally. Indeed, the Lord God is the One who will right the wrongs. He says, "Vengeance is Mine, and retribution" (Deuteronomy 32:35a).

However, in Matthew 5:39a, Jesus introduces a totally new concept for living in the Kingdom of Heaven. It totally goes against our natural responses and calls us to a higher standard.

2. What is Jesus challenging us to do in Matthew 5:39a, and what do you think it means?

3. According to James 4:7 and 1 Peter 5:8-9, who are we told to resist, and what can you conclude from what is communicated?

Can we deduce then that Jesus means that we are to react to evil people in a different manner than our natural responses? R.T. Kendall questions our natural impulses, "Whereas we cannot give in to sin or Satan, we can give in to an evil person whom God has allowed to test us. Retaliation belongs to God alone. Resist the devil and he will flee. Do not oppose evil people; leave them with God. Let God deal with them—He may change them." [14] Kendall continues with a real-life example:

> Hudson Taylor, the great missionary to China, went for years without conversions there. The Chinese hated him. For one thing, he always wore white (not very wise). But one day a person purposely rode a bicycle into a muddy puddle of water where Taylor was standing and splashed water on his white suit. Hudson Taylor fell to his knees and began to pray for the man on the bicycle. The Chinese saw this, and from that point his whole ministry changed. He began to win the Chinese and became a legend. [15]

After challenging His listeners not to resist evil people, Jesus proceeds to use four familiar illustrations from the first century about this principle. Living in the 21st century, we will not necessarily relate to all the situations. Our circumstances will probably be different, yet the Kingdom principle will apply—do not respond as the world does. Dallas Willard outlines a good strategy: "In every concrete situation we have to ask ourselves, not 'Did I do the specific things in Jesus' illustrations?' but 'Am I being the kind of person Jesus' illustrations are illustrations of?'" [16] Now we will examine each of these examples to discover what practical applications can be applied to our lives.

Insult

4. Describe the insult and Jesus' application to the situation in Matthew 5:39.

In the culture of Jesus' day, slapping someone across the face was one of the most egregious insults, comparable to spitting in someone's face today. It was often used to punish and humiliate a servant, and though the offended might choose to slap the person back, it would constitute a serious offense if the person held a superior position. Typical human behavior would be to flee or to respond in kind.

5. Examine Mark 15:16-20 and 1 Peter 2:23 and record what Jesus does when faced with insults.

And Jesus, with the infinite dignity of self-control and love, held His peace. He demonstrated His total refusal to retaliate by allowing them to continue their cruel mockery until they had finished. [17]

~ John Stott

Lawsuit

In that day, when faced with a financial need, a poor man might have to resort to using his clothing as collateral. Needless to say, he did not have a closet jammed packed with clothes, as we do today. Often, he only had his tunic and his cloak. If unable to repay the loan when requested, he could be taken to court. This is the background for Jesus' illustration.

6. What is Jesus' instruction in this situation? (Matthew 5:40)

7. How does the Old Testament Law address the issue in Exodus 22:26-27?

If someone takes something from us, the normal reaction is to cling to it. Those who understand the Kingdom provision are able to take a different approach: "Here is my shirt. Do you need my coat as well?" [18]

~ James Smith

Imposition

8. What imposition does Jesus mention in Matthew 5:41, and what challenge does He mention?

Palestine was an occupied territory having been conquered by the Romans. The Jews were resentful and inconvenienced when a Roman soldier conscripted them to carry his military equipment, but they had no choice. The Roman government only allowed the soldier to require assistance for one mile, but now Jesus is suggesting two miles. Can you imagine the consternation of His listeners?

9. Turn to Mark 15:21 for a biblical example of conscription. Explain the scene.

Are you a second miler? Are you willing to be inconvenienced? Plan to be inconvenienced to meet a need for someone else this week.

You will go the second mile, not for their sakes, but for Christ's sake. It would have been a sorry lookout for us if God had not gone the second mile with us. [19]
~ Oswald Chambers

Entreaty

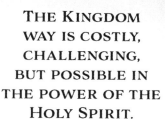

THE KINGDOM WAY IS COSTLY, CHALLENGING, BUT POSSIBLE IN THE POWER OF THE HOLY SPIRIT.

In this historical setting, Jews typically regarded giving as a service designated for family—certainly not for the world at large. Yet Jesus offers no such caveat. He suggests that they give to anyone who asks. Could He mean even the man at your exit on the expressway, the one you consider a "professional beggar"? Perhaps we find ourselves asking, "Is this person deserving of such a gift? Can I spare it?" We must remember though, "Every good and perfect gift is from above" (James 1:17, NIV). Warren Wiersbe suggests, "Verse 42 does not command us to give to everybody who asks whatever they desire, for in so doing we might do them harm. We must give them what they need the most and not what they want the most." [20]

10. How does Peter practice this principle in Acts 3:1-10?

11. What do you have that you could give to someone aside from money? Do you know of a need you can supply?

Nothing is given to us on the basis of ownership, only stewardship. [21]
~ Josif Tson

The Kingdom way is costly, challenging, but possible in the power of the Holy Spirit.

As we have worked our way through the fifth chapter of the book of Matthew, we have been challenged by Jesus to consider a different way of life, Kingdom living. Today we arrive at what could be described as the zenith of His appeal for selfless living. Jesus introduces His topic using His signature phrase, "you have heard," and by this point in our study, we understand that a call to greater commitment will follow. Take time now to familiarize yourself with Matthew 5:43-48.

1. In verse 43, what does Jesus say is the contemporary thinking of His day?

2. How does Jesus contradict that thinking? (v. 44)

To the average listener there on the mountain, Jesus' proclamation regarding enemies must have seemed astounding. It is our natural inclination to hate those who hurt us, or attempt to. In fact, in the Jewish culture, there was a whole list of people who were considered enemies—the Romans, the Samaritans, the Gentiles, etc. Though not found in the Old Testament Law, the idea was probably taught by the scribes and Pharisees. To the contrary, kindness was encouraged—"If you meet your enemy's ox or his donkey wandering away, you shall surely return it to him. If you see the donkey of one who hates you lying helpless under its load, you shall refrain from leaving it to him, you shall surely release it with him" (Exodus 23:4-5). Commentators consider that this teaching of hatred for enemies was derived from the influence of the imprecatory psalms and the account of the conquest of the Promised Land. Yet, Jesus presents a loftier way, the way of love.

3. Contemplate the word enemy. What thoughts immediately come to mind?

Did you think of a general category with a definition, or did you, perhaps, think of a person? If you live long enough, you will undoubtedly encounter an enemy. We could rate them on a scale from 1 to 10 based on the offense. Most of us will never confront a hurt that would rate a 10, but we can put a face, or faces, to the word "enemy". While our experiences will differ, Jesus' instruction is the same to all of us. We are to love our enemy.

In the English language, the word "love" has several definitions ranging from man's feeling for God to merely an attachment or interest in something. So we use the word to describe how we feel about everything from chocolate, to our new outfit, to our family. In the Greek, however, there are four words translated as love. Let's compare them using the notes of the lexical aids in the *Hebrew-Greek Key Word Study Bible*.

erao: Intense or passionate love.

storego: Natural love, family love, love which is native or inherent in man—especially denoting the love between parents and children.

phileo: A love of personal affection, fondness of something, often the love of friends.

agapao: A love rooted in the mind and will of the subject and means to value, esteem, prize, treat as precious, to be devoted to, of Christian's love for all men. Theologically, it represents God's action in sending His only Son to die for the world. [22]

Agapao or *agape* is the word Jesus uses in this passage. It is not the love that springs into your heart at the sight of your child or grandchild, for it does not come naturally. It is a matter of the will, and is a requirement if we are to love our enemies. Additionally, this is the kind of love God displays to mankind in salvation. "But God demonstrates His own love toward us, in that while we were yet sinners, Christ died for us" (Romans 5:8). Christ died for us while we were still His enemies. Can we, through the power of the Holy Spirit, love our enemies? Smith explains the process, "But the Greek word *agapao* (or *agape*) refers not to a feeling but to an action. To love (*agapao*) is *to will the good of another*. It does not entail an emotion, loving or even liking a person. We will their good and demonstrate it in action." [23]

4. What additional thing does the Lord say we should do for our enemy, and do you find that difficult? (v. 44)

5. What reasoning does Jesus give for praying for your enemy? (v. 45a)

R.T. Kendall explains it like this: "We must make a choice. It is when we cross over into the supernatural. We can cross over into the supernatural by being like Jesus—that is, praying for our enemy. Praying for those who have hurt us is Christ-likeness. Doing good to those we don't like is God-likeness. That is true godliness." [24]

Crossing over to the supernatural—what a concept. That is when, through the power of the Holy Spirit, we pray for our enemy as Jesus did. "But Jesus was saying, 'Father, forgive them; for they do not know what they are doing'" (Luke 23:34a). When we do good to our enemies, we emulate the Father who sends good to both His enemies and His children. "For He causes His sun to rise on the evil and the good, and sends rain on the righteous and the unrighteous" (Matthew 5:45b).

And the first step toward crossing over to the supernatural is forgiveness. Forgiveness is difficult. It is a process, but it is possible. The *Dictionary of Everyday Theology and Culture* defines it as follows:

> Forgiveness is not the same as approving what another person has done or even being tolerant of others. It's not the same as excusing a wrong, ignoring it, trying to forget it, or pretending a wrong didn't occur. Instead, it's a choice to bless someone who has done us wrong when there appears to be no sensible reason to do so. [25]

What does real-life forgiveness look like? We might take a page out of the life of the late Elisabeth Elliot to catch a glimpse. She and her husband, Jim, served as missionaries in Ecuador among the Indians. In an attempt to contact the unreached Auca tribe and hopefully share the gospel, Jim and four other missionaries flew into their territory where they were killed in 1956. Elisabeth remained in Ecuador and learned the Aucan language. In 1958, she and her three-year-old daughter along with Rachel Saint, whose husband had also been murdered, went to live with the Aucas to share the message of salvation through Jesus Christ. You probably are already familiar with Elisabeth's story, but may it remind us all of the power of forgiveness. Reflect on her compelling words, "When I looked at that person who had offended me through the 'spiritual eye,' I saw in him one of God's instruments to teach me, instead of one of the devil's to torment me. I saw something more. I saw a person God loves, and whom He wants to love through me." [26]

6. Have you put into practice the process of forgiveness? If so, describe the situation and the ultimate outcome.

7. Was prayer for your enemy a part of the forgiveness process, and did it change your attitude toward the one who hurt you?

8. Has the Lord pointed out anyone that you have neglected to forgive? If so, what will you do about it?

Jesus urges His listeners to love their enemies, for the believer has a higher standard in Kingdom living. He points out that even tax collectors and Gentiles, both greatly despised by the Jews, do that. We, too, must cross over to the supernatural.

The last verse in our passage today has the potential to overwhelm us. For it reads, "Therefore you are to be perfect, as your heavenly Father is perfect" (Matthew 5:48). Perfection seems such an impossible goal given our sinful nature. So let's investigate this Greek word *teleios*.

9. Record the meaning of *teleios* from your Greek dictionary or online site.

Do you feel relieved to discover that the meaning of perfect in this passage is maturity? I do. While gaining spiritual maturity is a life-long process, it is indeed attainable. We cannot plunge the depths of this subject today, so I want to leave you with a message from the Apostle Peter drawn from *The Message*.

> *So don't lose a minute in building on what you've been given, complementing our basic faith with good character, spiritual understanding, alert discipline, passionate patience, reverent wonder, warm friendliness, and generous love, each dimension fitting into and developing the others. With these qualities active and growing in your lives, no grass will grow under your feet, no day will pass without its reward as you mature in your experience of our Master Jesus.*
> 2 Peter 1:5-8

KINGDOM EXERCISE

The plane touched down in the middle of the night. Our group was amazingly alert despite the twenty-hour flight and the lateness of the hour. We were on a mission trip and had arrived at our destination—India, a totally unknown entity to most of us. As we moved into the sizeable lobby packed with people, I overheard many conversations, but did not understand a word. We had entered into a new culture with a different language, unfamiliar customs, unknown gods, and incomprehensible traffic laws. There was no confusion with our purpose, however. We had come to serve our fellow believers at a conference for women. It was not an easy process for the women to get there—some had to walk into the city from rural villages, one woman was beaten by a family member for her decision to come, some desiring baptism faced threats from governmental officials about repercussions, others encountered persecution because of their faith—yet they came. Their hunger to know God more intimately drove them there.

The excitement was tangible as I looked out over the sea of beautiful women dressed in the colors of India, with their faces upturned and their hearts waiting to hear from God's Word. Each day they filed into the outdoor amphitheater ignoring the heat. Despite the awkwardness of listening through a translator, we received their rapt attention as we taught from Colossians, developing the theme, *Christ in You, the Hope of Glory*. Though our way of life and culture were vastly different, our hearts melded together in Christ because we were all a part of His family—the Kingdom of God.

Perhaps my most vivid memory of our time in India was captured when a special presentation was made to the women who had learned to read in the previous year. Illiteracy is not unusual there among women, particularly in the rural areas. I was asked to assist in distributing a gift to honor them. I wish you could have seen the joy, often mingled with tears, on their faces as they were presented their very own Bibles and clutched them to their chests. They now had the potential to know God more intimately, and they had the skills and their Bibles to accomplish it. How glorious!

My heart was pierced at the thought of American Christians with shelves full of Bibles in numerous translations who rarely take the time to delve deeply into God's Word, much less consider it at all on a regular basis. I am so grateful, my friends, that the same sacrifice that provided our salvation also ripped the dividing curtain between God and believers, giving us entry into the Holy of Holies. I can still see those Indian ladies in my mind's eye. I long for that same passion to know Him. The Psalmist penned, "He made known His

> **ANY CASUAL OBSERVER CAN DETECT THE DEEDS OF GOD SUCH AS CREATION, BUT TO KNOW HIS WAYS DENOTES THE INTIMACY OF A CLOSE RELATIONSHIP.**

ways to Moses, His deeds to the people of Israel" (Psalm 103:7, NIV). Any casual observer can detect the deeds of God, such as creation, but to know His ways denotes the intimacy of a close relationship.

THE DISCIPLINE OF MEDITATION

Today we will put into practice the concept of meditation. This, of course, is not to be confused with practices in the New Age or Eastern religions. Our purpose will be to take time to reflect on God's Word in order to understand who He is and what His instructions are for living the Kingdom life. Synonyms for the verb meditate include consider, contemplate, reflect, and ponder. These words do not suggest a quick perusal, but careful consideration. It is not something you do at a fast pace in order to check it off your to-do list. It involves time and is the basis for knowing His ways.

We have already deduced from Psalm 103 that Moses' relationship with God exceeded the one the average citizen of Israel experienced. You might be thinking by now, "Well, he was Moses after all!" While God does call out some for specific responsibilities, He longs for intimacy with all believers. It is available to us, but we must enter into His presence and stay a while. Before we begin, take a moment to trace God's interaction with Moses through Scripture.

1. God revealed His name to Moses (Exodus 3:13-14, NIV).

   Moses said to God, "Suppose I go to the Israelites and say to them, 'The God of your fathers has sent me to you,' and they ask me, 'What is his name?' Then what shall I tell them?" God said to Moses, "I AM WHO I AM."

2. God revealed His Law to Moses that he might know His precepts (Exodus 20:1, 21, NIV).

   And God spoke all these words...The people remained at a distance, while Moses approached the thick darkness where God was.

3. God met with Moses on a regular basis, friend to friend (Exodus 33:9, 11, NIV)

   As Moses went into the tent, the pillar of cloud would come down and stay at the entrance, while the Lord spoke with Moses...The Lord would speak to Moses face to face, as one speaks to a friend.

4. God defended Moses when Miriam and Aaron opposed him (Numbers 12:6-8, NIV).

   He (God) said, "Listen to my words: When there is a prophet among you, I, the LORD, reveal myself to them in visions, I speak to them in dreams. But this is not true of my servant Moses; he is faithful in all my house. With him I speak face to face, clearly and not in riddles; he sees the form of the Lord."

Do you see the progression of intimacy between God and Moses? It was not instantaneous, but rather developed over time as Moses learned the nature and precepts of God. We will be striving to do the same in our activity today.

This kind of intimacy is not found through the experience of salvation alone, but through the ongoing desire of a longing heart, thirsting after God. [27]
~Wood Kroll

THE EXERCISE

Today, you will spend some time meditating on a passage of Scripture for the purpose of knowing the nature of God and hearing what He says to you through it.

I have chosen one of my favorite passages for us to consider today, Philippians 2:5-11. Set aside a generous amount of time in a place where you won't be interrupted. You might want to have your Bible software or Hebrew/Greek Dictionary close by for easy reference. The text is printed below. Feel free to make notes on it. Read it slowly. Think about every phrase. I am sure you are familiar with the word *selah* that you find frequently in the Psalms. The actual meaning is uncertain, though it could indicate a pause or a musical transition. One pastor suggested that the meaning was stop and think about it. That's what we want to do today.

Before you begin, pray these words from Psalm 25 back to the Lord: "Show me Your ways, O Lord, teach me Your paths; guide me in Your truth and teach me, for You are God my Savior, and my hope is in You all day long" (Psalm 25:4-5, NIV).

PHILIPPIANS 2:5-11
Have this attitude in yourselves which was also in Christ Jesus,

Who, although He existed in the form of God,

did not regard equality with God a thing to be grasped,

but emptied Himself,

taking the form of a bond-servant,

and being made in the likeness of men.

Being found in appearance as a man,

He humbled Himself by becoming obedient to the point of death,

even death on a cross.

For this reason also, God highly exalted Him,

and bestowed on Him the name which is above every name,

so that at the name of Jesus every knee will bow,

of those who are in Heaven and on earth and under the earth, and that every tongue will confess that Jesus Christ is Lord,

to the glory of God the Father.

REFLECTION QUESTIONS

1. What spoke to you about the character of Jesus Christ?

2. How were you impressed to emulate the Lord Jesus?

3. Compare your attitude to the one Jesus displayed.

4. What was the most meaningful part of your meditation today?

5. Will you make meditation a part of your regular schedule?

WEEK SIX
KINGDOM RIGHTEOUSNESS
—•——•——•—— MATTHEW 6:1-8 ——•——•——•——

Be careful not to practice your righteousness in front of others to be seen by them.
If you do, you will have no reward from your Father in Heaven.
MATTHEW 6:1, NIV

There is no pride so dangerous, so subtle and
insidious, as the pride of holiness. [1]
~ANDREW MURRAY

Method versus motive. In Matthew 6, Jesus speaks to the religious activities of giving, praying, and fasting. James Bryan Smith says, "He takes three righteous and holy actions and shows how the condition of a person's heart determines whether the discipline is a blessing or a hindrance. Jesus is a genius when it comes to how our hearts work." [2]

The idea of being noticed and praised for our good works can be referred to as vainglory. Smith describes it this way, "Vainglory—the need to have others think well of us in order to feel worthy."[3] He goes on to say, "When the devil sees someone who is serious about his or her spiritual life, he does not give up. He utilizes a special vice to destroy them: vainglory." [4]

Matthew 6 opens with Jesus giving a word of caution to the listener. I pray as you begin this week's study, you will lean in closely and allow Jesus' words to encourage and challenge your heart to be pure in motive in the specific areas of giving and prayer.

Today's lesson is an overview of the passage we are studying this week as Jesus begins to discuss Kingdom worship. We will see that it is not just a matter of *what* we do to worship God, but the reason *why*.

Read Matthew 6:1-4.

1. In your own words, what caution does Jesus give in verse 1?

In lovingkindness, Jesus tells us to be careful not to make a show of our acts of righteousness. If we do what we do to be recognized and praised by others, we will receive no reward in Heaven. The "feel good" that we experience will be all the reward we get. We like to be acknowledged, bragged on, and recognized for a job well done. It feels good to have a pat on the back.

Public acknowledgement is not wrong, nor do I think appreciating it is wrong. However, if the attitude of our heart (which only we and God truly know) is primarily a desire for human praise, we fall into the category of those mentioned in Matthew 6:1.

2. How does Jesus tell us to give? (vv. 2-4)

J. Vernon McGee cautions, "Giving is between you and God, and the very minute you get a third party involved, you don't get any credit in Heaven." [5] Jesus tells us not to give as the hypocrites (an actor playing a role) do, because they do it for the sole purpose of being honored by others.

3. What does He repeat in the latter part of verse 2 as it relates to our reward?

As good as it may feel to receive an accolade for our gift or service, it will be short-lived and temporary. In contrast, the heavenly reward that awaits us will be eternal and everlasting.

Read Matthew 6:5-8.

4. What does Jesus tell us <u>not</u> to do in these verses?

5. How <u>should</u> we pray?

Before we look at giving and prayer in more detail, let us spend today examining our hearts.

As I began to study this portion of Scripture, the Lord revealed to my heart that I struggle in one area more than I realized. (I don't even like typing out those words.) Giving and praying to be noticed are not specific struggles I face; however, He did reveal that human praise is more valuable to me than it should be. I do not long for it or wring my hands in hopes of it, but He showed me that it adds to my sense of self-worth and validation more than it should.

This excerpt from Smith's book, *The Good and Beautiful Life*, is powerful:

> The Kingdom narratives oppose the world's narratives: You are valuable to God. God loves you no matter what. Your worth is not dependent on your performance or on what others think of you. Your worth is found in the loving eyes of God. If you win, God loves you. If you lose, God loves you. If you fast and pray and give your money to the poor, God loves you. If you are sinful and selfish, God loves you. He is a covenant God, and His love never changes. You are valuable, precious and worth dying for—just as you are. [6]

6. Consider Jesus' words in Matthew 6:1-8 and reread the quote above. Do you struggle to believe your value to God? Do you place too much emphasis on the thoughts, opinions, and approval of others? Journal your thoughts.

Set your minds on things above, not on earthly things.
Colossians 3:2, NIV

MATTHEW 6:1-4

As we go deeper into our study of Matthew 6:1-4 today, we will see that Jesus makes it clear that our acts of "righteousness" are to be directed only toward God. And that doing something to be noticed by others invalidates the act with God. Here is the bottom line: If we do things to impress others, God will not be impressed. And we miss His reward.

The issue boils down to our motive. If we give a gift with the hope that someone will recognize or praise it, we are "pre-empting God's role in our life." [7] To be clear, Jesus is not saying that recognition or praise is wrong. We see Paul commending believers throughout the epistles. I enjoy giving words of encouragement and affirmation to those who have blessed me in various ways. Receiving these words is not sinful. This is all about the motive of our heart. As Dallas Willard writes, "What matters are the intentions of our heart before God." [8]

Oswald Chambers echoes this thought as he challenges, "Have no other motive in giving than to please God." [9]

Think of a gift you've recently given, whether it be monetary or otherwise. Ask yourself these questions and answer honestly. (Mark any of these areas with which you may struggle and commit them to prayer.)

- As I planned to give, did I hope to receive recognition or praise?
- Did I desire attention be given to me in a public setting so others would know?
- If no one knew about my gift, would I still have a desire to give it?

Read Matthew 6:1-4.

1. How do the hypocrites give to the needy? (v. 2)

> **THE WORLD FORGETS AND QUICKLY GETS OVER US. OUR HEAVENLY FATHER REMEMBERS AND FOREVER DELIGHTS IN US.**

In regards to this manner of giving, Willard observes, "What they wanted, they got. They wanted people to recognize their good deed, and people did. The ego is bloated and the soul shrivels." [10]

As previously noted, the Kingdom narrative and the world narrative differ vastly. The world is all about ego, pride, and looking good to others. As with anything the world offers, this is temporary. The commendation of others comes quickly and then it's over. The Kingdom of Heaven is always about eternity. Rather than a shriveled soul, it gives us a nourished soul, one that is satisfied with an audience of One and stores up eternal treasures that will not pass away.

The world forgets and quickly gets over us. Our Heavenly Father remembers and forever delights in us.

2. In what ways do we "blow trumpets" (Matthew 6:2) today?

One way I immediately think of is social media. (Disclaimer: I have posted on social media platforms many times to brag on my children.) Again, I do not find this, in and of itself, to be wrong; however, the intentions of our heart <u>can</u> be wrong if we are not careful. In today's world, I believe this is an area in which we must continually ask the Lord, "Search me, O God, and know my heart…point out anything in me that offends you…" (Psalm 139:23-24, NLT).

Social media offers a platform to advertise and promote ourselves in unprecedented ways. We can easily "announce it with trumpets" when we share with the world all that we have done. We must strive to keep a pure heart as we give money, time, talents, and services to others.

Read Colossians 3:23-24.

3. For whom should we work/serve/give?

No matter our work, service, gift, talent, or ministry, we should be doing all of it as "unto the Lord." If He were the only One who knew, the only One aware of our efforts, we should do it with everything we have, giving all of ourselves for the glory of God the Father. He is our Master. We are His servants.

4. What specific instruction does Jesus give in Matthew 6:3-4?

5. How do you interpret these verses?

Willard gives this insight on Matthew 6:3-4, "The kind of people who have been so transformed by their daily walk with God that good deeds naturally flow from their character are precisely the kind of people whose left hand would not notice what their right hand is doing." [11] As I read Willard's words, they made an impact on my heart and caused me to reflect in a way I had not done before. Oh, that my heart would be so pure, so in communion with the Father, chasing after Him with devotion and passion, that any good deed, service, or gift would be a natural outpouring from my life. I pray the Lord continues to reveal any dark corners of my heart and prune away any hint of self. I want my love for Him to be so great that money, gifts, service, and ministry cannot help but spring forth from my life onto the lives of those around me...all for HIS glory.

6. What are some examples of ways to give to others in a way that honors God?

2 Chronicles 16:9 (NLT) says, "The eyes of the LORD search the whole earth in order to strengthen those whose hearts are fully committed to Him." We need His strength to serve others, to give of our time, money, and talents. I imagine Him looking down from His throne, His holy hand above His brow scanning the earth for a faithful, selfless child to partner with as He reveals His glory.

Soli Deo Gloria! Glory to God alone! May this be the anthem ringing in our hearts.

MATTHEW 6:5-6

Have no other motive in prayer than to know Him. [12]
~OSWALD CHAMBERS

I must tell you that I am beyond excited to write today's lesson. Limiting my words will be a challenge!

Read Matthew 6:5-6.

Prayer has become my most treasured gift as a child of God. This did not come naturally or quickly. Under the teaching and leadership of precious mentors, I have learned how to pray and have become absolutely convinced of its power. I cannot go a day without it. I cannot survive life's stormy seas and deep valleys apart from it. It is my lifeline. It is as valuable and necessary as the air I breathe.

This was not always the case. I was a Christian for more than twenty years before I began to experience this intimate conversation with my heavenly Father.

1. What instruction do we receive in Matthew 6:5-6?

Jesus' words here are not speaking against public prayer. Jesus prayed both privately and publicly. God's Word tells us that when we are gathered together, He hears us and is in our midst. In Scripture, we are commanded to pray together, and we see examples of God's hand moving when His people pray. But apparently, the men Jesus refers to in these verses are praying in public, but not in private. Private conversation with the Father is essential.

Yes, we can pray anywhere and anytime, but there is something special about the secret place. The place behind a closed door. A quiet spot in the corner of your living room. That place that only you and God meet each day to commune with one another. In his book, *Secrets of the Secret Place*, Bob Sorge says, "The secret place is your portal to the throne, the place where you taste of Heaven itself." [13]

Setting aside a time and place for prayer is vital. Most commentaries I read suggest giving God the portion of your day that works best for you and befits your personality. For me, morning is best. It allows me to begin the day with my mind fixed on Him before thousands of distractions ensue. I can offer a convincing case for the morning, but, more importantly, I urge you to set a specific time and place aside each day to enter into the presence of God with minimal distraction.

2. Do you have a secret place and are you meeting God there daily to pray? (Consider sharing your place and routine with your small group.)

My secret place is in our formal living room in the corner of my sofa. Each morning, I brew a cup of coffee, grab my soft white throw, and settle into my spot. My Bible, books, and prayer box are all there and ready to use. I open the shutters that face me so I can see the sun as it rises or watch the rain gently fall on the trees. As my body settles in to that place, I literally inhale and slowly exhale. I close my eyes and I say to the Lord, "My heart has heard you say, 'Come and talk with me.' And my heart responds, 'LORD, I am coming'" (Psalm 27:8, NLT). I begin by thanking Him for something He did the day before or laying before Him a heavy burden that is already on my mind. I tell Him how much I love Him and thank Him for meeting with me. As I type these words, tears fill my eyes. As I visualize my morning routine with Him, my heart overflows with gratitude for how He draws me in close to His heart. I am overwhelmed with His love for me, with His mercy, grace, and patience with me.

Often times, we do not feel like praying. Perhaps we are tired (physically or spiritually), weary and worn from asking, discouraged because it seems our prayers are hitting the ceiling. Just as a fire must be continually stoked to keep burning, our prayer life ignites something within us as we pour our hearts out to God, and He pours Himself into us as He speaks.

Sorge describes it this way:

> When you approach God, you are drawing near to the great blazing inferno of the ages. To be set on fire, you must get close to God. When you feel cold, distant, and "out of it" spiritually, it's time to retreat to the closet, place yourself before the fireplace of His Word, and allow the intensity of His face to restore your fervency. The only sure source for staying white-hot is in devoting yourself consistently to the place-of-the-shut-door. [14]

If your prayer life is not where you want it to be, do not feel guilty or condemned. God is not sitting on His throne scowling and shaking His finger when you miss your time with Him. As Sorge says, "When you neglect the secret place, He's not disappointed *in* you, He's disappointed *for* you." [15]

He longs to reveal Himself to you. There is no limit to what He can do as a result of your prayers. If you already have a secret place, resolve today that you will protect this place and time. If you do not, commit today to find your secret place and determine to meet Him there each day, without compromise.

3. What promise does Jesus give in the latter part of Matthew 6:6?

There are not many guarantees in this earthly life, but there is one thing you can be sure. Your Father will see what you do in the secret place—where no one else sees—and He will reward you.

As you set aside a secret place, and make a priority of meeting with your heavenly Father on a daily basis, your life will be forever changed. You will long for more of Him. You will see Him move in ways that leave you speechless and in awe. You will become convinced of His nature and character. You will miss Him when you do not go. You will experience abundant life and burn with desire for others to know Him this way.

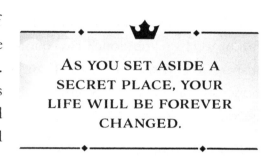

AS YOU SET ASIDE A SECRET PLACE, YOUR LIFE WILL BE FOREVER CHANGED.

4. What have you learned about God as a result of your personal prayer life with Him?

In addition to all the other work that gets done through prayer,
perhaps the greatest work of all is the knitting of the human heart
together with the heart of God. [16]
~JOHN ORTBERG

MATTHEW 6:7-8

This week, we have looked at giving and prayer as it relates to our intentions and motives. We are to be pure in heart and practice these things with a heavenly mindset while living in This Present Kingdom. God's reward and approval should be our only focus—the very thing that motivates us to give to those in need and to pray boldly and honestly before Him. If no one ever knows of our giving or hears our prayers, we should still commit to do these things simply because it pleases God.

Read Matthew 6:7-8.

How do we go about daily life, giving and praying, in a manner that ultimately brings glory and honor to His name alone? Two quotes that give insight to this subject are from Willard and Smith, respectively. Willard says, "If I am Jesus' disciple that means I am with Him to learn from Him how to be like Him." [17] Smith says, "Apprentices of Jesus learn how to be with Jesus in order to become like Jesus." [18]

1. Read Matthew 26:39-44. What difference do you notice in the way Jesus prays and the prayers of the Gentiles described in Matthew 6:7?

2. What are some modern day examples of "meaningless repetition"?

During the early years of my Christian walk, I was not discipled. Thankfully, I heard sound biblical preaching and teaching my entire life. This laid a firm foundation for which I am eternally grateful. But it has been my experience that discipleship (apprenticeship) goes far beyond sermons and group Bible studies. I do not see how we can read the verses from the Sermon on the Mount and have any hope to experience Kingdom living apart from a radical, personal devotion to Jesus Christ—to be "with Him to learn from Him how to be like Him." [19]

3. Read the following verses and record any insight on how we can be a committed disciple/apprentice of Jesus Christ. Practically speaking, how do we guard against Pharisaical giving and prayer?

Psalm 16:8

Colossians 3:1-2

Psalm 86:11b

Proverbs 4:23

Many Christians simply focus on the rules, doing or not doing certain practices. When we fall into this trap of legalism rather than focusing on our relationship with the Lord, it can lead us to do these things with impure motives. We give to the poor (making sure others know about it), or we lead prayer publicly (making sure to use all the right words, babbling to impress those who are listening) with the hopes of pleasing people or checking off our religious to-do list.

If we follow the instructions given in the list of scriptures we just read, we have minds fixed on Jesus, Spirit eyes that see as Jesus sees, childlike faith seeking to please the Father alone, and hearts that long to look more and more like Jesus. We give and pray the way Jesus tells us to because we are focused on the relationship, not the rules.

Read John 15:5.

4. What does Jesus say is the key to producing fruit?

5. What can we do apart from Jesus?

WHEN OUR INNER LIFE IS TRANSFORMED BY ABIDING IN HIM AND HIM IN US, WE BEGIN TO DO SUPERNATURAL ACTS NATURALLY.

Smith explains, "To abide, then, is not done by observing a set of outer activities...To abide in Christ involves spending time with Jesus." [20] When our inner life is transformed by abiding in Him and Him in us, we begin to do supernatural acts naturally. Our giving to others and our personal prayer life (for an audience of One) will become a natural way of life because we are becoming more and more like Jesus.

As I have studied and prepared to write this lesson, I have been so challenged to sit quietly before the Lord and ask Him to examine my heart. Giving and prayer have been this week's focus, but He has called me to look deep within and survey my devotion and commitment to Him.

6. Answer these questions honestly.

- Are you a devoted follower/disciple/apprentice of Jesus Christ?
- Are you giving to those in need from a pure heart that only wants God to notice?
- Are you spending time in prayer, in a secret and sacred place, pouring your heart out to God in a way that no one else sees or knows about?
- Do you notice a transformation in your life in the past six months, year, five, or ten years?
- Is your mind fixed on Jesus with an eternal perspective?

How we give and how we pray will be determined by who we follow. If we look to self or our fellow man, we will give and pray as the Pharisees did—seeking attention and with a prideful heart. If we look to Jesus Christ, we will give and pray as He did—for the glory of God and with a humble heart.

In the words of Dallas Willard, "One thing is sure: You are somebody's disciple...there are no exceptions to this rule. Who teaches you? Whose disciple are you?" [21]

KINGDOM EXERCISE

Jesus encourages us to do good things with absolutely no
concern about what others think about us. [22]
~JAMES BRYAN SMITH

THE DISCIPLINE OF GIVING

As I reflected on the spiritual discipline of giving, the following words came to mind.

> Develop the habit of having such a relationship to God that you do good without knowing it. Then you will no longer trust your own impulse or judgment—you will trust only the inspiration of the Spirit of God. The mainspring of your motives will be the Father's heart, not your own; the Father's understanding, not yours. [23]

I would like you to begin this week's exercise by positioning yourself before the Father. Maybe you want to kneel where you are. Perhaps you'd like to sit outside on your patio in the beauty of His creation. Come before Him with a still and quiet heart and ask Him to give you the motives of His heart as you prepare to give. Confess to Him any selfishness, greed, or desire to be known by men.

Before you begin today's Kingdom Exercise, write out Psalm 51:10 as a prayer.

THE EXERCISE

We will focus on giving in two ways.

This will, most likely, look differently for each of us. God has an incredible way of uniquely displaying His character and power when we come to Him with open hands, ready to say "yes" to whatever He speaks to our hearts. Smith says, "Any act of service that lightens someone's load will do." [24]

Do not put pressure on yourself to come up with some magnanimous and creative idea. Perhaps the Spirit will lead you this way, but most often, a simple act of service will minister greatly to the heart of one in need.

First, ask the Lord to allow someone to cross your path who simply needs help. Maybe that person has already come to mind as you consider this exercise. Pick up groceries, fill a tank with gas, watch someone's children for a couple hours, pay a bill, cook a meal, send an encouraging note, help your child/grandchild complete a task they cannot do on their own, give a restaurant gift card, clean a house, mow a yard, leave a generous tip, sit on the porch with someone and offer a listening ear.

Now the icing on the cake – make an attempt to do something for someone in secret. As you give, whether it be monetary or not, give in a manner that the recipient has no idea it came from you. If that is not possible, make sure that *only* the direct recipient knows it came from you. Do it from a pure and humble heart. Do it expecting nothing in return. Do it and tell no one else you did it. Give of your resources, give of yourself, and be able to genuinely say, "Not to us, LORD, not to us but to Your name be the glory..." (Psalm 115:1, NIV).

Secondly, I encourage you, as part of this week's exercise, to give of yourself in prayer. If you are not currently setting aside time for prayer (behind the closed door), please find a time that works for you and commit to do this daily. Consider asking a friend to hold you accountable until you are regularly doing this on your own. If you are faithfully spending time with God in prayer, consider an additional time this week to spend with Him apart from your regular prayer time.

As I think about giving, I cannot think of a more impactful way to give than to offer myself wholly to my Creator, the Author and Perfecter of my faith, the Lover of my soul. Not only will He reward me for what is done in the secret place, but He will assuredly reveal new ways about how I can give to others so that His name is glorified and honored. As John Ortberg writes, "When a mind is washed—when someone begins to be filled with the very thoughts of God—it is a gift to the world." [25]

To everyone who reads these words, this is my prayer for you: May your mind be washed as you immerse yourself in Scripture and bow before the throne in prayer. As you pray, may your thoughts become His thoughts. May He transform you into His likeness and use you to bring change to the world.

REFLECTION QUESTIONS

1. Did you give to someone else?

2. Were you able to give "in secret"?

3. What struggles did you face as you planned to give?

4. What commitment did you make or renew in the area of prayer?

5. In what ways did God speak or bring about change to your heart?

6. How would you describe this exercise of giving?

WEEK SEVEN

KINGDOM PRAYER
——— • —— • — MATTHEW 6:9-15 ——— • —— • ———

Your Kingdom come. Your will be done, on earth as it is in Heaven.
MATTHEW 6:10

*When Jesus gave His disciples this prayer, He was giving them part of
His own breath, His own life, His own prayer.* [1]
~N.T. WRIGHT

When Jesus was asked by His disciples to teach them to pray, He responded with what we call the "The Lord's Prayer" (Luke 11:1-4). This prayer is recorded in the Gospels of Matthew and Luke with some variation. The variation lends itself to the prayer being a model, not a prayer to be prayed verbatim. Certainly, there is no prohibition to praying it verbatim, but Jesus' intention was for it to be an example to be emulated when we pray.

In the passage we studied last week, Jesus had just completed instruction on how not to pray (Matthew 6:5-8). The word "therefore" (Matthew 6:8, KJV) shows that the teaching on prayer to follow in Matthew 6:9-15 is the conclusion of His previous instruction. The way Jesus instructs them to pray "is a direct contrast to the verbosity, self-centeredness, and poor view of God reflected in the praying that Jesus rejected in verses 5-8." [2]

There is no evidence in Scripture that Jesus actually prayed this prayer. He is teaching His disciples that, when they pray, these are the things they need to include. With that understanding, this prayer is more appropriately called "The Model Prayer". N.T. Wright gives us a concise summary of what the prayer includes:

> The Lord's Prayer is a prayer about God's honor and glory. It's a prayer about God's Kingdom coming on earth as in Heaven—which pretty much sums up what a lot of Christianity is all about. It's a prayer for bread, for meeting the needs of every day. And it's a prayer for rescue from evil. The prayer says: I want to be part of His Kingdom-movement. I find myself drawn into His Heaven-on-earth way of living. I want to be part of His bread-for-the-world agenda, for myself and for others. I need forgiveness for myself—from sin, from debt, from every weight around my neck—and I intend to

live with forgiveness in my heart in my own dealings with others. And because I live in the real world, where evil is still powerful, I need protecting and rescuing. And in and through it all, I acknowledge and celebrate the Father's Kingdom, power, and glory. [3]

As we delve into this prayer, ask the Lord for ears to hear and eyes to see truths He desires to reveal from a passage many of us have committed to memory and may otherwise just breeze by because of its familiarity. God's Word is living and active. He gave us this model for us to follow. May He take us deeper still into His perfect will as we come before His throne in prayer.

MATTHEW 6:9-15

In writing about The Lord's Prayer, John McArthur notes, "The prayer is a model not just a liturgy. It is notable for its brevity, simplicity, and comprehensiveness. Of the six petitions, three are directed to God (vv. 9-10) and three toward human needs (vv. 11-13)." [4]

Read Matthew 6:9-15.

1. How does the prayer begin?

2. Are you comfortable calling God your Father?

When we address God as "Our Father who is in Heaven," we are immediately aware of His transcendence, omnipotence, and omniscience. He is far above all rule and authority. He is holy and majestic. Wright notes, "This prayer starts by addressing God intimately and lovingly, as `Father'—and by bowing before His greatness and majesty. If you can hold those two together, you're already on the way to understanding what Christianity is all about." [5] Addressing Him in this manner should keep us from rushing thoughtlessly into His presence.

3. In what way does addressing God as being "in Heaven" put us in our place?

If God is your Father, He is also Father to all who have come to Him through salvation in His Son, Jesus Christ. He is Father to every person in Christ, regardless of ethnicity, nationality, socio-economic status, or education level.

4. How does being "in Christ" with God as our Father compel us to love our brothers and sisters in the faith?

In his first letter John writes, "Everyone who believes that Jesus is the Christ has become a child of God. And everyone who loves the Father loves His children, too" (1 John 5:1, NLT).

5. What are the personal implications for living out this verse?

6. Read back through Matthew 6:9-15 and list the six petitions Jesus teaches.

SCRIPTURE	PETITION
Matthew 6:9	
Matthew 6:10a	
Matthew 6:10b	
Matthew 6:11	
Matthew 6:12	
Matthew 6:13	

We will begin our study of The Lord's Prayer with a focus on the first of the petitions directed toward God.

7. After addressing God as Father, Jesus prays, "Hallowed be Your name" (Matthew 6:9). How do we hallow the name of God?

D.A. Carson writes, "In the semitic perspective, a person's name is closely related to what he is. Therefore, when God in the Old Testament reveals that He has this name or that, He is using His name to reveal Himself as He is. The names are explanatory, they are revelatory." [6] God revealed Himself to people throughout the Old Testament. Every name was linked to His character and provision.

8. What is one of your favorite names for God from the Old Testament and the situation in which it was revealed?

9. Now, using the name you chose, write out a prayer thanking God for Who He is according to His name.

In his book, *Pray Like it Matters,* Steve Gaines gives examples of ways to pray the Names of God. "We can pray and thank God for His provision and blessings by praying, 'Father, I bless you today that You are Jehovah-Jireh, the Lord My Provider! Thank You that You will supply all of my needs according to Your riches in glory in Christ Jesus' (Philippians 4:19)." [7]

Worship is the foundation for every other petition. As Jesus is teaching His disciples, they would "have understood the first petition of the model prayer as a petition that God would receive the glory that He deserves from His people here and now. This involved praising the name of God with one's lips from the heart. It also involved glorifying God through righteous deeds (Matthew 5:16)." [8] "Righteous deeds" are the result of obeying or "honoring" God's Word. As we honor His Word, we are honoring His name.

10. Why is it important to honor God's name by obeying His Word? Provide scriptural support.

How do we enter the presence of One so lofty and exalted? How do we extol His virtues and hallow His name? One way is through worshiping Him in song. One of my favorite hymns is *Immortal, Invisible, God Only Wise* by Walter Chalmers Smith. Allow these words to stir your soul.

Immortal, invisible, God only wise,
In light inaccessible hid from our eyes,
Most blessed, most glorious, the Ancient of days,
Almighty, victorious, Thy great name we praise. [9]

MATTHEW 6:10

The second petition, "Thy Kingdom Come" demonstrates our allegiance to God and to His Kingdom. It is only as we hallow or honor the name of God that we will desire His Kingdom to come on earth. As we immerse ourselves in Scripture and are filled with the Holy Spirit, our will is aligned with His.

Read Matthew 6:10. Spend some time meditating on what Jesus is saying.

F.B. Meyer gives meaningful insight into this section of The Lord's Prayer:

> In giving us the second petition of the Lord's Prayer—"Your Kingdom come"—Jesus further turns our attention to what interests God…We have seen that God has a prayer list of His own, and He puts His requests right at the beginning of this remarkable prayer. First on God's prayer list is that we will pray that His name will be treated as holy on the planet He has made. His second request is that we pray for the coming of His Kingdom. [10]

Jesus came to bring the Kingdom of God from Heaven to earth. James Smith notes, "For Jesus, the Kingdom was not simply a nice idea, but a very real place—life with God, which is available to all. Outside the Kingdom of God we are on our own." [11]

I don't know about you, but I do not want to live this life on my own! I need the help of the Holy Spirit and desire to want God's Kingdom above my own.

God's Kingdom narrative is very different from that of the world. The world is under the control of the evil one until the return of Christ. Revelation 11:15 states, "The Kingdom of the world has become the Kingdom of our Lord and of His Christ; and He will reign forever and ever." It is an unalterable fact! But we will not experience the full manifestation of His Kingdom until His return.

In the meantime, we are to live according to His Word and His Will in His Kingdom on this earth. One of the ways to experience God's Kingdom now, is to reject the false narratives of this world. In his book, *The Good and Beautiful Life*, Smith provides a chart contrasting the two worldviews. [12] In the following table, I am giving you the first two contrasts he uses.

1. Complete this table using your own experiences and temptations. How are you tempted to doubt God and His Word? Which false narratives seem to trip you up the most? Write down the false narratives you struggle with and then give the Kingdom narrative that refutes that view from God's Word.

FALSE IMPERATIVE NARRATIVES (WORLD)	KINGDOM NARRATIVES
I am alone.	You are never alone. Jesus is with you always.
I must be in control all of the time.	Jesus is in control.

Inside the Kingdom of God, life is different. What Kingdom thoughts are you thinking? For your family, your neighborhood, church, and city? Our God is able to do "exceedingly abundantly above all that we ask or think" (Ephesians 3:20, NKJV). Ask Him to enlarge your faith and enable you to see with Kingdom eyes! May His Kingdom come and His will be done and may you be an instrument of His will!

"To pray that His Kingdom may 'come' is to pray both that it may grow, as through the church's witness people submit to Jesus, and that soon it will be consummated when Jesus returns in glory to take His power and reign." [13]

The third petition directed toward God in The Lord's Prayer is for His will to be done "on earth as it is in Heaven." Jesus has us focus on the will of the Father, because His will is always best for us. We know according to Romans 12:2 that God's will is "good and acceptable and perfect." Yet, the enemy tries to convince us of just the opposite.

How many times have you heard the suggestion in your mind that God can't be trusted? Or maybe that He doesn't even exist? Or what if all you are believing is not true?

Why does the evil one work so hard to keep us in doubt? Because the one who is doubting is not living by faith. The power of the Spirit is granted to those who believe. Those who walk by "faith, not by sight" (2 Corinthians 5:7). "Without faith it is impossible to please God" (Hebrews 11:6, NIV). Remember the enemy has come to "steal and kill and destroy" (John 10:10). Christ has come that we might have life abundant, but we must believe!

Because we are no longer citizens of this world but of Heaven, we live by a different standard. Our standard is God's standard. We do not fit into this self-centered, secularized culture that has permeated our nation and world. "But in the Christian counter-culture our top priority concern is not our name, kingdom and will, but God's. Whether we can pray these petitions with integrity is a searching test of the reality and depth of our Christian profession." [14]

Reflect over the last year of your life. Have you lived for your will or for God's? (One way to discern is to ask how much of your time and resources have been spent on those things that are eternal—people, the Word of God, and prayer—versus those things that are temporal and passing away.)

When we walk with the Lord and love Him with our whole hearts, His will begins to envelop our own. He begins to open our eyes and ears that we might see and hear as He does. Suddenly the clamor of your flesh and the siren cry of the world are silenced by the voice of the One you love above all. He will call you to Himself and then out into His world.

My daughters and their children were at our home recently. The girls and I stayed up one night after the children were in bed and watched the movie, *Harriet*, about the well-known abolitionist, Harriet Tubman. Most of you will recognize her name and link her with the underground railroad. But did you know that she singlehandedly rescued over 70 former slaves, many family and friends, over an 11-year period? She would later serve the Union army in the Civil War and alternated her roles as nurse, scout, cook, and spy. Eventually, she became the first American woman ever to lead an armed raid into enemy territory. It was through serving in this capacity that she saw over 700 slaves come to freedom. In 1896, Tubman purchased twenty-five acres to establish a home and hospital for indigent, aged, and sick African Americans. [15] Writing about Harriet's trust in the Lord and seemingly miraculous answers to prayer she experienced, one person noted, it "never seemed to strike her as at all strange or mysterious; her prayer was the prayer of faith, and she expected an answer." [16]

I am praying for the Lord to call out "Harriets" to claim the next generation for Christ. In recent years, God has called me to free children from the chains of generational poverty. To see their souls set free by the gospel and their futures enriched through education. Our world needs more "Harriets" to run into our cities and claim them. To believe the Lord and to trust Him as their guide. Will you join me in saying "yes" to what God is calling you to?

2. How are you serving others and seeing God's will come from Heaven to earth?

3. Prayer is the vehicle that God has chosen to bring His will from Heaven to earth. How would you rate your prayer life?

It is in prayer that we learn to discern God's voice. God will primarily speak through Scripture, but He also speaks through promptings of His Spirit in our inner man.

4. Write about a time that He prompted you to do something or spoke to you through His Word.

Christ desires for each of us to surrender daily to His will. Jesus told His followers, "And He was saying to them all, 'If anyone wishes to come after Me, he must deny himself, and take up his cross daily and follow Me'" (Luke 9:23). Pause and surrender to His will. Ask the Lord to give you ears to hear and a willing spirit.

Before we know God's will, we must surrender ourselves to it. Are you willing to die to your selfish desires (Luke 9:23) and ask God to accomplish His perfect will in every area of your life? [17]
~STEVE GAINES

MATTHEW 6:11-12, 14-15

The Lord's Prayer, in many ways, is a simple prayer. So simple that a child can pray it. But in many ways, it is also a difficult prayer because of what it requires. As you begin today's study, read Matthew 6:11-12, 14-15 slowly. Consider each word, every phrase.

We are entering the section of The Lord's Prayer that directs its petitions to the one praying. In the fourth petition, Jesus teaches His disciples to pray for their daily needs. In fact, as we will see next week as we continue in Matthew 6, Jesus tells His disciples to "seek first His Kingdom and His righteousness, and all these things will be added to you" (v. 33). Right before that, He has been telling them that the Father would provide food and clothing for them just as He feeds the birds and arrays the flowers of the field.

1. What are your daily needs?

2. Are you currently trusting the Father to provide those needs?

I am not asking you about tomorrow or next week or next year. In fact, Jesus told His followers, "So do not worry about tomorrow; for tomorrow will care for itself. Each day has enough trouble of its own" (Matthew 6:34). Live for today. Don't miss anything the Father has for you to experience. Follow the advice of the great missionary, Jim Elliot, "Wherever you are, be all there! Live to the hilt every situation you believe to be the will of God." [18]

The fifth petition may roll easily off our tongues, but it is not so easily lived out. Jesus instructs us to pray, "Forgive us our debts, as we also have forgiven our debtors" (Matthew 6:12).

3. Write a paraphrase of Matthew 6:12 and journal your thoughts about this fifth petition of The Lord's Prayer.

Over the years, I have listened to many stories from women who were struggling with forgiveness. I understood their reluctance. I, too, would have struggled forgiving some of the very real abuse and offenses. But what we know from Scripture is that we will be forgiven as we forgive. I have told many women: "It is okay to choose forgiveness simply out of obedience to God and a desire to be personally forgiven. As you release the person and the offense, you will find that the Lord then begins to bring healing to your raw emotions and very real wounds."

I remember in one of our early church experiences being betrayed by someone that I had considered a very good friend. I was deeply wounded and cried out to the Lord. I told Him this was not fair and I didn't believe I deserved this. The Holy Spirit so gently spoke within, "You are right, you don't deserve this, you deserve hell, just like they do." I felt like the person in the parable that Jesus told. You remember the guy who had been forgiven the humongous debt by the king and then had required payment of a measly debt from another person (Matthew 18:21-35)? The king turned the unforgiving servant over to be tortured until he paid back all he owed. Jesus then said, "This is how my heavenly Father will treat each of you unless you forgive your brother or sister from your heart" (Matthew 18:35, NIV).

Forgiveness is serious stuff! Jesus said we must forgive from the heart. That is total forgiveness. So, I must ask myself how can I, who have been forgiven so much, not forgive others? Putting our sin in perspective provides the motivation to obey. R.T. Kendall said, "Totally forgiving someone doesn't necessarily mean we will want to spend our vacation with them, but it does mean that we release the bitterness in our hearts concerning what they have done." [19]

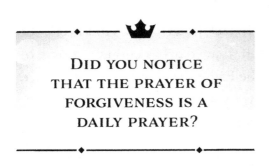

DID YOU NOTICE THAT THE PRAYER OF FORGIVENESS IS A DAILY PRAYER?

Did you notice that the prayer of forgiveness is a daily prayer? That means the comment your husband made that caused an offense, or the hurt you were hanging onto because your friend made an insensitive remark, needs to be forgiven daily. We must let it go. Commit it to the Lord. It doesn't mean that we don't discuss the situation, but it does mean that we cannot harbor unforgiveness. We cannot allow unforgiveness to fester and turn into bitterness.

4. What offense do you find yourself most easily giving into?

Kendall identifies the issue with true and total forgiveness, "It is no spiritual victory to think we are forgiving people when we are only avoiding facing up to their wrong behavior. It is, if anything evading true forgiveness…Total forgiveness is painful…Total forgiveness is a choice. It is not a feeling—at least at first—but is rather an act of the will." [20]

5. When we are confronted with truth, it requires action. What choices will you make to begin walking and living in forgiveness on a daily basis?

6. How do you think choosing forgiveness will impact your relationships?

Kendall challenges, "Keep no record of wrongs in your thoughts, and you will be less likely to expose such records by your words." [21]

7. How will choosing forgiveness impact your relationship with the Lord? (Matthew 6:14-15)

One of my favorite authors is Amy Carmichael, who served as a missionary to India in the first half of the 20th century. I have learned much from her writings. In her little book, *If*, she writes about Calvary love lived out daily. So much of what we struggle with as believers would be swept away if we truly understood Calvary love. One of my favorite quotes from her book deals with forgiveness:

> If I say, "Yes I forgive but I cannot forget," as though the God who twice a day washes all the sands on all the shores of all the world, could not wash such memories from my mind, than I know nothing of Calvary love. [22]

Dear sister in Christ, trust His perfect love. Choose forgiveness. Let it go. Allow the Holy Spirit to wash your soul with His healing presence as you obey His Word. He is faithful!

MATTHEW 6:13

The sixth and final petition of The Lord's Prayer is, "And do not lead us into temptation, but deliver us from evil" (Matthew 6:13). So much of what we deal with in the area of temptation takes place in our minds. The enemy is very crafty as he aims his fiery darts into the areas we are most susceptible. But the Lord makes it very clear that we are not struggling against flesh and blood. We must utilize the spiritual weapons He has given us.

1. Read 2 Corinthians 10:3-5. Write your own paraphrase of these verses.

Now, consider the words of Eugene Peterson's paraphrase:

> The world is unprincipled. It's dog-eat-dog out there! The world doesn't fight fair. But we don't live or fight our battles that way—never have and never will. The tools of our trade aren't for marketing or manipulation, but they are for demolishing that entire massively corrupt culture. We use our powerful God-tools for smashing warped philosophies, tearing down barriers erected against the truth of God, fitting every loose thought and emotion and impulse into the structure of life shaped by Christ (2 Corinthians 10:3-5, MSG). [23]

On Day Two, we discussed false narratives that are perpetrated by the world. These false narratives or stories cause us to live a lie. That is why we must immerse ourselves in God's Word so that we know the truth and will not fall for the lie of the evil one or those of the ones he has deceived.

We must tell the right story. The only way to do that is to control which narrative we believe and repeat it to ourselves. Wrong thoughts or stories lead to wrong emotions that end up controlling our behavior. We are to live Spirit-controlled lives.

WRONG THOUGHTS OR STORIES LEAD TO WRONG EMOTIONS THAT END UP CONTROLLING OUR BEHAVIOR.

This is a topic that we have discussed at length in our Bellevue Women Bible studies. And yet, I can still detect some of you saying, "I know the Bible answers, but how do I actually work this into my life?" This is where our scripture from 2 Corinthians comes into play. We must arrest every errant thought and replace it with the truth of

God's Word. If we don't want to be led into temptation, we must use the spiritual weapons the Lord has given us to protect us from the lies of the flesh, the world, and the enemy.

In her book, *Get Out of Your Head,* Jennie Allen writes, "The danger of toxic thinking is it produces an alternate reality, one in which distorted reasoning actually seems to make sense."[24] Allen describes a time in her life when the evil one ambushed her with an all-out assault against her faith. It was this 18-month battle that the Lord used to birth her book as He brought her out on the other side. She warns us, "But let's not be naïve: if our thought lives are the deepest, darkest places of stronghold within us, all hell will try to stop us from being free."[25]

The disciple John, in his epistles, is very clear that we are not of this world, "You are from God, little children, and have overcome them; because greater is He who is in you than he who is in the world" (1 John 4:4). We know we have the power of the Spirit living within us and the promises of Christ upon which to stand. So why are more of us not standing? Why are so many believers appearing to be caught up in the secularization of our culture, thinking and acting just like the world?

We have a choice to make. We must be alert and on guard. Our enemy is prowling about like a lion seeking someone to devour (1 Peter 5:8). Are you ready to do the hard work of taking your thoughts captive? Our choice is to think like Christ and be transformed as we spiral up toward Christlikeness; or to allow fleshly, demonic thoughts to capture our minds and spiral downward into sin, separation, and relational dysfunction.

Allen writes, "Every spiral can be interrupted. No fixation exists outside God's long-armed reach. Because we are a 'new creation' we have a choice."[26]

I highly recommend her book. I would differ a little on the cycle of the spiral. I believe the spiral begins with an errant thought. Thoughts fuel our emotions and lead to actions. That is why we must make choices based on the Word of God, and not on our feelings. As we focus on and think about the Word of God, and refuse entrance to any errant thought, our feelings will eventually line up with truth.

But, please hear me. I am not telling you not to feel! God created us in His image, and He gave us feelings. What I am asking you to do is explore your feelings and see what thoughts or past experiences trigger them. Are you responding in the Spirit or still reacting in the flesh?

Here is how I would outline the downward spiral into sin:

ERRANT THOUGHT

EMOTION

FIXATION ON THE THOUGHT AND EMOTION

SINFUL REACTION IN THE FLESH

RELATIONAL PAIN AND SEPARATION

Now, if I instead, take that errant thought captive and refuse to give it entrance into my mind, I have abruptly halted the spiral downward. I wield the Sword of the Spirit and speak out loud the truth of God's Word. It is then that I will experience what Romans 8:5-6 makes so clear:

> For those who are according to the flesh set their minds on the things of the flesh, but those who are according to the Spirit, the things of the Spirit. For the mind set on the flesh is death, but the mind set on the Spirit is life and peace.

When we "set our minds on the Spirit" the spiral will spiral up. Start at the bottom and follow the progression.

TRANSFORMATION

THEN YOU WILL EXPERIENCE HIS LIFE AND PEACE

EMOTIONS WILL EVENTUALLY LINE UP WITH TRUTH

CHOOSE – BEHAVIOR (ACTION)

REPLACE IT WITH GOD'S WORD

ERRANT THOUGHT – THE LIE

Learning to "spiral up" will require some work on our part. Because we are programmed in homes led by people with sin natures, none of us had a perfect home. We all learned certain behavior patterns that are so natural to us that we don't even notice them. Sometimes we have to go backwards before we can go forward.

In his book, Peter Scazzero states, "The work of growing in Christ (what theologians call sanctification) does not mean we don't go back to the past as we press ahead to what God has for us. It actually demands we go back in order to break free from unhealthy and destructive patterns that prevent us from loving ourselves and others as God designed." [27]

Anger and fear are legitimate emotions. Righteous indignation can lead to just change and action. Fear can protect you from impending danger. But when anger is damaging your relationships and fear is holding you captive, then you need to dig below the surface to the lie that is triggering the anger and the fear.

One of the lies we often believe is that we are not good Christians if we ever experience fear or anger. Instead of listening to the evil one who wants to shut you down, ask the Holy Spirit to expose the root or lie that is attached to his sinister whispers.

The reason we often fall for the lie is that we do not know who we are in Christ and do not use the weapons we have been given to take thoughts captive and live in the abundance Christ died to give us.

I was recently talking with a dear friend who hosts retreats for pastor's wives. At a recent retreat, she had the women attending fill out cards with the lies they had been believing. See if you resonate with any of these:

1. I don't measure up.
2. I am unworthy.
3. If anyone really knew me....
4. I will always be left alone.
5. Nobody will ever really love me.
6. I am unlovable.
7. People hate me.
8. I am never enough.
9. I am never good enough.
10. I need to work harder.
11. I am unloved.
12. I should be able to do it all.
13. I should always have it together.
14. I need someone to be my happiness.

15. I am better off dead.
16. It's all my fault.
17. I will never amount to anything.
18. No one really likes me.
19. I am never going to find peace.
20. I am not good at relationships.
21. I am not forgiven.
22. I am a bad mother.
23. I will be found out.
24. I have damaged my kids.
25. I don't deserve a good life.
26. I'm not smart enough.
27. I am a phony.
28. I'm not worthy.
29. I don't deserve to be happy.
30. Nothing will ever change.
31. What did I do wrong to have so many bad things happen to me?
32. I should have never married my husband.
33. I am lazy, I will never be close to God.
34. I am crazy.
35. I am not spiritual enough.
36. I feel guilty.
37. I am a failure.
38. I am afraid.
39. I don't believe that God could love me.
40. I want to go back to my sin.
41. I fear my past.
42. I am going to lose my mind.
43. My husband is going to leave me.
44. I will give in to my lustful thoughts.
45. I am just playing a role—I am not really saved.
46. I will never live up to the expectation that God has for me.
47. I am worthless.
48. I am a nobody.
49. I have no friends.
50. I always give up.
51. I am crazy and my sins will always haunt me.
52. I don't fit in.
53. I am not a good person despite my efforts.
54. I cannot resolve conflict.
55. I must be perfect.
56. I don't have a problem.

That last one may be the most damaging! This list is just a sample of about 400 cards that were submitted. Do any of these lies sound familiar? If not, what lie does the enemy feed you?

If you don't take these thoughts captive, you are opening the door for the enemy—see to it that you "do not give the devil an opportunity" (Ephesians 4:27). Believing the lie gives the enemy the opportuinity he is looking for to get a foothold in your mind. You will then act and make choices based on a lie. When you believe the lie, you are exchanging God's truth for altered reality orchestrated by the evil one who is scheming against you.

> **WHEN YOU BELIEVE THE LIE, YOU ARE EXCHANGING GOD'S TRUTH FOR ALTERED REALITY ORCHESTRATED BY THE EVIL ONE WHO IS SCHEMING AGAINST YOU.**

2. Think about your relationships. What issue keeps resurfacing in your marriage or close friendships?

- Examine your feelings. Ask the Lord to show you the lie or the errant thought at the root.

- Acknowledge the lie you have been believing and take it captive.

- Write out an upward spiral by listing the lie and then replacing it with the Word of God. Complete the spiral upward and the resulting life and peace that you will experience as you become more like Christ.

You cannot fight this battle for someone else. You can encourage, pray for, and exhort, but each individual must choose the reality of God's Kingdom and apply it. We come alongside each other in support. We were never intended to do it alone, that is why God gave us community within His church. There is power in agreement and tremendous freedom when the things that have been held in the dark are brought into the light as we confess the lies we have believed and pray with a sister in Christ for freedom.

Remember, "the thief comes only to steal and kill and destroy; I came that they may have life, and have it abundantly" (John 10:10). It is time to claim the abundant life that is rightfully yours.

3. Jesus told His followers that unless they became like little children they would not enter the Kingdom of Heaven (Matthew 18:3). What are some of the traits of children?

Now, read The Lord's Prayer as it is paraphrased for children by Sally Lloyd Jones, the author of *Jesus Storybook Bible*. Allow her words to penetrate your heart. Let down your guard. Allow the everlasting, never changing love of God to fill you and surround you. You are accepted in the Beloved!

Hello Daddy!
We want to know You.
And be close to You.
Please show us how.
Make everything in the world right again.
And in our hearts, too.
Do what is best – just like You do in Heaven,
And please do it down here, too.
Please give us everything we need today.
Forgive us for doing wrong, for hurting You.
Forgive us just as we forgive other people
when they hurt us.
Rescue us! We need You.
We don't want to keep running away
And hiding from You.
Keep us safe from our enemies.
You're strong, God.
You can do whatever You want.
You are in charge.
Now and forever and for always!
We think You're great!
Amen!
Yes we do!

At the conclusion of the prayer, Lloyd-Jones writes, "You see, Jesus was showing people that God would always love them—with a Never Stopping, Never Giving Up, Unbreaking, Always and Forever Love. So they didn't need to hide anymore, or be afraid, or ashamed. They could stop running away from God. And they could run to Him instead. As a little child runs into her daddy's arms." [28]

4. After reading this paraphrase, what is your response to the Father?

Living and swimming in the river of God's deep love for us in Christ is at the very heart of true spirituality. Soaking in this love enables us to surrender to God's will, especially when it seems so contrary to what we can see, feel, or figure out ourselves. This experiential knowing of God's love and acceptance provides the only sure foundation for loving and accepting our true selves. [29]

*~*PETER SCAZZERO

KINGDOM EXERCISE

THE DISCIPLINE OF PRAYER

Prayer is talking wth God. First and foremost, it is listening to Him, seeking to understand His will. And in doing so, the one praying is inevitably a participant of change. Change within oneself, and change in the ciricumstances and lives we pray for. Although prayer is a spiritual discipline, it is so much more. Dallas Willard writes, "It would be a low-voltage spiritual life in which prayer was chiefly undertaken as a discipline, rather than a way of co-laboring with God to accomplish good things and advance His Kingdom purposes." [30]

Prayer is an ongoing conversation with the Father. From early morning until we place our heads on the pillow at night. The more we pray, the more we are reminded to pray, and as we see prayers answered, our confidence in God's power spreads into other areas of our lives.

THE EXERCISE

Today, utilize the six petitions in The Lord's Prayer to guide your personal time of prayer. Write out your requests as you pray through these petitions.

1. Our Father, Who is in Heaven, hallowed be Your Name.

2. Your Kingdom come,

3. Your will be done, on earth as it is in Heaven.

4. Give us this day our daily bread.

5. Forgive us our debts, as we also have forgiven our debtors.

6. Do not lead us into temptation, but deliver us from evil.

Close your time of prayer with worship – "For Yours is the Kingdom and the power and the glory forever. Amen" (Matthew 6:13).

REFLECTION QUESTIONS

1. How did God speak to you as you were praying today?

2. Prayer, like the other spiritual disciplines, is a way of training and transforming our souls. Did you sense any change occurring within yourself during your time of prayer today?

3. As you were praying today, did you sense that you were "co-laboring with God" to see His Kingdom advanced? In what way(s)?

Prayer does not fit us for the greater work;
prayer is the greater work. [31]
~OSWALD CHAMBERS

We must believe that God, in the mystery of prayer,
has entrusted us with a force that can
move the Heavenly world,
and can bring its power down to earth. [32]
~ANDREW MURRAY

WEEK EIGHT
KINGDOM SEEKERS
——•—— MATTHEW 6:16-34 ——•——

But seek first His Kingdom and His righteousness, and
all these things will be added to you.
MATTHEW 6:33

It is only as we discover God's Kingdom, settle into it, and live its love that we
can properly walk with God as He intended—on earth as in Heaven. [1]
~DALLAS WILLARD

"I wonder what sort of a tale we've fallen into?," [2] muses Samwise Gamgee to his dear friend and master, Frodo Baggins, in J.R.R. Tolkien's epic trilogy, *The Lord of the Rings*. Sam, a seemingly ordinary hobbit, doesn't join the Fellowship because he is devoted to seeing the Ring destroyed or saving Middle Earth. He joins out of his devotion to Frodo. Sam freely chooses to follow Frodo in his quest, even when Frodo gives him several outs along the way. But throughout the difficult journey, Sam remains steadfast. Sarah Arthur notes,

> …the decisions are not easy for Sam. Even he feels the temptation of the ring for the brief time he carries it. He wrestles to discern what is the right road, the most loyal choice. He struggles to blend the various "departments" of his life into one unified whole in which his master's needs come first. But he does it one step at a time. He talks himself through it, he thinks out loud, he argues back and forth…until he finally pulls through. [3]

Self-preservation and creature comforts have no place in Sam's life. He has one purpose. To stick by his master. As Tolkien writes, "Now they were come to the bitter end. But he had stuck to his master all the way; that was what he had chiefly come for, and he would still stick to him." [4] He will not waver. He will not falter. He will not give up. Sam is convinced that his life is part of a larger story that will end well, no matter how his own story may end. If he ends up a hero in the finale, good. But if he doesn't, that's fine, too. As long as he fulfills the promise he made to remain close to his master, he is content with the ending.

Sam's single-hearted devotion sets the standard for us. We've heard the words many times. Perhaps we can even quote what Jesus said by heart, "If anyone wishes to come after Me, he must deny himself, and take up his cross and follow Me. For whoever wishes to save his life will lose it; but whoever loses his life for My sake will find it" (Matthew 16:24-25).

Why is it that single-hearted devotion is so difficult for us? What is it that keeps us from aligning every department in our lives under one Master?

Jesus is clear. Either we walk with Him in every aspect of our lives, or we don't walk with Him at all. Arthur continues:

> The single-hearted devotion of Sam is an ever-elusive goal in our spiritual lives. Yet here's the beauty of serving Jesus: When we mess up, when our loyalties are conflicted, when we make disloyal choices, there is grace to make everything right again. We have not lost our last and best chance to prove our faithfulness. We are given the wisdom and the power and the undivided heart to get up and try again. [5]

Tolkien's stories are but a pale shadow of the real adventure that God has called us into in This Present Kingdom. To "walk with God as He intended—on earth as is in Heaven" requires an undivided heart, a single-hearted devotion to our Master. May our prayer be that of the psalmist, "Teach me your way, Lord, that I may rely on your faithfulness; give me an undivided heart, that I may fear Your name" (Psalm 86:11, NIV). Kingdom Seekers, let the adventure begin!

MATTHEW 6:16-18

Immediately after Jesus finishes teaching the disciples how to pray, He transitions to the subject of fasting and links it with what He has just taught on giving and prayer. In Jesus' day, the scribes and Pharisees commonly flaunted their giving, praying, and fasting. They engaged in these practices solely for appearance's sake, so that others would notice and think well of them. Their lives were focused on Kingdom performing, not Kingdom living.

Read Matthew 6:16-18.

1. What instruction does Jesus give about fasting that He has already taught about giving and prayer in Matthew 6:1-8?

2. What word does Jesus use for people who make a public show of their fasting? (v. 16)

3. What reward awaits those who show off their fasting? (v. 16)

4. What reward awaits those who fast in secret? (v. 18)

Fasting is a fundamental spiritual discipline that allows us to practice self-denial and open up space in our body and soul to engage on a deeper level with God. It is a discipline that helps us to align every department in our lives under Him. Richard Foster notes that fasting is taught as a way of life throughout Scripture:

> Scripture has much to say about fasting that we would do well to look once again at this ancient Discipline. The list of biblical personages who fasted becomes a "Who's Who" of Scripture: Moses the lawgiver, David the king, Elijah the prophet, Esther the queen, Daniel the seer, Anna the prophetess, Paul the apostle, Jesus Christ the incarnate Son. [6]

5. Read Matthew 4:2-4 and John 4:31-32. Why did Jesus fast?

In short, fasting for Jesus was a feast. In the Father, He had a source of sustenance beyond food.

6. Read the following two Old Testament passages and make notes on what you learn about fasting.

Jonah 3:4-8

Psalm 35:13

7. In Zechariah 7, after their return from Babylonian captivity, the town of Bethel sends a delegation to Jerusalem to ask a question about fasting. In response, what pointed question does God ask in Zechariah 7:5?

In other words, "Are you seeking Me or trying to manipulate Me?" God addresses manipulation and fasting in Isaiah 58 in answer to the Israelites asking why their prayers go unanswered.

8. Read Isaiah 58:1-12 and answer the following questions.

- Why are the people fasting? (vv. 1-4)

- Are they walking in righteousness before God? (vv. 1-4)

- What kind of things are they doing when they fast? (v. 5)

- How does God describe the fast He chooses? (vv. 6-7)

- In verses 8-12, God uses words "then" and "if" to show the impact of a godly fast. What are the results of a godly fast?

Fasting is a spiritual discipline that calls us from the ordinary routines of everyday life into communion with God. And it is typically born out of need. In Matthew 9:14-15, the disciples of John the Baptist ask Jesus why His disciples are not fasting. Jesus responds that the Bridegroom is still with them supplying their needs. But the day is coming when He will be gone, and they will fast.

9. What are some examples of needs that have prompted you to fast?

Notice in Matthew 6:16 that Jesus says "Whenever you fast," not "if you fast." Kay Arthur writes about the reason more believers don't regularly fast:

> ...we're too busy, too self-sufficient. We'll work and get it ourselves. Or we will get involved in planning and scheming, and manipulating in order to bring about what we need. If we are that busy, who has time for fasting? Fasting is for those who will put aside all else, including food, to seek God on some particular issue or need. [7]

Kingdom Seeker, when is the last time you sought God earnestly in prayer and fasting?

MATTHEW 6:19-24

In the mid-1800's, Danish philosopher, Soren Kierkegaard, wrote a parable about two thieves who broke into a jewelry store. Instead of stealing anything, they simply switched the price tags around. The next day, the jewelry store opened for business as usual. No one noticed that the expensive jewelry pieces had suddenly become cheap, and the costume jewelry, which had been almost worthless before, was suddenly very expensive.

For several weeks, customers who thought they were purchasing valuable jewelry actually bought imitation jewelry. And those who could not afford the higher ticket pieces left the store with treasures.

Kierkegaard believed that his parable was an indictment of the day and age he lived in:

> My point is obvious, isn't it? The people of my day have no ability to tell the truly valuable from the virtually worthless. Not just in commerce but in the world of ideas too our age is putting on a veritable clearance sale. Everything can be had so dirt cheap that one begins to wonder whether in the end anyone will want to make a bid. [8]

And nothing has changed for the good since Kierkegaard's time. Our culture is just like that jewelry store. It's like someone has come in and switched all the price tags, and we can no longer discern what is of true value and what is not. In our world, a high value is placed on material wealth and the power that accompanies it. Popularity, fame, money, beauty, and social media followers all carry high price tags. But, as we will see today, Jesus teaches that these things are virtually worthless in the only "jewelry store" that matters: The Kingdom of God.

Read Matthew 6:19-21.

As Jesus continues to emphasize in His sermon, living in the Kingdom of God is not about not doing anything wrong. In fact, it is not even about checking all of the boxes for doing things right. The Kingdom goal for living is an "inward union of mind and heart with 'the heavens'." [9] Two desires war within to distract us in our pursuit of developing a Kingdom heart: the longing for the approval of others and a desire for material things. Repeatedly, Jesus has exposed the religious leaders' need for prominence, their drive to be noticed. And now He is revealing that they have an errant value system; they have been investing in all the wrong things. On the outside they appeared to have wealth and prominence, but on the inside, they were destitute.

We live in a consumer society that is relentless in telling us that life at its best belongs to those who have the most things. In fact, we hear that message so often that we have to remind ourselves that true riches are not measured by dollar signs and do not rise and fall with the stock market. The world's verdict on who is rich and who is poor is faulty. The price tags have been switched.

1. What are some examples of earthly treasures?

2. Can you think of a time when you saved to buy an earthly treasure only to encounter the truth of Matthew 6:19? Write about your experience and what you learned.

Let's face it. Accumulating things can be seductive. Luring. Possessions can be an evil mistress. Always demanding more. But it doesn't have to be that way. Jesus is not saying that we cannot have possessions; He is saying that we cannot be possessed by our possessions.

3. Read Proverbs 30:7-9. What two things does Agur ask God to keep from him?

-

-

4. In regard to riches, what is Agur's request?

In Matthew 6:21, Jesus reveals the core issue, "where your treasure is, there your heart will be also." Our lives organize themselves around our heart. What the heart deems as treasure is where our time, money, and talents will be drawn.

Jesus is continuing to lay His axe to the religious value system of the day. He has already exposed wrong motives for fasting, giving, and prayer. And in doing so, He goes to the heart of the matter, motive. Let's fast forward this a couple of millennia. Jesus is saying that if your motive is to be seen, to be noticed, to be valued by others—you have had your reward in full now (see Matthew 6:2; 6:5; 6:16). That's it—your post went viral on Facebook, you received a lot of likes on Instagram, you amassed a huge following on Twitter. Enjoy it now, because there is nothing more.

But. If your motive is simply to serve your Father and Redeemer, if being noticed by men means nothing to you—then you have the smile of the Godhead awaiting you! One day, the only thing that matters will be your motive! "Therefore, do not go on passing judgment before the time, but wait until the Lord comes who will both bring to light the things hidden in the darkness and disclose the motives of men's hearts; and then each man's praise will come to him from God" (1 Corinthians 4:5). One way we can train our motives is through the discipline of secrecy, "do not let your left hand know what your right hand is doing" (Matthew 6:3). Doing things in secret will help to break the grip of our need for the approval of others.

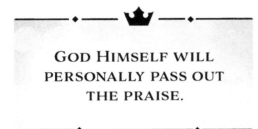

GOD HIMSELF WILL PERSONALLY PASS OUT THE PRAISE.

Remember, your life will organize itself around your heart. Your plans for the day are inextricably linked to what you treasure. And what you treasure is connected to your reward. Do you treasure what Heaven treasures? For those who align their value system with Heaven, Paul says, "each man's praise will come to him from God." Somehow, and this is a great mystery, God will praise you individually because of who you are and what you have done. Not Gabriel. Not Michael. God Himself will personally pass out the praise.

So, how do we keep from laying up treasures on earth? Jesus answers that question next.

Read Matthew 6:22-23.

5. Rewrite Matthew 6:22-23 in your own words.

We have had an eye problem since Satan enticed Eve in the Garden of Eden.

6. Read Genesis 3:6. Where does Eve's sin begin?

Eve's downfall came when she took her focus off God and placed it on the fruit of the tree. She saw. She liked what she saw. She took what she liked. She ate what she liked. And then she shared it with her husband. Her sin became a transmittable disease that still has us reeling!

We see a similar sin pattern in the book of Joshua. When God gave the Israelites victory over Jericho, He was clear in His instruction. The city was under ban and all of the possessions in the city belonged to the Lord. They were to take no spoils of war (Joshua 6:18). But, one of Joshua's commanders, Achan, just could not keep from being allured by all the things he saw. And that spelled trouble for Israel. God withdrew His hand, and they could not even conquer the small town of Ai.

7. Read Joshua 7:19-25 and notice the similarities between Achan and Eve. Where does Achan's sin begin?

David has the same problem in 2 Samuel 11. He sees Bathsheba. He desires Bathsheba. He takes Bathsheba. Is it any wonder that Jesus says the eye is the lamp of the body?

8. Read the following verses and make notes on what they say about where to focus our eyes.

2 Corinthians 4:18

Hebrews 12:2

It is all a matter of our perspective. Our focus. Are we focused on things that can be destroyed by moth and rust and stolen by thieves? Or do we value what Heaven values? In the moment we live on earth, it is easy to forget that we are just strangers and pilgrims here and that our real "citizenship is in Heaven, from which also we eagerly wait for a Savior, the Lord Jesus Christ" (Philippians 3:20).

Read Matthew 6:24.

There is no dual citizenship in God's Kingdom. You cannot serve two masters. There is only room for one King on the throne of your heart. You cannot "fix your eyes" in two different directions. Which master are you pursuing?

One day, all the achievements of man will be burned up and all that will remain is what was done by the Spirit of God through human hands (2 Peter 3:10-12). These will become our treasures in Heaven. The things done by the Spirit through us for the glory of God and God alone.

As we wind up today's lesson, take a minute and think about some of the people Jesus celebrated. The Good Samaritan. The widow who gave two mites. The four friends who brought their paralytic friend to Jesus. A little boy who gave five loaves and two fish. A woman who broke open an alabaster jar of perfume. Do you know what all of these people have in common? We don't know their names. But Jesus celebrated them! You see, we don't have to make the news headlines or see our names in bright lights to make a difference.

As citizens of Heaven, we are to live for an audience of One. We are to long solely for the applause of the nail-scarred hands. Here is a Kingdom training challenge for you. Will you intentionally plan to do something this week in secret? Do something for someone and tell no one. That sound you will hear as you are secretly investing in the Kingdom of God will be His hands celebrating you.

MATTHEW 6:25-30

In Matthew 6:19-24, Jesus explains that a person's attitude toward material possessions is an indicator of his or her spiritual condition. And that attitude has nothing to do with whether someone is wealthy, poor, or somewhere in the middle. Those who "have" are tempted to trust in their possessions for satisfaction, security, or standing; those who "have not" are tempted to doubt God's provision for what they believe is necessary to "really live". On the heels of His warning about seeking material things, Jesus seamlessly transitions to the next point in His sermon—anxiety—with the phrase "For this reason" (v. 25). This transitional phrase is connected to verse 24. He is saying, "Because God is your Master, do not be worried." Notice that Jesus does not say, "You don't have to be worried." He says, "Do not be worried." His instruction is not a consoling statement meant to give comfort; it is a direct command meant to be obeyed.

Jesus is addressing the kind of destructive anxiety that eats into our souls, robbing us of our peace and joy by thrusting us into an imaginary future where we lack what we need and are gripped by fear. Think about it. How many times have you allowed yourself to worry and get stressed about a situation, only for that scenario to never happen?

When given the opportunity, worry will assume a position of power in our life. It will try to change the unchangeable and control the uncontrollable. But the truth of the matter is that worry is impotent when it comes to fixing the future; it only contributes to us fearing it. Corrie ten Boom said it well, "Worry is a cycle of inefficient thoughts whirling around a center of fear." [10] It is like a mental hurricane that only yields destruction.

Corrie ten Boom certainly had opportunity to be overcome with worry and anxiety. During Hitler's reign in Germany, she and her family, Dutch reformed believers, sheltered hundreds of Jews by hiding them in a secret room in their house. Her well-known book, *The Hiding Place,* describes her life during World War II, including the time she and her sister, Betsie, spent in concentration camps.

In May 1940, the German Blitzkrieg invaded the Netherlands and the "Nazification" of the Dutch people began. The quiet and peaceful life the ten Boom family had known ceased to exist. Almost overnight, their home became a refuge for Jews, intellectuals, and others that the Gestapo wanted to eliminate. A secret room the size of a small closet was built into Corrie's bedroom behind a false wall. When Nazi security sweeps came through their neighborhood, a buzzer in the house would signal danger, and the refugees had just moments to make it to the hiding place.

It would be hard not to battle worry and anxiety in the face of the Nazi regime and all of its horrors. But Corrie discovered that "Worrying does not empty tomorrow of its sorrow; it empties today of its strength." [11] So she emptied herself into God's hands and became emboldened with a courage beyond her own. It was a courage she would repeatedly draw upon. On February 28, 1944, a Dutch informant turned the ten Boom family in to the Nazis, and the Gestapo raided their home and arrested the family. Her father died within two weeks of his arrest. Corrie and her sister, Betsie, were eventually sent to Ravensbrück concentration camp, near Berlin. Betsie died there on December 16, 1944. Twelve days later, Corrie was miraculously released due to a clerical error. After the war, her story of faith, courage, and conviction began to emerge. With a Kingdom perspective, she committed the remainder of her life to Kingdom purposes. From her experience she wrote, "Never be afraid to trust an unknown future to a known God."[12] What words of spiritual wisdom for us to embrace and hold on to!

Read Matthew 6:25-30.

1. What two references to nature does Jesus make in this passage?

2. Why do you think Jesus uses these two examples?

Jesus is teaching about trusting God with the ordinaries of life. Our daily needs. Worry is a signal that we do not really believe that God can or will take care of us. In this passage, Jesus is basically asking, "Have you forgotten Who your Father is?"

The Greek word for worry is *merimnaó* and means "to be apprehensive, have anxiety, be anxious, be (unduly) concerned," [13] which conforms to the English definition, "a feeling of worry, nervousness, or unease, typically about an imminent event or something with an uncertain outcome." [14]

3. Think about Corrie's statement, "Never be afraid to trust an unknown future to a known God." Is there a situation in your life that you need to trust your Father with? Take a moment and journal how God is speaking to you.

4. Read Job 33:4; Psalm 145:16-17; Colossians 1:17; and Hebrews 1:3. Summarize the comprehensive message of these verses in 1-2 sentences.

God is not only the Creator of the Universe; He is the Sustainer of the Universe. I am pretty sure that you are nodding your head right now agreeing with what you just read. But do our actions line up with what you say we believe? We say we believe in God and trust in God, but our actions unravel our professed beliefs. Too often, an end of the day reflection reveals where our trust and confidence are actually placed—in ourselves. And there it is. The source of our anxiety and worry—reliance upon self rather than God.

WE SAY WE BELIEVE IN GOD AND TRUST IN GOD, BUT OUR ACTIONS UNRAVEL OUR PROFESSED BELIEFS.

5. What are some of the emotional indicators in your life that let you know you are trusting in yourself rather than God?

When these emotions manifest themselves, it is time for us to change the narrative in our minds. From faith in ourselves to trust in God. From confidence in ourselves to dependence upon God. It is time for us to step down from the elevated position to which we have ascended, the manager of the world. Putting our trust in self is the source of worry, but pride is the root. Acting as if what happens is ultimately in our hands is pride.

6. What does Jesus say about the folly of this line of thinking? (v. 27)

Peter gives a powerful word on worry and anxiety, "Therefore humble yourselves under the mighty hand of God, that He may exalt you at the proper time, casting all your anxiety on Him, because He cares for you" (1 Peter 5:6-7). If we want to address our anxious thoughts, the place to begin is by dealing with our pride, because humility provides the ultimate release from anxiety. It is vital for us to be able to distinguish between the voices of pride and humility. Pride says, "What happens is up to me." It is a sinful mindset that feeds anxiety. Humility, on the other hand, says, "Lord, every matter concerning me is in Your hands." Humility opens the door to peace.

The secret to Corrie ten Boom's peace in the midst of horrific circumstances was that she knew her life was out of her hands. Out of her hands, and into the hands of her loving Father, Who she trusted to make "all things to work together for good to those who love God, to those who are called according to His purpose" (Romans 8:28).

7. What does Jesus say worrying about the basics of life demonstrates? (v. 30)

Worry strikes a blow at the character of God. How is it that we can say we trust God with our eternal destiny but fail to believe that He will provide our daily needs?

In Philippians 4:6-8, Paul explains the steps to escape worry's grip:

> Be anxious for nothing, but in everything by prayer and supplication with thanksgiving let your requests be made known to God. And the peace of God, which surpasses all comprehension, will guard your hearts and your minds in Christ Jesus. Finally, brethren, whatever is true, whatever is honorable, whatever is right, whatever is pure, whatever is lovely, whatever is of good repute, if there is any excellence and if anything worthy of praise, dwell on these things.

#1 Pray. Give your anxious thoughts to God. Don't allow them to rattle around in your mind. Take your cares and turn them into prayers to your Father.

#2 Pray with thanksgiving. Thank God for what He has done in the past. Praise is the language of faith.

#3 Flip your thoughts. Change the narrative in your mind. Dwell on good and noble thoughts that give you peace rather than topics that make you worried and fearful. This process requires discipline but produces peace.

We will continue this study tomorrow. For today, spend a few minutes in prayer, walking through the three steps Paul gives in Philippians 4:6-8. Discipline your mind throughout the day. Shut out anxious thoughts and instead, dwell on things that are "worthy of praise."

MATTHEW 6:31-34

Control and certainty are myths. The only thing certain is that life is full of uncertainties and situations totally beyond our control. And when we try to govern the uncertain and the uncontrollable, anxiety is the result.

A recent study indicates that anxiety has reached epidemic proportions in the United States, with more than 40 million adults having it as a medical diagnosis. The most common treatment, anti-anxiety prescriptions, increased by 67% between 1996 and 2013 and overdoses from these drugs quadrupled between 2002 and 2015. Anxiety is not just an epidemic, it has become a deadly epidemic. [15]

Let's take a pause here and wade briefly into the subject of believers and anti-anxiety medication. To be clear, whether or not to take an anti-anxiety medicine is a personal decision between a patient and that person's physician. Some disorders related to anxiety require medical attention. At times, believers do not get the help they may need because they feel not being able to cope with anxiety is a spiritual failure. Here is a scenario to consider. If you break your ankle, you will need a crutch to help you walk until the break heals. However, if you are still using a crutch ten years after the break has healed, there is a problem. You have become dependent upon the crutch. While your doctor may determine that a crutch is the only option for you, all of us want to walk in the greatest freedom we can.

The issue is dependence. When an anxiety crisis occurs, where do we turn? Do we immediately reach for a pill? Or do we pray first? A medical diagnosis does not minimize our dependence upon God, it increases it.

Worry, stress, and fears are a part of our daily life. If we attempt to address those issues apart from God, they will overtake us. Willard writes,

> The words anxious and worry both have reference to strangling or being choked. Certainly that is how we feel when we are anxious. Things and events have us by the throat and seem to be cutting off our life. We are being harmed, or we fear what will come upon us, and all our efforts are insufficient to do anything about it. Perhaps more energy has gone into dealing with this human situation than into anything else—from songs about "Don't Worry! Be Happy!" to $250-an-hour sessions with a therapist.

> Because we have the option, in reliance upon Jesus, of having abundant treasures in the realm of the Heavens, Jesus gives us another of His "therefores". Life is not about food, He continues to say, or the body about clothes. It is about a place in God's immortal Kingdom now. Eternity is, in part, what we are now living. [16]

As Jesus continues teaching on the mountainside, He makes His instruction personal. Just as children rely upon their parents to meet their needs, we also, as God's children, are dependent upon Him for every need we have. That dependence is how Jesus says we are to address our anxious thoughts.

Read Matthew 6:31-34.

1. What things are the Gentiles (unbelievers) anxious about? (vv. 31-32)

Kent Hughes explains,

> The Gentiles, the secular world, seek material things because they overestimate their significance. The characteristic tendency of those without Christ is to be bound by the horizons of earth. Everything is crammed into the visible. This, in turn, promotes worry about secondary matters such as food and clothes. [17]

Not only are unbelievers focused on the visible things of this earth, but they also misunderstand God's character. They think of God as far off, removed from the difficulties of life.

2. What distinguishes the way believers think from that of unbelievers? (v. 32)

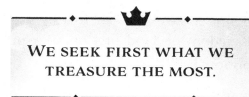

WE SEEK FIRST WHAT WE TREASURE THE MOST.

People are always seeking after something. Two different Greek words are used for the word "seek" in Matthew 6:32-33. The word *epizēteō* is used in verse 32 to describe the Gentiles' quest and means "to be seriously interested in or have a strong desire for, wish, wish for." [18] The Greek verb *zēteō* used in verse 33 has a slightly different connotation, "to devote serious effort to realize one's desire or objective, strive for, aim (at), try to obtain, desire, wish (for), desire to possess (something)." [19] Having a "serious interest" versus expending "serious effort" seems to be a distinguishing factor between the seeking of unbelievers and believers. And the issue once again appears to be focus. The Gentiles are focused on temporal things. Not necessarily bad things, but things that distract from the Source of those things—God Himself. They are seeking after the essentials while they lack the one true Necessity.

3. Read Matthew 13:22. What does Jesus say chokes out the Word?

Matthew 6:33 makes it clear that our priorities must be in the right order. Remember Matthew 6:21? "For where your treasure is, there your heart will be also." We seek first what we treasure the most.

4. What does it mean to seek first the Kingdom of God and His righteousness?

Joel Green gives an insightful paraphrase of Matthew 6:33:

> Let the Kingdom of God be at the center of your life…not at the top. Let the Kingdom of God set the standards for your life. Let the Kingdom of God determine how you live, how you work, how you communicate, how you play. [20]

Green goes on to note that the Greek word *proton* translated "first" is not used to "denote the first in a series but also that upon which everything else hinges. In other words, do not put the Kingdom of God first on your priority list; rather, let the Kingdom of God determine your priority list!"

5. What would you say are the top five priorities in your life?

6. Now take a minute and think about the way you have spent the last 24 hours. Do your priorities line up with the way you spend your time?

Matthew 6:33 is an invitation to live in the Kingdom of God, in the present, with Jesus at the very center of everything. And Matthew 6:34 is a reminder to do so one day at a time. "So do not worry about tomorrow; for tomorrow will care for itself. Each day has enough trouble of its own." Certainly, there is nothing wrong with wise planning for the future. But one of the things we must be cautious about is spending so much time fixating on the future that we totally miss the present. This is the "When…then" syndrome. You know how that goes. "When I get married, then…" "When I get a new job, then…" "When I get a new house, then…".

7. Is there a "When…then" scenario impacting your life right now? If so, what is it?

Here is the issue. Once we finally achieve our "then", we find out that is has its own set of problems. Regardless of how hard we try, "tomorrow" will have trouble. It is futile to think that we can live a problem-free life. To worry about what may or may not happen in the future will sabotage your life for God in the present. George MacDonald put it this way: "No man ever sank under the burden of the day. It is when tomorrow's burden is added to the burden of today, that the weight is more than a man can bear." [21] The truth is, God will give us the strength to bear the trouble when it comes. But He does not give us the strength to bear worrying about it. Think about it in mathematical terms.

Today's Troubles + Tomorrow's Troubles = An Unbearable Burden

8. What are some ways you can consciously live in the "present" this week?

> **ALTHOUGH SOME PEOPLE MAY BE ABLE TO MULTI-TASK, NO ONE IS ABLE TO MULTI-SEEK.**

Although some people may be able to multi-task, no one is able to multi-seek. In closing today, spend a few moments with the Lord, asking Him to purify your priorities and to align your life with His purposes. As that occurs, the reality of Matthew 6:33 will breakthrough in your life.

Aim at Heaven and you will get earth "thrown in":
aim at earth and you will get neither. [22]
~C.S. Lewis

KINGDOM EXERCISE

We live in an age of consumerism where self-fulfillment is the popular norm. This consumer economy relies on keeping our desires fueled and satisfied. Sadly, we have become so accustomed to having what we want, when we want it, that we really can't imagine living another way. Media messaging that says "you deserve this" has infiltrated our minds, and even worse, invaded our souls. Consequently, self-denial has been categorized as an antiquated notion, even among believers. A recent article in *The Boston Globe* makes this convicting observation:

> In purging self-denial from the tradition, American Christians play into the hands of corporate merchandisers, who hope we'll spend more and more year-round to quench unquenchable desires. Yet the highest price we pay is spiritual. Self-denial…fosters humility. It blunts the insidious delusion of entitlement. It shapes compassion for the poor and hungry by raising at least a measure of awareness of their circumstances. It breeds courage as we tell our lowest desires: No, you are not my master. I answer to a higher authority. With God's help, it opens a way for higher desires to take root—for the creation of a new heart, in biblical parlance. To trade the inherited wisdom of this way for the cheap platitudes of self-help therapy is costly indeed.

> Strangely, Americans recognize the value of sacrifice in pursuing material goals, such as prosperity via education. Yet we tell ourselves that spiritual growth can be cost-free. [23]

Sacrifice and self-denial, once the heart of Christianity, rarely make their appearance in our conversations anymore. After all, if something makes life less enjoyable, why should we do it? And the answer is…because it pleases God.

THE DISCIPLINE OF FASTING

What spiritual discipline comes to mind when we think about self-denial? Fasting. Hang on. Please don't stop reading. Sure, none of us really has the desire to fast. But, perhaps that is exactly the reason that we should.

Fasting has been part of the Judeo-Christian tradition for millennia. Throughout history, God's people have made fasting a significant part of their worship. The Bible mentions fasting over sixty times and as we have seen, the list of Biblical characters who have fasting interwoven in their narratives reads like a Who's Who List: Moses, Elijah, David, Ezra, Esther, Daniel, Anna, Paul, Jesus.

Yet today, this discipline has almost been forgotten.

Willard describes fasting as the discipline that "confirms our utter dependence upon God by finding in Him a source of sustenance beyond food." [24] Fasting helps us to focus on God and matters of the Spirit. It enables us to gain control of our appetites so that we can direct all of our energies on Him.

In *Spiritual Disciplines Handbook: Practices That Transform Us*, Adele Calhoun summarizes the purpose of fasting:

> Fasting is not a magical way to manipulate God into doing our will; it's not a way to get God to be an accomplice to our plans. Neither is fasting a spiritual way to lose weight or control others. Fasting clears us out and opens us up to intentionally seeking God's will and grace in a way that goes beyond normal habits of worship and prayer. While fasting, we are one on one with God, offering Him the time and attentiveness we might otherwise be giving to eating, shopping, or watching television.
>
> Fasting is an opportunity to lay down an appetite—an appetite for food, for media, for shopping. This act of self-denial may not seem huge—it's just a meal or a trip to the mall—but it brings us face to face with the hunger at the core of our being. Fasting exposes how we try to keep empty hunger at bay and gain a sense of well-being by devouring creature comforts. Through self-denial we begin to recognize what controls us. Our small denials of the self show us just how little taste we actually have for sacrifice or time with God. [25]

Biblical fasting always has a spiritual purpose. It involves giving up physical comforts and desires to gain spiritual insight. Calhoun provides a definition of fasting, "A fast is the self-denial of normal necessities in order to intentionally attend to God in prayer. Bringing attachments and craving to the surfaces opens up a place for prayer. This physical awareness of emptiness is the reminder to turn to Jesus who alone can satisfy." [26]

A true fast is giving up food for a predetermined purpose for a predetermined period of time. Certainly, you can fast from other things like media or television, but in a biblical sense, fasting is always about giving up food. It is a way to say to God that we crave Him more than we crave food. We are more hungry for Him than food. And that is why fasting is so powerful, it reminds us that we do not live on bread alone. And can we be honest? If we can say "no" to food, we can say "no" to anything else.

THE EXERCISE

Jesus saw fasting as so important and basic to a life of worshiping God that He taught it as one of three main disciplines for the spiritual life. Setting it alongside giving and prayer in the Sermon on the Mount, He says, "When you fast…" (Matthew 6:16) not "If you fast…"

This week, seek God as to whether He would have you to fast. It can be one meal, two meals, an entire day, or more. If God leads you to fast, please step out and obey. Some people are unable to fast from food for medical reasons. Perhaps you could consider a Daniel type fast (vegetables and fruit). Please do not misunderstand, this is not an exercise in legalism. Fasting is a discipline meant to deepen our relationship with God.

REFLECTION QUESTIONS

1. In our study this week, what did you learn about fasting?

2. Why do you think "doing without" draws us closer to God?

3. If you felt God leading to you fast this week, how did He speak to you during your time?

*Like all the Spiritual Disciplines, fasting hoists the sails of the soul in
hopes of experiencing the gracious wind of God's Spirit.
But fasting also adds a unique dimension to your spiritual life and helps you grow in Christlikeness
in ways that are unavailable through any other means.
If this were not so, and if the blessings of fasting could be experienced by other
means, Jesus would not have taught and modeled fasting.* [27]
~DONALD WHITNEY

WEEK NINE
KINGDOM DOERS
— MATTHEW 7:1-12 —

*In everything, therefore, treat people the same way you want them
to treat you, for this is the Law and the Prophets.*
MATTHEW 7:12

*The perfect love of the Heavenly Father is most reflected in His children
when they treat others as they themselves wish to be treated.* [1]
~JOHN MACARTHUR

We live in a conflicted time. In a world that loudly shouts the message of tolerance, we find very little of it in day-to-day life. Daily, people face-off on social media, emboldened by the perceived anonymity, and in other settings to battle over a variety of topics—politics, theology, social issues, etc. Acrimony reigns. It appears that it is no longer acceptable to agree to disagree. The standard must be conformity. Nothing else. It grieves me to see such mean-spiritedness, particularly when it involves Christians. Kingdom living suggests a better way. This week, our study in the Sermon on the Mount will examine Jesus' teaching on interpersonal relationships, culminating in a look at the Golden Rule.

Animosity has been a part of the human condition since sin entered the world in the Garden of Eden. It was certainly a part of the Jewish culture in the time frame of this sermon. The Jews hated all things Gentile. The Pharisees despised all who did not conform to their man-made rules. In His message, Jesus offers a different mind-set, one free of judgment. John MacArthur notes the contrast,

> But Jesus is here talking about the self-righteous, egotistical judgment and unmerciful condemnation of others practiced by the scribes and Pharisees. Their primary concern was not to help others from sin to holiness, but to condemn them to eternal judgment because of actions and attitudes that did not square with their own worldly, self-made traditions. [2]

In this setting, Jesus delivers His message of no condemnation and selfless love.

MATTHEW 7:1-2

In last week's study, Jesus encourages His listeners to "seek first His Kingdom and His righteousness" (Matthew 6:33). While that familiar verse might slip easily off our tongues, the reality of living it out in the Kingdom is more challenging, but necessary, as we contemplate the next bit of instruction from Jesus in Matthew 7 on judging others.

Read Matthew 7:1-2.

The judging spoken of here is not what you would find in a court of law. Rather it is, unfortunately, what we often encounter within the framework of interpersonal relationships, even among Christians.

1. Summarize the content of Matthew 7:1-2.

2. What additional insights are found in the following verses concerning judging?

    Luke 6:37

    Romans 2:1-2

    James 4:11-12

> **A CRITICAL SPIRIT IS IN DIRECT CONTRADISTINCTION TO THE WAY OF JESUS.**

Despite the warning from Jesus of impending judgment for us when we judge, whether now or in the world to come, there is something within our human nature, or more correctly our sin nature, that draws us into criticism. And a critical spirit is in direct contradistinction to the way of Jesus. Think about the manner in which He interacted with people, even those immersed in sin. Love was the hallmark of His exchanges.

James Smith describes the opposite approach:

> When we see someone who is at fault, caught in sin or behaving badly, we often turn to the method the world commonly uses to "fix" people: condemnation engineering. A verbal assault, we think, will set them straight, and it appears to work. We reason, If I give so and so a good talking to, they will shape up. It is a very powerful weapon in our arsenal. [3]

MacArthur comments on the results of judging with a critical spirit: "Whenever we assign people to condemnation without mercy because they do not do something the way we think it ought to be done or because we believe their motives are wrong, we pass judgment that only God is qualified to make." [4]

3. Have you been confronted with "condemnation engineering"? How did it make you feel? Did it result in positive change?

4. Are you ever tempted to play God in someone's life through judging? Don't rush to answer this question. Ask God to reveal your heart. Be gut-level honest. Try to think of an example.

5. If so, which of these factors motivates your move to make a judgment?

____ genuine concern

____ anger

____ biblical truth

____ jealousy

____ restoration

____ spite

____ other_____

Finding fault in others is usually an easy endeavor. There will always be that person whom you genuinely dislike or disagree with—the one that rubs you the wrong way, the one to whom you feel morally or intellectually superior. But these attitudes are not the way of the Kingdom. Dallas Willard points out, "Condemnation always involves some degree of self-righteousness and of distancing ourselves from the one we are condemning. And self-righteousness always involves an element of comparison and of condemnation." [5] Jesus highlights this sinful tendency in His parable in Luke 18.

6. Read Luke 18:9-14. Contrast the prayers of the Pharisee and the tax collector. What key concept does Jesus relate?

Most of us are not confronting people on a regular basis, although we might from time to time; nor, hopefully, are we the recipients of regular, continuous criticism. There is another form of judgment that should be avoided, yet unfortunately flourishes—gossip. Some find it harmless, but it should never be a part of Kingdom living. Smith explains,

> Perhaps the most pervasive form of judgment is gossip. I define gossip as (1) speaking negatively (2) about someone who is not present. [6]

> If we don't feel good about ourself, one way to feel better is to knock someone else down. When we judge others, we feel superior to them. This explains why gossip feels so good. Gossip allows us to escape into a world where we are superior to those we are gossiping about. Their faults are laid bare, and as we focus on their weaknesses and failures we are spared from admitting our own. [7]

Participation in gossip should not be the lifestyle of a believer. Whether we couch it in concern or a prayer request, down deep we know it is judging and not pleasing to the Savior. Proverbs warns us about the fruit of gossip:

> A troublemaker plants seeds of strife; gossip separates the best of friends (Proverbs 16:28, NLT).

> A gossip goes around telling secrets, but those who are trustworthy can keep a confidence (Proverbs 11:13, NLT).

> A gossip goes around telling secrets, so don't hang around with chatterers (Proverbs 20:19, NLT).

Do not be a party to gossip. What steps can you take to avoid it? Choose encouragement rather than criticism.

Let's make Tim Keller's prayer our prayer.

> Lord, save me from the sins of my tongue and the flaws of character that fuel them. Make my words honest (by taking away my fear), few (by taking away my self-importance), wise (by taking away my thoughtlessness), and kind (by taking away my indifference and irritability). Amen. [8]

MATTHEW 7:3-6

In our lesson yesterday, we contemplated the danger of judging others. Unfortunately, our natural tendency is to be blind to our own faults and to be quick to judge others. Jesus warns that a critical, judgmental spirit sets us up for not only judgment in this world but also by God in the world to come. Indeed, God is the one to judge the motives and hearts of everyone. This does not mean that we are not to be discerning where sin and false teaching are involved. And sometimes, we will need to confront some who have fallen into sin as God leads, but never in a self-righteous, condescending manner and with much trepidation. MacArthur notes: "The Savior does not call for men to cease to be examining and discerning, but to renounce the presumptuous temptation to try to be God." [9]

1. Read Matthew 7:3-5. What rebuke does Jesus give to one who would judge another?

2. In verses 3-5, Jesus uses a figure of speech called a hyperbole, an exaggerated statement to make a point. Note the significance of its use in this passage.

Jesus describes the person in these verses as a hypocrite. The Greek word, *hypokrites*, is defined as "one who acts pretentiously, a counterfeit, a man who assumes and speaks or acts under a feigned character." [10] You recall, of course, that Jesus frequently referred to the Pharisees using that moniker. Clearly the disdain Jesus held for one who judged others without first judging himself is evident. Let's peruse an example from the Old Testament.

3. Examine 2 Samuel 12:1-10, and record what David's response to Nathan revealed about him.

Jesus does not forbid us from helping our brother to remove the speck from his eye. Once we have dealt with our own sin, our own self-righteousness, our own critical spirit, then we become a usable vessel to come alongside someone else—not to condemn but to minister. However, it is a very delicate process requiring much humility and prayer.

4. According to Galatians 6:1-5, who may approach one caught in sin, and what caution does the Apostle Paul give?

John Stott shares a pertinent quote from early church father, Chrysostom, "'Correct him,' said Chrysostom, alluding to someone who has sinned, 'but not as a foe, nor as an adversary exacting a penalty, but as a physician providing medicines,' yes, and—even more—as a loving brother anxious to rescue and restore." [11] Jesus is our example in this process. He is always so compassionate and personal as He addresses a sinner. Remember how He offered the Samaritan woman Living Water as she came to the well in John 4, giving her exactly what she needed? May we do likewise if indeed the Lord sends us on a restoration assignment.

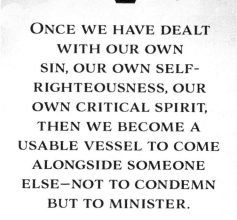

ONCE WE HAVE DEALT WITH OUR OWN SIN, OUR OWN SELF-RIGHTEOUSNESS, OUR OWN CRITICAL SPIRIT, THEN WE BECOME A USABLE VESSEL TO COME ALONGSIDE SOMEONE ELSE—NOT TO CONDEMN BUT TO MINISTER.

In his book, *The Divine Conspiracy*, Willard gives some guidelines for correcting others. Here are some excerpts for you to consider.

- We don't undertake to correct unless we are absolutely sure of the sin.

- Not just anyone is to correct others. Correction is reserved for those who live and work in a divine power not their own.

- The "correcting" to be done is not a matter of "straightening them out." It is not a matter of hammering on their wrongness and on what is going to happen to them if they don't change their ways. It is a matter of restoration.

- The ones who are restoring others must go about their work with the sure knowledge that they could very well do the same thing that the person "caught" has done, or even worse. This totally removes any sense of self-righteousness or superiority, which, if it is present, will certainly make restoration impossible. [12]

5. What wisdom can you derive from the following verses to assist you as you go?

1 Corinthians 13:4-8a

Colossians 3:12-14, 4:6

Take time now to read Matthew 7:6. Many might find this verse seemingly out of place wondering what dogs, pigs, and pearls have to do with judging others. Now understand that the dogs referred to here are not the household pets we think of in our culture nor are pigs what we would see on the farm—or choose as pets, though I have a hard time comprehending that concept. In the first-century Jewish culture, these animals, considered unclean, were usually wild scavengers, dirty, dangerous, and detested. Therefore, no one would have considered giving the sacred sacrifice from the burnt offering meant for God alone to dogs nor precious pearls to pigs. Nor is Jesus suggesting that certain groups of people such as Gentiles were unworthy of salvation. Commentators offer more than one suggestion. Some propose that the pigs and dogs refer to false teachers and those adamantly opposed to the gospel who refuse the gospel message. Another suggestion proposes that it denotes those who do not find what is offered helpful or digestible, such as those who are being judged. Nevertheless, each option calls for great discernment on our part. Ponder this illustration from the Book of Acts.

6. Review Acts 13:44-46 and record the result of Paul's interaction with the Jews in Pisidian Antioch.

One last thing to contemplate is how we would respond when a needed correction is brought to our attention. Will you react gratefully and positively or defensively? An example is found in the life of the early church.

7. How did Apollos respond to correction as recorded in Acts 18:24-28, and what can you learn from his example?

We cannot play the role of judge—passing sentence as if we were God. We cannot play the role of superior—as if we were exempt from the same standardswe demand of others. We must not play the hypocrite—blaming others while we excuse ourselves. [13]
~JOHN MACARTHUR

Today in our study, the narrative of Jesus seems to digress into what seems to be a change in subject matter. It is stepping away from the complexities of judging ourselves and others toward a discussion on prayer. This deviation appears surprising since Jesus had discussed prayer in chapter 6 as He presented what we call The Lord's Prayer. Could it be that Jesus has a new dimension to be introduced about prayer—one beyond our prayers for forgiveness and daily provisions? Could it be that continuous prayer for ourselves and those we are trying to encourage would help us to plumb the depth of God's wisdom for living life in the Kingdom? Perhaps Jesus has not changed the subject at all. John MacArthur observes, "God's wisdom is among our greatest needs. We cannot be discerning and discriminating without divine counsel from our Heavenly Father; and the primary means for achieving wisdom is petitioning prayer." [14]

1. Read Matthew 7:7-8 and the corresponding passage in Luke 11:9-10. What three imperative words do you find? Note the progression in their use.

The imperative verbs are in the present tense so literally they can be read as "keep on asking," "keep on seeking," and "keep on knocking."

2. Essentially what is Jesus urging us to do, and what will be the result?

Dallas Willard reminds us, "Prayer is never just asking, nor is it merely a matter of asking for what I want. God is not a cosmic butler or fix-it man, and the aim of the universe is not to fulfill my desires and needs." [15] Prayer is a quest to know God and understand His purpose. God longs for us to come into an intimate relationship with Him as we seek His face.

R.T. Kendall elaborates,

> A good definition of prayer is asking God to act. Three things—asking, seeking, knocking—come to the same thing but are nonetheless slightly different. You ask because you want to receive; you seek because you want to find; you knock because you feel you need to get God's attention when He could be hiding His face or testing your earnestness and sincerity in wanting more of Him. [16]

3. What do these verses relate concerning our effectiveness in prayer?

James 1:5

James 1:6-8

James 4:3

1 John 3:21-22

1 John 5:14

4. Are you ever tempted to give up when you do not receive an immediate response to your prayer? Describe a time when God answered after persistent prayer.

When you long for wisdom, go to the Lord. When your heart aches, leave it at His feet. When you are lonely, He will be by your side. When you are afraid, He will cover you with His wings. When you don't know what to do, He will guide. There is no situation for which He is not infinitely more than adequate. Pray. Pray fervently, persistently, unceasingly. Pray.

MacArthur sums up this section, "Here Jesus says, in effect, 'If you want wisdom to know how to help a sinning brother and how to discern falsehood and apostasy, go to your heavenly Father. **Ask**, **seek**, and **knock** at the door of Heaven, and you will receive, find, and have the door opened.'" [17]

In the last segment of our passage for today, Jesus compares the provisions of an earthly father to that of the heavenly Father. I don't know about you, but I am highly suspicious that if you have children or grandchildren, you love to meet their needs or desires. It is within the fabric of the nature of parents to give good gifts to our children. But God, on the other hand, has the wisdom to give us what we truly need.

5. How does Jesus describe an earthly father, and how does He contrast him to the heavenly Father in Matthew 7:9-11?

Jesus confirms that though we inherited a sinful nature, we seek to provide good things for our children and would not entertain giving them something harmful. The stones He refers to were the small limestones found on the seashore. Though they appear to be similar in size and shape, they provide no nourishment. And the snake, probably an eel, is unclean by Jewish ceremonial law and is not appropriate. Jesus reminds His listeners of the nature of God and His perfect provisions when He exclaims, "how much more will your Father who is in Heaven give what is good to those who ask Him!" (Matthew 7:11b). This verse introduces us to the "How Much More Principle" found in other passages. Let's investigate a few.

> GOD'S GIFTS ARE INCOMPARABLE—GOD THE SPIRIT INDWELLING THE BELIEVER, THE SUPERIORITY OF HEAVEN TO OUR EARTHLY EXISTENCE, THE SUFFICIENCY OF THE ATONING SACRIFICE TO THE IMPOSSIBILITY OF KEEPING THE LAW.

6. Record the "how much more" phrases in these verses.

Matthew 12:12

Luke 12:24

Hebrew 9:11-14

7. Read the companion verse found in Luke 11:13. What "how much more" gift does God bestow on His children?

God's gifts are incomparable—God the Spirit indwelling the believer, the superiority of Heaven to our earthly existence, the sufficiency of the atoning sacrifice to the impossibility of keeping the Law. He gives us so much more, my friend, so much more.

MATTHEW 7:12

Today we come to the pinnacle of Jesus' treatise on interpersonal relationships in the Sermon on the Mount. What we commonly call the Golden Rule states, "So in everything, do to others what you would have them do to you, for this sums up the Law and the Prophets" (Matthew 7:12, NIV). Notice that the sentence begins with "so" or "therefore" in other translations, which alerts us to the fact that Jesus is referring to what He has said previously to give credence to what He is about to say. The companion scripture found in Luke offers some insight.

1. Review Luke 6:27-31. What concepts for Kingdom living precede the Golden Rule in this passage?

2. What is the scope of the application of the Golden Rule?

Interestingly, similar phrases were found in other cultures of the day, including Greek, Roman, and the Rabbinical writings, yet with a noticeable difference. Here are a few for you to peruse:

- "What is hateful to yourself do not do to someone else." Rabbi Hillel
- "What thou thyself hatest, to no man do." *Book of Tobit, Apocrypha*
- "What you do not want done to yourself, do not do to others." Confucius
- "Do not do to others the things which make you angry when you experience them at the hands of other people." Nicocles, ancient Greek king
- "What you avoid suffering yourself, do not afflict on others." Epictetus, Greek philosopher
- "What you do not want to be done to you, do not do to anyone else." [18] The Stoics

3. What distinctive difference do you find in Jesus' statement in Matthew 7:12 from those popular in the culture of His day?

4. From your perspective, what prevents mankind from heeding Jesus' command?

The Knowing Jesus Study Bible has some pertinent insight:

> What Jesus taught was revolutionary at the time—and would be considered fully as radical if it had first been announced in our own day and culture. The generally accepted political tactic throughout all ages, as well as our natural human instinct, is to hate our enemies and look for ways to belittle, deride or injure them—physically, financially, in terms of reputation—in any way we can. Jesus instead promoted the unthinkable, urging people to love their enemies and choose not to fight back after having been cheated or hurt. His teaching goes against the grain of our common sense, because common sense is based on our faulty, unregenerate human nature, untouched by the grace and power of Jesus. [19]

No doubt, we all acknowledge the selfishness that is innately a part of the human condition. We have watched it in action in toddlers, in adults, and, if we are honest, in ourselves. Why is it so difficult to be unselfish and to follow Jesus' design for Kingdom living? It simply boils down to wanting our own way. "What we have in this verse is the self-love principle put in reverse. It is when selfish love should become absolutely unselfish." [20] Avoiding doing harm to someone does not rise to the level of actually doing good to him. Whether for friend or foe, doing good necessitates personal involvement, taking on a selfless, sacrificial mindset. Paul reminds us, "Let no one seek his own, but each one the other's well-being (1 Corinthians 10:24, NKJV).

WHETHER FOR FRIEND OR FOE, DOING GOOD NECESSITATES PERSONAL INVOLVEMENT, TAKING ON A SELFLESS, SACRIFICIAL MINDSET.

5. Investigate these passages to collect wisdom for implementing the Golden Rule. Record what you find.

Ephesians 4:29, 32

1 John 3:17-18

1 Peter 3:15

Jesus communicates at the end of Matthew 7:12 that the sacrificial giving of oneself to meet the needs of others sums up the Law and the Prophets. The Law signifies the first five books of the Old Testament, an impossible standard for sinful man to meet, while the Prophets denote the remainder of the Testament outlining God's plan to do for us what we could not do for ourselves. So Jesus' coming did not negate the Law and the Prophets; rather it fulfilled the Old Testament. Answering a question regarding which is the greatest commandment, Jesus responds,

> You shall love the Lord your God with all your heart and with all your soul and with all your mind. This is the great and first commandment. And a second is like it: You shall love your neighbor as yourself. On these two commandments depend all the Law and the Prophets (Matthew 22:37-40, ESV).

Jesus presents the challenge for us today—love God and serve your neighbor sacrificially, treating him as you would like to be treated, exemplifying the Golden Rule.

6. Let's practice our Golden Rule principle by evaluating and documenting how you would like to be treated if:

You have a financial need.

You are ill.

Someone you love died.

You suffered public humiliation.

You have fallen into sin.

You received an award.

Your child is in trouble.

Your husband left you.

You made a bad decision.

You hold a different worldview.

Meditating on your response to these potential real-life situations helps to clarify ways you can minister to those God places in your path. John Stott sums up the Golden Rule principle well, "It transforms our actions. If we put ourselves sensitively into the place of the other person, and wish for him what we would wish for ourselves, we would never be mean, always generous; never harsh, always understanding; never cruel, always kind." [21]

A classmate of mine from college, Bill Cates, wrote this song while we were still students. It was published and became a part of the Baptist Hymnal. May his question penetrate your heart.

"Do You Really Care?"

I look around in the place that I live; I see people with so much to give;

Yet there are those who are dying to know just that somebody cares.

I see people just longing to know what they can live for and where they can go;

We have the hope and the purpose to share, but do we really care?

People grope in darkness, searching for a way,

Don't you know of someone you can help today?

Do you really care? Do you know how to share with people everywhere?

Do you really care?

Will you take the dare? Spread Good News everywhere?

The cross of Christ to bear?

Do you really care? [22]

KINGDOM EXERCISE

She was a tiny woman. Some may have viewed her as frail and slightly stooped. But to me she was a giant. Her name was Emily Colvette. Our lives intersected while I was in high school when my mother came home from a volunteer meeting and announced that I would be working with her that summer. She was the director of the Woody Barton Goodwill Center in my hometown of Nashville. The center was located in a once-fashionable neighborhood that had fallen on hard times. The stately homes had been sub-divided into apartments. Though I came from a background of modest means, this was my first encounter with true poverty. It was in this forgotten neighborhood that Miss Colvette lived and worked and modeled for me what it meant to be a servant. There was never a task too menial for her attention nor one too challenging for her abilities. She could cleverly accomplish the most marvelous things using just a miniscule of money. I never heard her complain; she merely placed her confidence unreservedly in her Savior and served Him with abandon.

The Goodwill Center was a lighthouse in that community. Its name was most appropriate since it spread good will throughout the neighborhood. It was where the residents came when they needed food and clothing, a class for practical life skills, truth from the Bible, or even a shoulder to cry on. Then came summer, Day Camp arrived, providing a wonderful pastime for children who needed something wholesome to do. And that is where my job as a camp counselor came in. From 9 a.m. until 3 p.m., we met under the mature trees in the neighborhood park and poured our lives into scores of children sharing with them the love of Jesus. I loved it. I returned the next summer, and the next, when I served as Miss Colvette's assistant. It certainly wasn't the salary that drew me there. Don't laugh hysterically, but my pay was $2.00 a day. Though it seems like an eternity ago, it was a laughable amount even then. What I gained through this experience was far more valuable than a paycheck. It prepared me for the plans God had for me in the future—it was invaluable.

I loved to engage Miss Colvette in conversation as she had her morning Coke—no coffee drinking for her. In those interactions, her wisdom, gleaned from walking faithfully with the Lord, overflowed, making a lasting impression on me. She was selfless; she did not have to have her own way. Her goal was to serve her Lord and others in the center of His will. It didn't matter to her that she labored in relative obscurity. Did she ever sit me down and explain the ins and outs of absolute submission to God? No, she didn't have to for she lived it out before me.

THE DISCIPLINE OF SUBMISSION

Today, we will be contemplating the spiritual discipline of submission. For most of us, the life of submission does not come easily. From toddlerhood, the longing to have your own way and control your destiny is ingrained into the fabric of our psyche. We desire to sing along with Frank Sinatra, "I did it my way." Such is not the way of Kingdom living. Submission requires placing ourselves under the control of someone else. Synonyms include obedience, compliance, surrender, acquiescence, and deference. For the Christian, it means submitting to God first and then to others.

JESUS IS OUR GUIDE IN THIS PROCESS OF SUBMISSION. THOUGH GOD THE SON, HE BECAME A SERVANT TO PROVIDE THE SALVATION FOR MANKIND THAT NO ONE ELSE COULD DO.

Jesus is our Guide in this process of submission. Though God the Son, He became a Servant to provide the salvation for mankind that no one else could do. Let's consider the words of our example, Jesus.

> For I have come down from Heaven, not to do My own will, but the will
> of Him who sent Me (John 6:38).

> During the days of Jesus' life on earth, He offered up prayers and petitions
> with fervent cries and tears to the One who could save Him from death,
> and He was heard because of His reverent submission (Hebrews 5:7, NIV).

> Now My soul has become troubled; and what shall I say,
> "Father, save Me from this hour"? But for this purpose I came to this hour.
> Father glorify Your name. Then a voice came out of Heaven: "I have both glorified it,
> and will glorify it again" (John 12:27-28).

> And He went a little beyond them, and fell on His face and prayed,
> saying, "My Father, if it is possible, let this cup pass from Me;
> yet not as I will but as You will" (Matthew 26:39).

THE EXERCISE

The life that Jesus led on earth exemplified absolute submission to God the Father. Today I would like us to reflect on the measure of our own submission in our pursuit to emulate Jesus. We will begin by examining the concept of the bond-slave as described in Exodus 21:2, 5-6 (NKJV).

> If you buy a Hebrew servant, he shall serve six years; and in the seventh he shall go
> out free and pay nothing...But if the servant plainly says, "I love my master, my wife,
> and my children; I will not go out free," then his master shall bring him to the judges.
> He shall also bring him to the door, or to the doorpost, and his master shall pierce his
> ear with an awl; and he shall serve him forever.

This permanent, irrevocable relationship is how the Apostle Paul describes his wholehearted devotion and affiliation to the Lord Jesus Christ. "Paul, a bondservant of Jesus Christ, called to be an apostle, separated to the gospel of God (Romans 1:1, NKJV). The question is: Have you relinquished the control of your life unreservedly to the Savior?

Josef Tson, the Romanian pastor who suffered greatly under communist rule, makes an observation about the hesitancy some Christians have regarding the call to be a bond-slave. His explanation raises a point that I have never considered before.

> Christian *surrender* means that a person lifts his or her hands and says to God, "Here I am; I surrender; You take over; I belong to You; You dispose of me!"

> But this is America, the country of the independent people! This is the place of "Nobody should command me!…I belong only to myself!"

> A call to surrender, and even more, to full surrender, simply doesn't go well with such people. Therefore, the preachers, who wanted "results", and wanted them in big numbers, felt (and gave in to) the temptation to soften the demand, to reduce the cost, to make the message more "palatable". And they hit the word "commitment".

> You see, *commitment* means "I engage myself to do something for you," or even lighter, "I promise to do something for you," but I remain myself and I may keep my promise or not. We can speak of weaker or stronger commitment, but be it strong as possible, it is still my independent self that engages itself in a tentative promise. [23]

Which word, surrender or commitment, represents your response to Jesus? Have you relinquished control and submitted to His will alone? Are you afraid of His plans for you—what if it's not what you desire? Jesus says, "Whoever does not take up their cross and follow Me is not worthy of Me. Whoever finds their life will lose it, and whoever loses their life for My sake will find it" (Matthew 10:38-39, NIV).

Let's hear from two missionaries who submitted to fulfilling God's will for them:
But don't talk to me about sacrifice. It is no sacrifice. In the face of the superlative joy of that one overwhelming experience, the joy of flashing that miracle word, Savior, for the first time to a great tribe that had never heard it before, I can never think of these forty years in terms of sacrifice. I saw Christ and His Cross and I did this because I loved Him. [24]
~WILLIS HOTCHKISS, Pioneer Missionary, East Africa, Late 1800s

*I need to be so utterly God's that He can use me or hide me,
as He chooses, as an arrow in His hand or in His quiver. I will ask
no questions: I relinquish all rights to Him who desires my
supreme good. He knows best.* [25]
~HELEN ROSEVEARE, Missionary Doctor, Belgian Congo, Mid 1900s

REFLECTION QUESTIONS

1. How does the position of bond-slave resonate with you?

2. Describe any area of your life you are unwilling to surrender to God's purpose.

3. Where do you stand—surrender or commitment? Elaborate.

4. Journal your thoughts, then share them with the Lord.

Anything, Anytime, Anywhere, Lord—your bond-slave.

WEEK TEN
KINGDOM WISDOM
—— • —— • —— • —— MATTHEW 7:13-29 —— • —— • —— • ——

Enter through the narrow gate.
MATTHEW 7:13

The resurrection of Christ is at the very heart of the gospel! Any
departure from this truth is a corruption of our minds and has its origin in the subtlety
of Satan. Aware of this danger, Paul expressed his
utmost concern: "I fear, lest somehow, as the serpent deceived Eve
by his craftiness, so your minds may be corrupted from
the simplicity that is in Christ (2 Corinthians 11:3). [1]
~MAJOR IAN THOMAS

This week we will be looking at the closing words of the Sermon on the Mount. Jesus expounds on two ways (broad and narrow), two teachers (false and true), and two foundations (sand and rock). In each instance, the hearer (or reader as in our case) is called upon to make a choice between the kingdom of Satan or the Kingdom of God. Jesus unapologetically demands a response without softening the implied hardship accompanying the decision to follow Him.

John MacArthur makes some observations about this passage:

> From here through the rest of the sermon (vv. 13–29) Jesus repeatedly points out two things: the necessity of choosing whether to follow God or not, and the fact that the choices are two and only two. There are two gates, the narrow and the wide; two ways, the narrow and the broad; two destinations, life and destruction; two groups, the few and the many; two kinds of trees, the good and the bad, which produce two kinds of fruit, the good and the bad; two kinds of people who profess faith in Jesus Christ, the sincere and the false; two kinds of builders, the wise and the foolish; two foundations, the rock and the sand; and two houses, the secure and the insecure. In all preaching there must be the demand for a verdict. Jesus makes the choice crystal clear. [2]

Jesus has been setting forth God's standards for Kingdom living. In broad strokes, He has painted a portrait of His Kingdom and laid it alongside the self-righteous, hypocritical standards typified by the scribes and Pharisees. The contrast is staggering to a people steeped in the Law and determined to live accordingly. By and large, the rabbinical teachers and the Pharisees have mistaken their strict religiousness for righteousness. They have believed sinful man could find favor with God through a works-based, man-made righteousness by strict adherence to religious ritual and the Law. The pretense of such heresy is tragic, considering the sinfulness of unregenerate man and the weakness of the flesh.

As Jesus begins His ministry, the rabbis have been adding their interpretations and traditions to the Scriptures. As those oral teachings are written down, the Talmud (as these writings were named) results and nearly eclipses the Torah (the written law given by God through Moses). The rabbis and religious leaders have been captured by the self-effort of a religious, legalistic, rule-keeping, systematic adherence to the Law, which was never intended to produce righteousness. They are relying on their personal Jewish pedigrees, their religious education, and their good works to gain God's favor and secure entrance into Heaven.

The Law was designed to expose the lostness of mankind and reveal the need for a Savior. The Law could only reveal, not redeem. As Paul writes, "Therefore the Law has become our tutor to lead us to Christ, so that we may be justified by faith" (Galatians 3:24).

Christ gave His life for us (substitutionary atonement) so that we "may be found in Him, not having a righteousness of my own derived from the Law, but that which is through faith in Christ, the righteousness which comes from God on the basis of faith" (Philippians 3:9). This relationship is initiated in our lives by a personal surrender to Christ as Lord, and we are judicially declared righteous (called justification). He now lives His life through us, and we are progressively changed into His image (sanctification) by "the power of His resurrection and the fellowship of His sufferings, being conformed to His death" (Philippians 3:10). One day He will take us to Heaven (glorification) where we "may attain to the resurrection from the dead" (Philippians 3:11).

In the remaining portion of the Sermon of the Mount, we are reminded that there are false prophets in the world. Therefore, we must be careful of being deceived, perhaps the most dangerous element is self-deception. It is possible for people to know the right language, believe intellectually the facts of the gospel, participate in religious rituals, strictly adhere to high standards of behavior, and still not be saved. Jesus uses two ways (broad and narrow), two teachers (false and true), and two foundations (sand and rock) to set forth the options facing each of us. Choose Jesus!

As we begin our study this week, we have arrived at the portion of the message where Jesus begins to draw the net. He presses in on the inevitable decision every person must make, bringing us to the crossroads where each must decide on the way he/she will take. Jesus has been leading up to this appeal throughout the Sermon on the Mount. We can become a citizen of God's Kingdom and inherit eternal life or remain a citizen of this fallen world, a decision which leads to eternal damnation. "There is a way which seems right to a man, but its end is the way of death" (Proverbs 14:12).

The Lordship of Jesus demands a decision. There are only two possibilities: receive Him or reject Him. A choice is required which will determine both your direction and your destination, so choose carefully.

Man's right to choose began in the Garden. Genesis 2:16-17 says, "The Lord God commanded the man, saying, 'From any tree of the garden you may eat freely; but from the tree of the knowledge of good and evil you shall not eat, for in the day that you eat from it you will surely die.'" During the wilderness wanderings God instructed Moses to say to the people, "I call Heaven and earth to witness against you today, that I have set before you life and death, the blessing and the curse. So choose life in order that you may live, you and your descendants, by loving the Lord your God, by obeying His voice, and by holding fast to Him" (Deuteronomy 30:19-20).

After Israel entered the Promised Land, Joshua confronted the people with a choice. They must choose between continuing to serve the Egyptian and Canaanite gods they had adopted or turn to the Lord. Joshua emphatically said, "Choose for yourselves today whom you will serve; whether the gods which your fathers served which were beyond the River, or the gods of the Amorites in whose land you are living; but as for me and my house, we will serve the Lord" (Joshua 24:15).

On Mount Carmel the prophet Elijah confronted the people of Israel saying, "How long will you hesitate between two opinions? If the Lord is God, follow Him; but if Baal, follow him" (1 Kings 18:21).

God gives us the freedom to choose.

Read Matthew 7:13-14.

Jesus has repeatedly shown the narrowness of God's standard of righteousness in contrast to the broad way. The narrow gate is Christ Himself. In John 14:6, Jesus said, "I am the Way, and the Truth, and the Life; no one comes to the Father but through Me."

1. What command does Jesus give in Matthew 7:13?

2. How does Jesus describe the two gates? (v. 14)

We were born on the broad way. David wrote, "Behold, I was brought forth in iniquity, and in sin my mother conceived me" (Psalm 51:5). The Bible teaches that all men are sinners by birth, by nature, and by practice. No decision on our part is required to remain on the broad way.

John Phillips describes the broad path:

> The broad path offers pleasure, promotion, possessions, power, and piety of a sort; customs and culture; and a varied menu of distractions and delights. Gifted men and great are on this road, as are all kinds of vices, vanities, and violence. Ever amid the violets lurk the vipers.

> The broad way gets narrower as it goes along. It is brooded over by a lord whose realm is darkness, whose rule is bondage, and whose reign is characterized by revenge against God—revenge in the form of the ruin and damnation of mankind. This road offers no real joy, no genuine or lasting pleasure, and only fleeting moments of happiness at best. [3]

Leaving the broad way and entering the narrow gate requires a decision to receive Jesus through repentance and faith. This transaction sets us on the narrow path defined by personal holiness and practical righteousness.

Keeping in mind the two paths mentioned in the Sermon on the Mount. The writer begins with the word "blessed". In the original language, the psalmist chose to use the plural form of this word. This reminds us that God does not mete out His blessings one at a time. Rather, He pours them out, lavishing them on us in abundance. The psalmist contrasts "the way of the righteous" with "the way of the wicked" (Psalm 1:6). We are blessed when we walk in His path of righteousness.

Read Psalm 1:1-6.

3. According to this Psalm what should we avoid?

4. How should we invest our time and energy?

5. What is the result of a life lived for the Lord?

Untold blessings await the one who chooses to follow Jesus. Proverbs 28:20 says, "A faithful man will abound with blessings."

6. Take a minute to count your blessings. Make a list of ten blessings (either tangible or spiritual) you have received from the Lord.

#1

#2

#3

#4

#5

#6

#7

#8

#9

#10

Beloved, there are two paths. They intersect at Calvary, where the invitation to follow Jesus has been extended. A decision is required. Leave the path of destruction, accept Christ as Savior, and start along the narrow way or follow the broad way to eternal damnation. Christ's invitation to everyone to "enter through the narrow gate" (Matthew 7:13) remains in effect today. Choose wisely. Choose well. Choose Jesus!

MATTHEW 7:15-23

The listeners sitting on the hillside include those with various belief systems ranging from religious Pharisees to irreligious pagans. His intention is to confront His hearers face-to-face with truth, forcing each hearer to make an intelligent moral decision to receive or reject the gospel message. His discourse on Kingdom living is so radically different from the religious rituals touted by the Pharisees or from the pagan worship of idols that every hearer is forced to reexamine his/her belief system in light of His divine revelation. We can only imagine the systemic shift in understanding that His hearers experienced as His words landed, rattling the souls and shaking the hearers to the core.

On the heels of His stern warning of two doors, two directions, and two destinations, the Lord addresses the danger of false prophets "who come to you in sheep's clothing, but inwardly are ravenous wolves" (Matthew 7:15).

Read Matthew 7:15-23.

1. What does Jesus say to "beware" of? (v. 15)

2. What metaphor does Jesus use to describe false prophets?

We learn from this metaphor that false prophets are both dangerous and deceptive. False prophets often misrepresent the need for salvation, even denying the existence of Heaven or hell. They typically believe there are a number of paths to God, most, if not all, require self-effort of some sort. Typically, false teachers rely heavily on the love of God while dismissing God's righteous judgement on sin and our need for repentance.

False teachers were, and continue to be, a source of concern for followers of Christ. They assume the identity of sheep in order to gain admittance and win acceptance by the people of God. Their well-honed messages carry just enough truth to make their teachings plausible.

Read 2 Timothy 3:1-7.

3. How does Paul describe the general condition of the prevailing culture "in the last days"? (vv. 2-5)

4. False teachers will target certain women. How does Paul describe them? (vv. 6-7)

5. How devastating to be numbered among this group. How can you avoid being deceived by those who intentionally distort the truth of the Word of God for the purpose of gaining converts for their false religion?

False prophet are no merely mistaken, confused, or lacking solid Biblical training. They intentionally set about to infiltrate the church. They target those who are in the seeking phase or immature believers who are not grounded in the truth of the Word. Peter warned "there will also be false teachers among you, who will secretly introduce destructive heresies, even denying the Master who bought them, bringing swift destruction upon themselves" (2 Peter 2:1).

6. In 2 Timothy 2:15, Paul admonishes Timothy to stay true to his calling. What instructions did he give to his protégé?

Beloved, our defense against false teachers is to have a working knowledge of the Word of God and an unwavering dependence on the Holy Spirit of God. Paul wrote, "All Scripture is inspired by God and profitable for teaching, for reproof, for correction, for training in righteousness; so that the man of God may be adequate, equipped for every good work" (2 Timothy 3:16-17).

In order to blend in among the Christian community, false prophets adopt an outward behavior that is similar to those they seek to deceive. In time their facade will fade, exposing their true nature. Jesus said, "You will know them by their fruits" (Matthew 7:16). While the fruit of the

Spirit identifies true believers' alignment with Christ, false prophets reveal their true nature by their doctrines and their deeds.

As I am finishing up my writing assignment for this study, I have just returned from a week with our grandchildren. My husband and I kept four of our grandchildren while mom and dad slipped away for a much-needed time of refreshment. We were thrilled to be able to move into their home and get the time with our grands! Our charges ranged from age 11 to age 3. At the onset of the week, I decided I would like to get them to memorize Galatians 5:22-23, "The fruit of the Spirit is love, joy, peace, patience, kindness, goodness, faithfulness, gentleness, [and] self-control." I intended to work on this memory work all week, crowning their success at the end of the week with a much-anticipated celebratory meal. I thought it would be a good basis for conversations over mealtime and a standard we might all seek to achieve in our words and our behaviors.

I was delighted, and a little bit surprised, when the older three memorized the whole passage on the first day. I was equally surprised when the three-year-old wanted in on the action. Each day at lunch I would ask each child, "What are the fruit of the Spirit?" In turn each one would recite the passage with increasing speed. When it was the youngest one's turn, he would lock his sparkly blue eyes on mine and with his blond head bobbing up and down with excitement he would joyously shout, "Jesus!" Each child, in turn, would patiently recite the fruit of the Spirit in order, urging him to repeat each word. With great delight he would say each one again in his chirpy toddler voice.

> BELOVED, JESUS IS THE ANSWER! HE IS THE ANSWER TO EVERY HURT AND HEARTACHE, EVERY SICKNESS AND SORROW, EVERY DISAPPOINTMENT AND DISTRESS. JESUS IS THE ANSWER, REGARDLESS OF THE QUESTION.

He provided no end of enjoyment as he struggled wrapping his mouth around those compound words. Although he gradually got more and more of the phrases in order, he never stopped initially answering, "Jesus", to my query. In fact, due to my strong reaction of delight at his initial answer, nearly every question I asked during my stay was answered the same way, "Jesus!" My reply remained the same, "You're right, buddy. Jesus is always the right answer, regardless of the question." Beloved, Jesus is the answer! He is the answer to every hurt and heartache, every sickness and sorrow, every disappointment and distress. Jesus is the answer, regardless of the question.

As followers of Christ, we are gradually becoming conformed to His image. Consequently, the fruit of His indwelling Spirit is progressively manifested through our words and works. In like manner, the fruit of the false confessors of faith will reveal their true nature. No tree can hide its identity for long. Eventually, it betrays itself by the fruit it produces. "Every good tree bears good fruit, but the bad tree bears bad fruit" (Matthew 7:17).

Jesus follows His narrative regarding fruit with the lengths some will go in order to veil their deviousness. On the Day of Judgment, some will use their involvement with prophesying, exorcism, and any number of miracles as proof positive of their right standing with God. I can't help but think that Judas was among the listeners that day. While he became one of the twelve disciples and participated in these types of ministry, he was not a true believer. In time, the fruit of his choices became manifestly evident, confirming he was never one of Jesus' followers. John explains, "They went out from us, but they were not really of us; for if they had been of us, they would have remained with us; but they went out, so that it would be shown that they all are not of us" (1 John 2:19).

7. Who does Jesus say will enter the Kingdom of Heaven? (Matthew 7:21)

The Day of Judgment will reveal the lost state of those who falsely profess Christ without possessing Him; those who have not met His terms for salvation which are repentance and faith. Therefore, Jesus will declare to them, "I never knew you; depart from Me, you who practice lawlessness" (Matthew 7:23).

Intellectual acknowledgment of the facts of the gospel cannot gain anyone God's favor. James writes, "The demons also believe, and shudder" (James 2:19). Self-effort cannot bring anyone into a personal relationship with Christ. Titus 3:5 says, "He saved us, not on the basis of deeds which we have done in righteousness, but according to His mercy." Repentance and faith must be activated in order to seal the transaction between the sinner and the Savior. The burning question is not, "Do you know Jesus?" The more pressing issue is, "Does Jesus know you?"

This solemn warning against false prophets is not license to become suspicious of everybody engaged in ministry or to verbally bash preachers and teachers, a pastime that has seemingly become an acceptable hobby on social media platforms. Rather, it is a solemn reminder that false teachers are joining churches and we must be on guard. Luke affirms the faith of the Bereans who "were more noble-minded than those in Thessalonica, for they received the word with great eagerness, examining the Scriptures daily to see whether these things were so" (Acts 17:11). May we follow their example, becoming more intentional students of the Word of God!

Jesus, as He is drawing the Sermon on the Mount to a close, addresses two paths (narrow and wide) and two prophets (false and true). Tomorrow we will turn our attention to two foundations.

Having dramatically upended the belief system of most who heard the Sermon on the Mount, Jesus brings His discourse to a close with the parable of the wise and foolish builders. The emphasis of the story is not on the men or their materials; the emphasis is on the foundations of their structures.

In 1994, we built a home on ten acres. While I am a city girl at heart, the decision to move to a rural area was a wise one. The biggest drawback was the additional driving required to get the boys to and from school, to pick up groceries and other necessities, and the regular treks to our home church. I soon learned to make the extended travel time profitable by listening to untold hours of sermons, and I greatly expanded my repertoire of Christian music. My well-traveled corridor to get to town led me past a large home under construction. Because we had just recently built our home, I watched with great interest as the foundation was poured and the construction progressed. Each day, I would pray for the safety of the construction crew and for the family that would soon take up residence.

During the summer months of 2003, we had a rash of pop-up storms, a weather pattern that is common to our area. One of those cloudbursts, which became locally known as Hurricane Elvis, was accompanied by straight-line winds over 100 mph. Our home did not sustain any damage. However, as I drove in that morning, I was horrified to see that the home under construction had totally collapsed, unable to sustain the gale force winds. The 2x4 lumber used in the construction were piled haphazardly, resembling a game of pickup sticks gone awry. I immediately began to pray for the family, knowing this set-back would seriously delay the finished product, and, especially for the lady of the house, the destruction would be devastating. As I drove on, I couldn't help but ponder the image and reflect on this passage which immediately came to mind. "The rain fell, and the floods came, and the winds blew and slammed against that house; and it fell—and great was its fall" (Matthew 7:27).

Read Matthew 7:24-27.

In this parable, we have two builders. On the surface, they appear to be similar: same place, same plan, same pursuit.

1. What difference is there between the two structures? (vv. 24-27)

Luke 6:46-49 adds a bit more information about the construction of the wise man's house.

2. How does Luke describe what the wiseman did? (v. 48)

The foolish man "built a house on the ground without any foundation" (v. 49). He took some shortcuts, probably saving some time and money. The finished product may have looked similar to that of the wise builder. It wasn't until a storm broke out that the fallacy of the foolish man's design was revealed.

3. What happens to the house built without a foundation? (v. 49)

4. How does Jesus describe the devastation of the collapsed house? (v. 49)

The storm comes and immediately it is reduced to a pile of rubble. Sudden ruin. Proverbs 6:15 says, "Therefore his calamity will come suddenly; instantly he will be broken and there will be no healing." Stuart Weber writes of this parable, "The first man was wise; the second man was foolish. The first man found stability and blessing in this life and in eternity; the second experienced calamity in this life and in eternity (the rain, floods, and winds can represent both hardships in this life and God's final judgment)." [4]

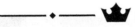

THERE ARE TWO THINGS NECESSARY FOR A FIRM FOUNDATION: HEARING THE WORD AND HEEDING THE WORD.

There are two things necessary for a firm foundation: hearing the Word and heeding the Word. The wise builder hears the truth and responds, activating saving faith. Jesus explains that the wise builder hears His words "and acts on them" (Matthew 7:24) while the foolish man hears them but "does not act on them" (Matthew 7:26) or mix them with faith. Jesus said, "He who has My commandments and keeps them is the one who loves Me; and he who loves Me will be loved by My Father, and I will love him and will disclose Myself to him" (John 14:21).

While hearing the Word is an important part of our sanctification, obedience is the benchmark for spiritual maturity.

Read James 1:22-25.

James was quite likely among the crowd that heard Jesus preach the Sermon on the Mount. That passage seems to echo this parable.

5. What admonition does James give us?

James makes the distinction between the superficial Christian and the supernatural believer.

6. To what does he liken the one who is merely "a hearer of the word and not a doer"? (James 1:22)

7. What characteristic is evident in the effectual doer?

James 2:17 says, "Even so faith, if it has no works, is dead, being by itself." Saving faith, an internal decision, is demonstrated by works of righteousness, an external display of a transformed life. This truth is demonstrated by Jesus' parable. Faith and obedience to God's divine revelation was the foundation of the wise man's house while disobedience, fueled by unbelief, was the foundation of the foolish man's structure.

8. What are some of the storms of life you have experienced?

9. How did you weather the storm, and, if you did not manage well, what might you have done differently?

In a sermon on this passage Dr. Adrian Rogers said,

> We can speculate that most likely a man named Simon Peter and a man named Judas were standing in the crowd when Jesus gave the Sermon on the Mount. They heard Jesus give the parable of the two foundations. Judas was there. Simon Peter was there. Two kinds of builders—very similar: they both erected a spiritual house. Peter built one, and Judas built one. And, had you looked at the two houses, you know what you would have said? You would have said, "Judas can build a better house than Simon Peter."
>
> Do you know who was the best man outwardly? Do you know who had the prettiest house? Not Peter. Judas had the best-looking house. He did, didn't he? Do you know what they did with Judas? They made Judas the treasurer. Now, who do you get for the treasurer? The best. I mean, the most trustworthy. When Jesus said, "One of you is going to betray me," (see Matthew 26:21; Mark 14:18; John 13:21) not a one of them said, "Oh, I know who it is. It's that rascal Judas." Not a one of them said that. They said, "I wonder if it's me." None of them said, "I know it's Judas"—not a one! You know why? He had a good-looking house. I mean, a good-looking house! He knew how to build a house—almost.
>
> But there was a difference. Jesus said, "Peter, who do you say that I am?" Peter said, "[You are] the Christ, the Son of the living God" (Matthew 16:16). And, Jesus said, "That's right. And, upon this rock I'll build my house; I'll build my Church. The very gates of hell will not prevail against it" (see Matthew 16:18). Peter knew who Jesus was. Peter was weak, just like I am and like you are. He wasn't much of a house builder, but boy did he have a good foundation! He laid his faith on a firm foundation.
>
> Now, I want to tell you that a storm came, and it blew through the life of Judas; and a storm came, and it blew through the life of Simon Peter. And, when the storm was over, Judas's house was gone—it was gone. And, Judas died and went to hell. You say, "Did Judas lose his salvation?" He never had it. The Bible says that Jesus, speaking of Judas, said, "Did I Myself not choose you, the twelve, and yet one of you is a devil?" (John 6:70). The Bible says that "Jesus knew from the beginning who they were who

did not believe and who it was that would betray Him" (John 6:64). Judas never ever had real faith. Simon Peter did. Jesus said to Simon Peter, "Simon, Simon, behold, Satan has demanded permission to sift you like wheat; but I have prayed for you, that your faith may not fail" (Luke 22:31–32). Peter had faith, and the Savior interceded for him. You know, when the storm hit ole Simon, a few windows were broken out. Did you know that? And, some shingles blew off the roof, and some things happened to that house. I want to tell you something: after the storm, he was still standing. And, he became the flaming apostle of Pentecost, and do you know why? I'll tell you why: he had the real thing—he had the real thing. He knew God. He had heard the Word of God. He believed the Son of God. He bowed his knee to Jesus Christ. Weak, yes; failing, yes—but the house stood that was built on a rock. [5]

Paul writes, "For no man can lay a foundation other than the one which is laid, which is Jesus Christ" (1 Corinthians 3:11). Storms are coming to all of us, saved and unsaved. God "sends rain on the righteous and the unrighteous" (Matthew 5:45). The storms reveal the foundation of our lives. A genuine faith in Christ will endure, not only in the storms of this life, but also in the final judgment.

The narrow gate and the narrow path are found and followed by obedience to God's Word and dependence on God's Spirit. Good fruit is produced by obedience to God's Word and dependence on God's Spirit. The solid foundation for a life that can endure the storms of life is built upon the Solid Rock, Jesus Christ. As we meditate on the application of this parable to our lives personally, may we make a fresh commitment to live a life fashioned on the firm foundation of Jesus Christ.

MATTHEW 7:28-29

The Sermon on the Mount is the largest body of Jesus' teaching that is consecutively recorded in the Word of God. John Phillips poetically notes, "There is nothing to compare with it in all the literature of the world. Even the greatest of the world's moral, religious, and philosophical statements blush and stammer in the presence of this sublime declaration." [6] In His sermon, the Lord challenges His followers to draw from the supernatural resources of the Kingdom of God and live lives set apart for His glory. This lifestyle is categorically contrary to the natural response of unredeemed humanity and serves to validate our genuine conversion experience.

Phillips adds,

> The multitudes had never heard anything like the Sermon on the Mount. Their rabbis gave wearisome, often false, and often frivolous exposition of the law…God's law was made void by rabbinic traditions, and the spirit of the law was crushed under an outward load of ordinances and observances. Judaism was no longer the pure religion of the Old Testament. The common people were oppressed by tradition and confused. [7]

Into this world, the King of Glory burst onto the scene, speaking with the authority of the living God and bringing a refreshing new message concerning the practical aspects of redemption.

As they listen, those sitting on the hillside are silently processing what they have heard and comparing it to the wearisome message touted by the scribes and Pharisees. Jesus' words are both powerful and profound. His message transcends religion and ritual. He speaks of a vital living relationship with God through Jesus Christ. The end result of a personal relationship with the Lord is a dramatically different life. He speaks to the laws of behavior for those who are saved. Their right standing with God through Jesus, which is at the core of Kingdom living, will be manifestly evident in their relationships and in their daily choices. Obviously, only people born again and indwelt by the Holy Spirit can live the kind of life Jesus is proclaiming.

Read Matthew 7:28-29.

1. As Jesus concludes His sermon, what is the crowd's response?

Stuart Weber notes, "Matthew used the Greek imperfect tense to denote an ongoing effect in Jesus' listeners. They just could not get over it." [8] Some two thousand years later His words are still having the same effect!

Using our sanctified imagination, just imagine with me what it must have been like for those hearing the message. The religious crowd is confounded. The Pharisees, huddled together in small groups, wag their heads and cluck their tongues in disgust, making no effort to mask their disdain for the message or the Messenger. The seekers are confused. The skeptics are intrigued. His followers are excited. The life Jesus has described is drastically different from the stale religious rituals and rule-keeping the Pharisees espoused and endorsed. The entire message is disruptive!

One of the first things the crowd notes is that Jesus doesn't hold Himself aloof from the crowd. Instead He leans in, His words fueled by power and passion. His eyes sparkle as they dart from face to face. A smile spreads across His face as He speaks of His heavenly Kingdom coming to earth through the radical reformation of the hearts of those who would follow Him. His tone is reverent as He speaks of the things of God, yet full of joy, a welcomed relief from the stylistic Jewish teachers of the Law. The words seem to spill out of Him, yet they are carefully measured and deliberate. His manner was easygoing. He is approachable, but there is no denying that the mark of the Divine emanates from His being. How can they not but stand amazed?

However, the thing that stands out the most to the audience who has heard His sermon is the authority with which He speaks. The other rabbis and religious leaders they are used to hearing quote various rabbis and experts of the Law to lend authority to their teachings, but Jesus speaks as the final authority on truth. His words resonate with His hearers. The teaching of the scribes and Pharisees can not begin to compare to the clearly delineated message of the newly arrived King.

Read John 7:40-46.

2. After Jesus has been teaching in the temple during the Feast of Booths, a great division arises among the people. Who do they say He is?

3. The chief priests and Pharisees send officials to arrest Him. When the temple police return empty-handed, what do they say concerning the Lord? (v. 46)

The words of Jesus have their origin in the Father. He needs no human teacher to add authority or authenticity to His words. Jesus speaks as the Son of God, co-equal with the Father (see Philippians 2:5-11).

4. Read John 14:10. What does Jesus say about His words?

5. Read John 16:5-15. What is the role of the Holy Spirit?

In the Sermon on the Mount, Jesus cites no human authorities or tradition. He speaks with candor and the confidence that comes from bringing God's message as "the mediator of a new covenant" (Hebrews 9:15).

KINGDOM EXERCISE

Richard Foster states, "Celebration comes when the common ventures of life are redeemed." [9] We, the redeemed of God, have much to celebrate! "He rescued us from the domain of darkness, and transferred us to the Kingdom of His beloved Son, in whom we have redemption, the forgiveness of sins" (Colossians 1:13-14). He "made us alive together with Christ (by grace you have been saved), and raised us up with Him, and seated us with Him in the Heavenly places in Christ Jesus" (Ephesians 2:5-6). In Christ, we have much to celebrate! Therefore, we should "rejoice in the Lord always; again I say, rejoice!" (Philippians 4:4).

Joy is a fruit of the Spirit (Galatians 5:22) and the birthright of every believer, one of the many endowments our salvation ensures. Joy is available, but not automatic. To access His joy, we must practice the presence of Jesus and remain in communion with Him. This Kingdom reality requires us to actively pursue faith-based obedience. Willard writes, "Kingdom obedience is Kingdom abundance." [10] The psalmist exclaims, "I have set the Lord continually before me; because He is at my right hand, I will not be shaken. Therefore, my heart is glad and my glory rejoices…In Your presence is fullness of joy; in Your right hand there are pleasures forever" (Psalm 16:8-9; 11). When we choose to abide in the Lord, joy becomes the by-product of a life consumed by Jesus Christ.

THE DISCIPLINE OF CELEBRATION

I am reminded of a time when I was challenged to choose joy in the midst of difficult circumstances. About ten years after building our home in Fayette County, we discovered time was taking a toll on our house. On a Sunday morning, we were getting ready to attend church. Standing in our master bathroom, I heard running water. The sound was coming from our closet! It took a few minutes, but I located the source of the leak. Water was coming from a cracked plumbing joint in our closet. Panicked, I called for Craig. In one fluid motion, he shut off the water valve and pulled up the wet carpet. He set up several fans in hope of salvaging the carpet. Surveying the wet mess, we both decided to continue with our plans and go to church. In light of what had just happened, we felt we needed church, lest we lose our religion! We managed to arrive in time for the sermon and picked up some plumbing supplies on the way home. When we arrived, Craig immediately set about trying to repair the leak. Fortunately, the fix was not difficult. Satisfied the repair was secure, we both sat down in the den. Only then did we discover the water had run under the wall from the closet to the den. Nearly one-third of the den carpet was soaked. Furniture was moved. Wet carpet was pulled up. More fans were set out. Earlier that morning, I had consciously determined not to lose my joy over the big wet mess in my house. I reaffirmed my heart's desire to the Lord.

I would not cave to my frustration. After what Jesus had done for me on the cross, I determined to stay in His presence and choose joy!

On the following Saturday, I was getting ready to attend a baby shower for my daughter-in-law. Obviously excited over the event, I was preoccupied with anticipation. I was in front of my vanity, applying my makeup, when I suddenly realized the carpet I was standing on was wet. Again, I called for Craig. I am known for large doses of recurring drama, but the high pitch of my voice revealed my panic. "The carpet is wet," I squealed. "Again? Are you serious?" he replied in genuine shock. Further investigation revealed a leak behind the shower stall that was running out under the drain pan. The shower stall had to be pulled out along with the vanity and mirror. Saturated drywall and insulation had to be removed down to the studs. The closets were emptied. The bathroom was gutted. The carpet was ruined. Walls were removed. Wallpaper was damaged. Even the light fixtures had to be taken down. Again, I was faced with a decision. Would I lose my joy in this plumbing journey? I am happy to report my joy remained intact. After what Jesus did for me on the cross, I determined the loss of some wood, hay, and stubble was of little consequence. I appropriated His joy by faith. I rose above the downward pull of my flesh. I fixed my mind on Jesus. I ran to my Strong Tower. I chose joy!

For several weeks, we lived in chaos. The contents of our closets were stacked in our bedroom. Shoe racks lined the walls. Accessories were haphazardly draped on doorknobs and drawer pulls. My scarves and Craig's ties were piled on our dresser. Purses were stacked in the corner. When I was tempted to give in to frustration, I forced myself to do the mental gymnastics necessary to cast down "speculations and every lofty thing raised up against the knowledge of God, and [take] every thought captive to the obedience of Christ" (2 Corinthians 10:5). With the Lord's help, I kept my joy intact.

As we were going to bed one night, Craig and I joked, "What else can happen?" Around 1:00 a.m. that question was answered. We were startled awake by the sound of ripping drywall. The ceiling in our master bedroom collapsed! Our upstairs water-heater sprang a leak and dumped 50 gallons of water and wet insulation in our bedroom. Thankfully, the bulk of the ceiling landed on our armoire and not on our heads. Water sheeted down the front of the armoire and the television housed in the cabinet. The sound of the collapse was frightening; the sight was staggering. Craig turned off the water and then ran upstairs. When he returned to our bedroom, I was sitting upright in the bed with the covers clutched to my throat. My mouth was still open. My eyes were riveted to the hole in our ceiling and the wet piles of pink insulation.

When I could pull myself from my perch, I discovered splatters of wet insulation had settled in my shoes, spotted my sweaters, and soaked stacks of our clothes still awaiting closet repairs before they could be stored. The carpet was steadily soaking up water like a dry sponge. The oriental rug under my bed appeared to be ruined. The dyes on the once-beautiful rug were bleeding together and forming puddles of mottled colors. I stood in the doorway of my bedroom and surveyed the scene. A decision was required. Would I experience the joy of the Lord or would I sell out eternal reward for earthy remnants? Would I maintain my spiritual equilibrium or fall in the pit of despair? The choice was mine to make. I chose joy!

After what Jesus has done on my behalf, I have no right to lose my joy. The manifestation of the joy of Jesus, especially in the midst of difficult circumstances, validates the presence and power of Christ in the believer.

In John 15:13 Jesus said, "Greater love has no one than this, that one lay down his life for his friends." I cannot speak for you, I cannot choose for you, but I have made my decision. After what Jesus has done on my behalf, I intend to live in His presence. I am determined to stay filled to the overflow with His joy. I choose joy!

THE EXERCISE

Today, we are going to practice the presence of the Lord and enter into His joy.

Select a verse or Bible passage that speaks to the joy that is ours in Christ. Write it out. Memorize it. Meditate on it.

REFLECTION QUESTIONS

1. In order to sustain the joy of the Lord, what steps are necessary when your joy is challenged by difficult circumstances?

2. Can you think of a time when your joy in the Lord was challenged? How did you respond?

3. Could improvement be made to the way you typically handle frustrations or distractions? What can you do in order to (more often) choose joy?

The unbelieving world may know periods of happiness, generally based on their circumstances at the moment. Only Jesus followers can know joy. Unspeakable joy. Unshakable joy. Undeniable joy. In the midst of our circumstances, joy. Through the ups and downs and the twists and turns of life, joy. And that beloved, gives us cause to celebrate!

Dallas Willard observes:

> Celebration is a life of "walking and leaping and praising God" (Acts 3:8). God loves to celebrate and loves even more when we, as His people, join Him in celebrating all the wonderful things He has done for us. Joy that is exhibited in celebration keeps everything else going, produces energy and makes us strong. This genuine and sustaining joy is achieved through obedience to God. Celebration manifests in endless ways: singing, dancing, laughing, as well as taking advantage of celebrating festivals, holidays, and the milestones of life. [11]

And just like that, we have come to the end of our study. Thank you for taking this journey with us to the shores of Galilee where we have sat at the Master's feet and listened to "The Disruptive Message of the Sermon on the Mount."

If you are outside a personal relationship with Jesus Christ, our prayer for you is to know the Lord Jesus Christ as Lord and Savior. Anything less would be an exercise in futility. Knowing about the Lord without having come to know the Lord is little more than the accumulation of facts, having never been mixed with faith. If you would like to become a follower of Jesus, we have prepared a handout entitled, "How to Become a Christian" on page 237. It is our sincere desire that you "enter through the narrow gate" (Matthew 7:13) into the saving knowledge of Jesus Christ!

Our prayer for all of us is that we would examine our hearts by the standards Jesus set out in His sermon. Ignoring the shouts of culture and the luring taunts of the world. Just our lives measured against the Jesus-shaped life. Like those who sat on the hillside listening, may we continue to be amazed by His words. And may our amazement turn into surrender to this Kingdom way of living "on earth as it is in Heaven." That, dear friend, is what it means to live in *This Present Kingdom*.

Until He comes,

The Lord bless you, and keep you; the Lord make His face
shine on you, and be gracious to you; the Lord lift up
His countenance on you, and give you peace.
NUMBERS 6:24-26

How to Become a Christian

Dear one, has there ever been a time that you have given your heart to the Lord? Do you have the assurance that if you were to die right now, you would go straight to heaven to spend all eternity in the presence of the Lord Jesus Christ and all His followers? If not, please let me share with you how you can be saved.

Admit Your Sin

First, you must understand that you are a sinner. The Bible says, "All have sinned and fall short of the glory of God" (Romans 3:23). In Romans 6:23 the Bible says, "For the wages of sin is death." That means that sin has separated us from a Holy God and we are under the sentence of eternal death and separation from God.

Abandon Self-Effort

Secondly, you must understand that you cannot save yourself by your own efforts. The Bible is very clear that it is "not by works of righteousness which we have done, but according to His mercy He saved us" (Titus 3:5, KJV). Again, in Ephesians 2:8-9 the Bible says, "For by grace you have been saved through faith; and that not of yourselves, it is the gift of God; not as a result of works, so that no one may boast."

Acknowledge Christ's Payment

Thirdly, you must believe that Jesus Christ, the Son of God, died for your sins. The Bible says, "God demonstrates His own love toward us, in that while we were yet sinners, Christ died for us" (Romans 5:8). That means He died a sacrificial death in your place. Your sin debt has been paid by the blood of Jesus Christ, which "cleanses us from all sin" (I John 1:7).

Accept Him as Savior

Fourthly, you must put your faith in Jesus Christ and Him alone for your salvation. The blood of Christ does you no good until you receive Him by faith. The Bible says, "Believe in the Lord Jesus, and you will be saved" (Acts 16:31).

Has there been a time in your life that you have taken this all-important step of faith? If not, I urge you to do it right now. Jesus Christ is the only way to heaven. He said, "I am the way, the truth, and the life. No one can come to the Father except through me" (John 14: 6, NLT).

Would you like to become a Christian? Would you like to invite Jesus Christ to come into your heart today? Read over this prayer and if it expresses the desire of your heart, you may ask Him into your heart to take away your sin, fill you with His Spirit, and take you to home to Heaven when you die. If this is your intention, pray this prayer.

"Oh God, I'm a sinner. I am lost and I need to be saved. I know I cannot save myself, so right now, once and for all, I trust You to save me. Come into my heart, forgive my sin, and make me Your child. I give you my life. I will live for You as You give me Your strength. Amen."

If you will make this your heartfelt prayer, God will hear and save you! Jesus has promised that He will never leave nor forsake anyone who comes to Him in faith. In John 6:37 He said, "The one who comes to Me I will certainly not cast out."

Welcome to the family!

END NOTES

INTRODUCTION

1. Wright, N.T. (2006). *Simply Christian*, p. 102. New York, NY: Harper One Publishing.

2. Smith, J. B. (2009). *The Good and Beautiful Life*, p. 37. Downer's Grove, IL: InterVarsity Press.

3. Smith, J. B. (2009). *The Good and Beautiful Life*, p. 37. Downer's Grove, IL: InterVarsity Press.

4. Wright, N.T. (2006). *Simply Christian*, p. 100. New York, NY: Harper One Publishing.

5. See Micah 5:2; Isaiah 9:6-7; and Psalms 22:27-31.

6. Wright, N.T. (2006). *Simply Christian*, p. 101. New York, NY: Harper One Publishing.

7. Crisler, B.C. (1976). "The Acoustics and the Crowd Capacity of Natural Theaters in Palestine," *The Biblical Archaeologist, 39*(4), pp. 128-41.

8. Hughes, R. K. (2001). *The Sermon on the Mount: The Message of the Kingdom*, p. 16. Wheaton, IL: Crossway Publishing.

9. Smith, J. B. (2009). *The Good and Beautiful Life*, p. 10. Downer's Grove, IL: InterVarsity Press.

10. Willard, D. (1998). *The Divine Conspiracy*, p. 35. London: William Collins Publishing.

11. Wright, N.T. (2006). *Simply Christian*, p. 92. New York, NY: Harper One Publishing.

12. Smith, J. B. (2009). *The Good and Beautiful Life*, p. 10. Downer's Grove, IL: InterVarsity Press.

13. Willard, D. (1998). *The Divine Conspiracy*, p. 33. London: William Collins Publishing.

14. Willard, D. (1998). *The Divine Conspiracy*, p. 35. London: William Collins Publishing.

15. Colson, C. (2007). *God and Government: An Insider's View on the Boundaries Between Faith and Politics*, p. 95. Grand Rapids, MI: Zondervan Publishing.

16. Luther, M. (n.d.) A Mighty Fortress. *The Baptist Hymnal*, p. 40. Nashville: TN: Convention Press.

17. Wright, N.T. (2006). *Simply Christian*, p. 222. New York, NY: Harper One Publishing.

18. Spangler, A. and Tverberg, L. (2009). *Sitting at the Feet of Rabbi Jesus*, p. 92. Grand Rapids, MI: Zondervan Publishing.

WEEK 1

1. Lewis, C.S. (1952). *Mere Christianity*, p. 54. NewYork, NY: MacMillan Publishing.

2. Smith, J.B. (2009). *The Good and Beautiful Life*, p. 56. Downers Grove, IL: InterVarsity Press.

3. Smith, J.B. (2009). *The Good and Beautiful Life*, p. 54. Downers Grove, IL: InterVarsity Press.

4. Smith, J.B. (2009). *The Good and Beautiful Life*, p. 53. Downers Grove, IL: InterVarsity Press.

5. Smith, J.B. (2009). *The Good and Beautiful Life*, p. 55. Downers Grove, IL: InterVarsity Press.

6. Smith, J.B. (2009). *The Good and Beautiful Life*, p. 56. Downers Grove, IL: InterVarsity Press.

7. Willard, D. (1998). *The Divine Conspiracy*, pp. 114-115. London: William Collins.

8. Willard, D. (1998). *The Divine Conspiracy*, pp. 116-117. London: William Collins.

9. Willard, D. (1998). *The Divine Conspiracy*, p. 132. London: William Collins.

10. Wiersbe, W. (1976). *Live Like a King*, p. 34. Chicago, IL: Moody Press.

11. Wiersbe, W. (1976). *Live Like a King*, p. 34. Chicago, IL: Moody Press.

12. Wiersbe, W. (1976). *Live Like a King*, p. 54. Chicago, IL: Moody Press.

13. Wiersbe, W. (1976). *Live Like a King*, p. 54. Chicago, IL: Moody Press.

14. Smith, J.B. (2009). *The Good and Beautiful Life,* p. 58. Downers Grove, IL: InterVarsity Press.

15. Willard, D. (1998). *The Divine Conspiracy*, p. 132. London: William Collins.

16. Elliot, E. (2019). *Suffering Is Never for Nothing*, pp. 2, 9. Nashville, TN: B&H Publishing Group.

17. Wiersbe, W. (1976). *Live Like a King*, p. 48. Chicago, IL: Moody Press.

18. Compilation by Richard A. Kauffman. (July 2007). *Christianity Today*. Retrieved from https://www.christianitytoday.com/ct/2007/july/22.50.html

19. Wiersbe, W. (1976). *Live Like a King*, p. 83. Chicago, IL: Moody Press.

20. Wiersbe, W. (1976). *Live Like a King*, p. 67. Chicago, IL: Moody Press.

21. Wiersbe, W. (1976). *Live Like a King*, p. 68. Chicago, IL: Moody Press.

22. Wiersbe, W. (1976). *Live Like a King*, p. 78. Chicago, IL: Moody Press.

23. Wiersbe, W. (1976). *Live Like a King*, p. 83. Chicago, IL: Moody Press.

24. Wiersbe, W. (1976). *Live Like a King*, p. 87. Chicago, IL: Moody Press.

25. Wiersbe, W. (1976). *Live Like a King*, p. 89. Chicago, IL: Moody Press.

26. Wiersbe, W. (1976). *Live Like a King*, p. 90. Chicago, IL: Moody Press.

27. Wiersbe, W. (1976). *Live Like a King*, p. 93. Chicago, IL: Moody Press.

28. Wiersbe, W. (1976). *Live Like a King*, pp. 95-96. Chicago, IL: Moody Press.

29. Wiersbe, W. (1976). *Live Like a King*, p. 99. Chicago, IL: Moody Press.

30. Foster, R.J. (n.d.) *Renovare*. Retrieved from https://renovare.org/about/ideas/spiritual-disciplines

31. Foster, R.J. (n.d.) *Renovare*. Retrieved from https://renovare.org/about/ideas/spiritual-disciplines

32. Foster, R.J. (n.d.) *Renovare*. Retrieved from https://renovare.org/about/ideas/spiritual-disciplines

33. Ortberg, J. (1997). *The Life You've Always Wanted*, pp. 77, 79. Grand Rapids, MI: Zondervan.

WEEK 2

1. Chambers, O. (2016). *Studies in the Sermon on the Mount: God's Character and the Believer's Conduct*, p. 15. Grand Rapids, MI: Our Daily Bread Publishing.

2. MacArthur, J.F., Jr. (1985). *Matthew, Vol.1*, p. 187. Chicago, IL: Moody Press.

3. MacArthur, J.F., Jr. (1985). *Matthew, Vol.1*, pp. 188-189. Chicago, IL: Moody Press.

4. Rogers, A. (2017). *It Pays to Serve Jesus, In Adrian Rogers Sermon Archive Matthew 19:29-20:16*. Signal Hill, CA: Rogers Family Trust.

5. Hendriksen, W., (1973). *Exposition of the Gospel According to Matthew*, p. 275. Grand Rapids, MI: Baker Book House.

6. MacArthur, J.F., Jr. (1985). *Matthew, Vol. 1*, pp. 190-191. Chicago, IL: Moody Press.

7. Smith, J.B. (2009). *The Good and Beautiful Life*, p. 91. Downers Grove, IL: InterVarsity Press.

8. Christian, I. (n.d.) *Bible.org*. Retrieved from https://bible.org/seriespage/blessed-are-pure-heart-matthew-58

9. MacArthur, J.F., Jr. (1985). *Matthew, Vol. 1*, p. 204. Chicago, IL: Moody Press.

10. MacArthur, J.F., Jr. (1985). *Matthew, Vol. 1*, pp. 205-206. Chicago, IL: Moody Press.

11. Christian, I. (n.d.) *Bible.org.* Retrieved from https://bible.org/seriespage/blessed-are-pure-heart-matthew-58

12. Smith, J.B. (2009). *The Good and Beautiful Life*, p. 91. Downers Grove, IL: InterVarsity Press.

13. Ezell, R. (n.d.) *Lifeway.* Retrieved from https://www.lifeway.com/en/articles/sermon-blessed-peacemakers-sons-god-matthew-5

14. Rogers, A. (2017). *It Pays to Serve Jesus, In Adrian Rogers Sermon Archive Matthew 19:29-20:16.* Signal Hill, CA: Rogers Family Trust.

15. MacArthur, J.F., Jr. (1985). *Matthew, Vol. 1*, p. 209. Chicago, IL: Moody Press.

16. Wiersbe, W., (2007). *Heirs of the King: Living in the Beatitudes*, p. 127. Grand Rapids, MI: Daily Bread Ministries.

17. Stott, J.R.W. (1985). *The Message of the Sermon on the Mount*, p. 50. Downers Grove, IL: InterVarsity Press.

18. Vine, W.E., Unger, M.F., & White, W., (1996). *Vine's Complete Expository Dictionary of Old and New Testament Words, Vol. 2*, p. 468. Nashville, TN: T. Nelson.

19. Bobai Agang, S. (March 2020). *Christianity Today.* Retrieved from https://www.christianitytoday.com/ct/2020/march-web-only/nigeria-pastor-partners-christ-suffering-persecution.html

20. Bobai Agang, S. (March 2020). *Christianity Today.* Retrieved from https://www.christianitytoday.com/ct/2020/march-web-only/nigeria-pastor-partners-christ-suffering-persecution.html

21. *Open Doors U.S.A.* (2020). Retrieved from https://www.opendoorsusa.org/2020-world-watch-list-report/

22. Stott, John. (1978). *The Message of the Sermon on the Mount*, p. 55, Downers Grove, Il: InterVarsity Press.

23. Stott, John, (1978), *The Message of the Sermon on the Mount*, p. 54. Downers Grove, Il: InterVarsity Press.

24. *The Daily Hatch.* (7/09/13). Retrieved from https://thedailyhatch.org/2013/07/09/adrian-rogers-why-i-believe-the-bible-is-true/

25. Swindoll, C. (1998). *Swindoll's Ultimate Book of Illustrations & Quotes*, p. 50. Nashville, TN: Thomas Nelson Publishers.

26. Phillips, J. (2009). *Exploring the Gospel of John: An Expository Commentary*, p. 286. Kregel Publications; WORDsearch Corp.

WEEK 3

1. Muggeridge, M. (1976). *Jesus the Man Who Lives*, p. 61. San Francisco, CA: Harper & Row.

2. Hughes, K. (2001). *The Sermon on the Mount: The Message of the Kingdom*, p. 77. Wheaton, IL: Crossway Books.

3. Salary. (n.d.) *Vocabulary.com*. Retrieved from https://www.vocabulary.com/dictionary/salary

4. Morris, L. (1992). *The Pillar New Testament Commentary, The Gospel According to Matthew*, p. 104. Grand Rapids, MI: Inter-Varsity Press.

5. Carson, D.A. (1987). *Jesus's Sermon on the Mount and His Confrontation with the World: A Study of Matthew 5-10*, pp. 37-38. Grand Rapids, MI: Baker Books.

6. Blomberg, C.L. (1992). *The New American Commentary: Matthew*, p. 102. Nashville, TN: Broadman & Holdman Publishers.

7. Jankovic, R. (2019). *You Who? Why You Matter and How to Deal with It*, p. 231. Moscow, ID: Canon Press.

8. Jankovic, R. (2019). *You Who? Why You Matter and How to Deal with It*, p. 4. Moscow, ID: Canon Press.

9. Arthur, Kay. (1985). *How Can I Be Blessed*, p. 155. Old Tappan, NJ: Fleming H. Revell Company.

10. MacArthur, J. (1985). *The MacArthur New Testament Commentary: Matthew 1-7*, p. 244. Chicago: Moody Bible Institute.

11. Willard, D. (1998). *The Divine Conspiracy: Rediscovering Our Hidden Life in God*, pp. 141-142. San Francisco, CA: Harper Collins Publishers.

12. Willard, D. (1998). *The Divine Conspiracy: Rediscovering Our Hidden Life in God*, p. 142. San Francisco, CA: Harper Collins Publishers.

13. Darkness. (n.d.) *Lexico*. Retrieved from https://www.lexico.com/en/definition/darkness

14. Beacon. (n.d.) *Dictionary.com*. Retrieved from https://www.dictionary.com/browse/beacon

15. Willard, D. (1998). *The Divine Conspiracy: Rediscovering Our Hidden Life in God*, p. xvii. San Francisco, CA: Harper Collins Publishers.

16. Lewis. C.S. (1950). *Mere Christianity*, pp. 196-197. New York, NY: Harper Collins Publishers.

17. Voskamp, A. (2016). *The Broken Way*, p. 73. Grand Rapids, MI: Zondervan.

18. Voskamp, A. (2016). *The Broken Way*, p. 215. Grand Rapids, MI: Zondervan.

19. Willard, D. (1988). *The Spirit of the Disciplines: Understanding How God Changes Lives*, p. 7. San Francisco, CA: Harper Collins Publishers.

20. Whitney, D.S. (1991). *Spiritual Disciplines for the Christian Life*, p. 122. Colorado Springs, CO: NavPress.

WEEK 4

1. Willard, D. (1998). *The Divine Conspiracy*, p. 6. London: William Collins Publishing.

2. Smith, J. B. (2009). *The Good and Beautiful Life*, p. 10. Downer's Grove, IL: InterVarsity Press.

3. Willard, D. (2006). *The Great Omission*, p. 226. New York, NY: Harper Collins Publishing.

4. *The Nelson Study Bible: New King James Version*. (1997). p. 1601. (D. Radmacher et al, eds.) Nashville, TN: Thomas Nelson.

5. Arthur, K. (1985). *How Can I Be Blessed*, p. 181. Old Tappan, NJ: Fleming H. Revell Company.

6. Vine, W.E. (1996). *W. E. Vine's New Testament Word Pictures: Matthew to Acts*. p. 48. Nashville, TN: Thomas Nelson.

7. Welch, E. (2017). *A Small Book About a Big Problem: Reflections on Anger, Patience, and Peace*, p. 232. Greensboro, NC: New Growth Press.

8. *ESV Gospel Transformation Bible*. (2013). p. 1274. Wheaton, IL: Crossway Publishing.

9. Lucado, M. (1999). *When God Whispers Your Name*, p. 134. Nashville, TN: Thomas Nelson.

10. MacArthur, J. (1985). *The MacArthur New Testament Commentary: Matthew 1-7*, p. 297. Chicago: Moody Bible Institute.

11. Willard, D. (1998). *The Divine Conspiracy*, p. 174. London: William Collins Publishing.

12. Chambers, O. (1960). *Studies in the Sermon on the Mount*, p. 32. Grand Rapids, MI: Discovery House Publishers.

13. Dickens, C. (2014). *The Christmas Carol*, p. 58. New York, NY: Global Classics.

14. Dickens, C. (2014). *The Christmas Carol*, p. 59. New York, NY: Global Classics.

15. Willard, D. (1998). *The Divine Conspiracy*, p. 176. London: William Collins Publishing.

16. Willard, D. (1998). *The Divine Conspiracy*, p. 177. London: William Collins Publishing.

17. *Aviation Knowledge*. (n.d.) Varig Flight Downed by a Decimal Point. Retrieved from http://aviationknowledge.wikidot.com/asi:varig-flight-254:downed-by-a-decimal-point

18. Smith, J. B. (2009). *The Good and Beautiful Life*, p. 90. Downer's Grove, IL: InterVarsity Press.

19. Hull, M. (1/27/20). Pornography Facts and Statistics. *The Recovery Village*. Retrieved from https://www.therecoveryvillage.com/process-addiction/porn-addiction/related/pornography-statistics/

20. Arthur, K. (1985). *How Can I Be Blessed*, p. 183. Old Tappan, NJ: Fleming H. Revell Company.

21. Smith, J. B. (2009). *The Good and Beautiful Life*, p. 94. Downer's Grove, IL: InterVarsity Press.

22. Blitz, M. (October 28, 2019). WiFi Is Illegal in This American Town. *Popular Mechanics*. Retrieved from https://www.popularmechanics.com/space/telescopes/a29589714/town-wifi-illegal/

23. Nouwen, H. (1981). *The Way of the Heart*, pp. 17-18. New York, NY: Ballantine Books.

24. Pascal, B. (2008). *Pensées and Other Writings*, p. 234. (A. Levi, ed.). New York, NY: Oxford University Press.

WEEK 5

1. Lewis, C.S. (1952). *Mere Christianity*, p. 163. New York, NY: Harper Collins Publishers.

2. *The ESV Study Bible*. (2008). p. 1785. Wheaton, IL: Crossway Bibles.

3. *The ESV Study Bible*. (2008). p. 1785. Wheaton, IL: Crossway Bibles.

4. Stott, J. (1978). *Christian Counter-Culture*, p. 94. Downers Grove, IL: InterVarsity Press.

5. Willard, D. (1998). *The Divine Conspiracy: Rediscovering Our Hidden Life in God*, p. 191. San Francisco, CA: HarperCollins Publishers.

6. Stott, J. (1978). *Christian Counter-Culture*, p. 94. Downers Grove, IL: InterVarsity Press.

7. Kendall, R.T. (2011). *The Sermon on the Mount*, p. 145. Bloomington, MN: Chosen Books.

8. Smith, J. (2009). *The Good and Beautiful Life: Putting on the Character of Christ,* p. 109. Downers Grove, IL: InterVarsity Press.

9. Willard, D. (1998). *The Divine Conspiracy,* p. 194. San Francisco, CA: HarperCollins Publishers.

10. Jamieson, R., Fausset, A. R., & Brown, D. (1997). *Commentary Critical and Explanatory on the Whole Bible* (Vol 2, pp.23-24). Oak Harbor, WA: Logos Research Systems, Inc.

11. Smith, J. (2009). *The Good and Beautiful Life: Putting on the Character of Christ,* p. 108. Downers Grove, IL: InterVarsity Press.

12. Smith, J. (2009). *The Good and Beautiful Life: Putting on the Character of Christ,* p. 110. Downers Grove, IL: InterVarsity Press.

13. Stott, J. (1978). *The Message of the Sermon on the Mount,* p. 102. Downers Grove, IL: InterVarsity Press.

14. Kendall, R.T. (2011). *The Sermon on the Mount: A Verse-by-Verse Look at The Greatest Teaching of Jesus,* p. 151. Bloomington, MN: Baker Publishing Group.

15. Kendall, R.T. (2011). *The Sermon on the Mount: A Verse-by-Verse Look at The Greatest Teaching of Jesus,* p. 151. Bloomington, MN: Baker Publishing Group.

16. Willard, D. (1998). *The Divine Conspiracy: Rediscovering Our Hidden Life in God,* p. 201. San Francisco, CA: HarperCollins Publishers.

17. Stott, J. (1978). *Christian Counter-Culture,* p. 106. Downers Grove, IL: InterVarsity Press.

18. Smith, J. (2009). *The Good and Beautiful Life: Putting on the Character of Christ,* p. 124. Downers Grove, IL: InterVarsity Press.

19. Chambers, O. (1995). *Studies in the Sermon on the Mount,* p. 44. Grand Rapids, MI: Discovery House Publishers.

20. Wiersbe, W.W. (1992). *Wiersbe's Expository Outlines on the New Testament,* pp. 30-31. Wheaton, IL: Victor Books.

21. Kendall, R.T. (2011). *The Sermon on The Mount,* p. 156. Bloomington, MN: Chosen Books.

22. Zodhiates, S., ed., (1996). *Hebrew-Greek Key Word Study Bible,* p. 1571. Chattanooga, TN: AMG Publishers.

23. Smith, J. (2009). *The Good and Beautiful Life: Putting on the Character of Christ,* p. 127. Downers Grove, IL: InterVarsity Press.

24. Kendall, R.T. (2011). *The Sermon on the Mount: A Verse-by-Verse Look at The Greatest Teaching of Jesus,* p. 172. Bloomington, MN: Baker Publishing Group.

25. Demarest, B., Matthews, K., eds. (2010). *Dictionary of Everyday Theology and Culture,* p. 161. Colorado Springs, CO: NavPress.

26. Elliot, E. (1985). *A Lamp Unto My Feet,* p. 176. Ventura, CA: Regal.

27. Kroll, W. (2000). *7 Secrets to Spiritual Success,* p. 49. Sisters, OR: Multnomah Publishers.

WEEK 6

1. Murray, A. (2001). *Humility,* p. 64. Minneapolis, MN: Bethany House.

2. Smith, J.B. (2009). *The Good and Beautiful Life,* p. 145. Downers Grove, IL: InterVarsity Press.

3. Smith, J.B. (2009). *The Good and Beautiful Life,* p. 142. Downers Grove, IL: InterVarsity Press.

4. Smith, J.B. (2009). *The Good and Beautiful Life,* p. 141. Downers Grove, IL: InterVarsity Press.

5. McGee, J.V. (1983). *Thru the Bible with J. Vernon McGee Vol. IV,* p.36. Nashville, TN: Thomas Nelson Publishers.

6. Smith, J.B. (2009). *The Good and Beautiful Life,* p. 147-148. Downers Grove, IL: InterVarsity Press.

7. Willard, D. (1998). *The Divine Conspiracy,* p. 209. London: William Collins.

8. Willard, D. (1998). *The Divine Conspiracy,* p. 210. London: William Collins.

9. Chambers, O. (1960). *Studies in the Sermon on the Mount: God's Character and the Believer's Conduct,* p. 50. Grand Rapids, MI: Our Daily Bread Publishing.

10. Willard, D. (1998). *The Divine Conspiracy,* p. 211. London: William Collins.

11. Willard, D. (1998). *The Divine Conspiracy,* p. 213. London: William Collins.

12. Chambers, O. (1960). *Studies in the Sermon on the Mount: God's Character and the Believer's Conduct,* p. 51-52. Grand Rapids, MI: Our Daily Bread Publishing.

13. Sorge, B. (2017). *Secrets of the Secret Place,* p. 8. Kansas City, MO: Oasis House.

14. Sorge, B. (2017). *Secrets of the Secret Place,* pp. 38, 39. Kansas City, MO: Oasis House.

15. Sorge, B. (2017). *Secrets of the Secret Place,* p. 62. Kansas City, MO: Oasis House.

16. Ortberg, J. (1997). *The Life You've Always Wanted,* p. 106. Grand Rapids, MI: Zondervan.

17. Willard, D. (1998). *The Divine Conspiracy*, p. 303. London: William Collins.

18. Smith, J.B. (2009). *The Good and Beautiful Life,* p. 207. Downers Grove, IL: InterVarsity Press.

19. Willard, D. (1998). *The Divine Conspiracy*, p. 303. London: William Collins.

20. Smith, J.B. (2009). *The Good and Beautiful Life,* p. 209. Downers Grove, IL: InterVarsity Press.

21. Willard, D. (1998). *The Divine Conspiracy*, p. 297. London: William Collins.

22. Smith, J.B. (2009). *The Good and Beautiful Life,* p. 146. Downers Grove, IL: InterVarsity Press.

23. Chambers, O. (1960). *Studies in the Sermon on the Mount: God's Character and the Believer's Conduct,* p. 51. Grand Rapids, MI: Our Daily Bread Publishing.

24. Smith, J.B. (2009). *The Good and Beautiful Life,* p. 151. Downers Grove, IL: InterVarsity Press.

25. Ortberg, J. (1997). *The Life You've Always Wanted*, p. 185. Grand Rapids, MI: Zondervan.

WEEK 7

1. Wright, N.T. (1996). *The Lord and His Prayer*, p. 2. Grand Rapids, MI: Wm. B. Eerdmans Publishing Co.

2. Quarles, C. (2011). *Sermon on the Mount: Restoring Christ's Message to the Modern Church*, p. 3838. Nashville, TN: B&H Publishing Group.

3. Wright, N.T. (2006). *Simply Christian*, p. 160. New York, NY: Harper-Collins Publishers.

4. MacArthur, J. (2006). *The MacArthur Study Bible,* p. 1371. Nashville, TN: Thomas Nelson.

5. Wright, N.T. (1996). *The Lord and His Prayer*, p. xiv. Grand Rapids, MI: Wm. B. Eerdmans Publishing Co.

6. Carson, D.A. (1987). *Jesus's Sermon on the Mount and His Confrontation with the World: A Study of Matthew 5-10*, p. 84. Grand Rapids, MI: Baker Books.

7. Gaines, S. (2013). *Pray Like it Matters,* p. 24. Tigerville, SC: Auxano Press.

8. Quarles, C. (2011). *Sermon on the Mount: Restoring Christ's Message to the Modern Church*, p. 3942. Nashville, TN: B&H Publishing Group.

9. Smith, W.C. (n.d.) Immortal, Invisible. *The Baptist Hymnal,* p. 43. Nashville, TN: Convention Press.

10. Meyer, F.B. (1959). *The Sermon on the Mount*, p. 229. Grand Rapids, MI: Baker Book House.

11. Smith, J.B. (2009). *The Good and Beautiful Life*, p. 76. Downers Grove, IL: InterVarsity Press.

12. Smith, J.B. (2009). *The Good and Beautiful Life*, p. 76. Downers Grove, IL: InterVarsity Press.

13. Stott, J. (1978). *Christian Counter-Culture*, p. 147. Downers Grove, IL: InterVarsity Press.

14. Stott, J. (1978). *Christian Counter-Culture*, p. 148. Downers Grove, IL: InterVarsity Press.

15. Larson, K.C. (2005). *Bound for the Promised Land*, pp. 302-304. New York, NY: Random House.

16. Larson, K.C. (2005). *Bound for the Promised Land*, p. 187. New York, NY: Random House.

17. Gaines, S. (2013). *Pray Like it Matters*, p. 27. Tigerville, SC: Auxano Press.

18. Elliot, J. (1978). *The Journals of Jim Elliot*, p. 278. Grand Rapids, MI: Baker Publishing Group.

19. Kendall, R.T. (2002). *Total Forgiveness*, p. 20. Lake Mary, FL: Charisma House.

20. Kendall, R.T. (2002). *Total Forgiveness*, pp. 20-21. Lake Mary, FL: Charisma House.

21. Kendall, R.T. (2002). *Total Forgiveness*, p. 129. Lake Mary, FL: Charisma House.

22. Carmichael, A. (2003). *If*, p. 36. Fort Washington, PA: CLC Publications.

23. Peterson, E. (2002). *The Message Bible*, pp. 1959-1960. Grand Rapids, MI: Zondervan.

24. Allen, J. (2020). *Get Out of Your Head*, p. 23. Colorado Springs, CO: Waterbrook.

25. Allen, J. (2020). *Get Out of Your Head*, p. 34. Colorado Springs, CO: Waterbrook.

26. Allen, J. (2020). *Get Out of Your Head*, p. 41. Colorado Springs, CO: Waterbrook.

27. Scazzero, P. (2017). *Emotionally Healthy Spirituality: It's Impossible to be Spiritually Mature While Remaining Emotionally Immature*, p. 27. Grand Rapids, MI: Zondervan.

28. Lloyd-Jones, S. (2007). *Jesus Storybook Bible*, p. 115. Grand Rapids, MI: Zondervan.

29. Scazzero, P. (2017). *Emotionally Healthy Spirituality: It's Impossible to be Spiritually Mature While Remaining Emotionally Immature*, p. 49. Grand Rapids, MI: Zondervan.

30. Willard, D. (1988). *The Spirit of the Disciplines: Understanding How God Changes Lives*, p. 184. San Francisco, CA: Harper Collins Publishers.

31. Chambers, O. (1935). *My Utmost for His Highest*, p. 291. New York, NY: Dodd, Mead & Company.

32. Murray, A. (2004). *Daily in His Presence*, p. 309. Colorado Springs, CO: Multnomah Books.

WEEK 8

1. Willard, D., Nouwen, H. J., Buechner, F., Tozer, A. W., Wright, N. T., Smith, J. B., . . . Manning, B. (2018). *Faith That Matters: 365 Devotions from Classic Christian Leaders*, p. 153. New York, NY: HarperOne.

2. Tolkien, J.R.R. (1965). *The Two Towers*, p. 362. New York, NY: Ballantine Books.

3. Arthur, S. (2003). *Walking with Frodo: A Devotional Journey Through the Lord of the Rings*, p. 71. Carol Stream, IL: Tyndale House.

4. Tolkien, J.R.R. (1965). *The Two Towers, p. 273*. New York, NY: Ballantine Books.

5. Arthur, S. (2003). *Walking with Frodo: A Devotional Journey Through the Lord of the Rings*, p. 73. Carol Stream, IL: Tyndale House.

6. Foster, R. (1988). *Celebration of Discipline*, p. 48. New York, NY: Harper Collins.

7. Arthur, K. (1985). *How Can I Be Blessed,* p. 217. Old Tappan, NJ: Fleming H. Revell Company.

8. Quoted in *Our Daily Bread*. (July 8, 1994). *ODB*. Retrieved from https://odb.org /1994/07/08/rearranging-the-price-tags/

9. Willard, D. (1998). *The Divine Conspiracy*, p.187. London: William Collins Publishing.

10. Ten Boom, Corrie. (1983). *Clippings form My Notebook*, p. 33. Waterville, ME: Thorndike Press.

11. Ten Boom, Corrie. (1985). *Jesus is Victor*, p. 60. Grand Rapids, MI: Revell Books.

12. Ten Boom, Corrie. (1977). *Each New Day: 365 Reflections To Strengthen Your Faith, p. 61*. Grand Rapids, MI: Revell Books.

13. *Merimnao.* (n.d.). *The New Testament Greek Lexicon.* Retrieved from http:// classic.studylight.org/lex/grk/view.cgi?number=3309>

14. Anxiety. (n.d.). *Dictionary.com*. Retrieved from https://www.dictionary.com/ browse/anxiety

15. Garrison, A. (8/02/18). Antianxiety Drugs Fuel the Next Deadly Drug Crisis in US. *CNBC*. Retrieved from https://www.cnbc.com/2018/08/02/antianxiety-drugs-fuel-the-next-deadly-drug-crisis-in-us.html

16. Willard, D., Nouwen, H. J., Buechner, F., Tozer, A. W., Wright, N. T., Smith, J. B., . . . Manning, B. (2018). *Faith That Matters: 365 Devotions from Classic Christian Leaders*, p. 148. New York, NY: HarperOne.

17. Hughes, R. K. (2001). *The Sermon on the Mount: The Message of the Kingdom*, p. 223. Wheaton, IL: Crossway Publishing.

18. *Epizeteo.* (n.d.). *The New Testament Greek Lexicon.* Retrieved http://classic. studylight.org/lex/grk/view.cgi?number=1934

19. *Zeteo.* (n.d.). *The New Testament Greek Lexicon.* Retrieved from http://classic. studylight.org/lex/grk/view.cgi?number=2212

20. Green, J. (1989). *The Kingdom of God in Meaning and Mandate,* pp. 68-69. Wilmore, KY: Bristol Books.

21. Quoted in Harris, A. (1965). *Better than Gold,* p. 45. New York, NY: Macmillan Company.

22. Lewis, C.S. (1980). *Mere Christianity*, p. 118, New York, NY: Harper Collins Publishers.

23. MacDonald, G. J. (2011). Why Lent Must Rise Again. *The Boston Globe.* Retrieved from http://archive.boston.com/lifestyle/articles/2011/03/13/why_ lent_must_rise_again/

24. Willard, D. (1999). *The Spirit of the Disciplines*, p. 166. New York, NY: HarperOne.

25. Calhoun, A. (2015). *Spiritual Disciplines Handbook: Practices That Transform Us*, p. 246. Downers Grove, IL: InterVarsity Press.

26. Calhoun, A. (2015). *Spiritual Disciplines Handbook: Practices That Transform Us*, p. 246. Downers Grove, IL: InterVarsity Press.

27. Whitney, D. (2014). *Spiritual Disciplines for the Christian Life*, p. 219. Colorado Springs, CO: Tyndale House.

WEEK 9

1. MacArthur, J. (1985). *The MacArthur New Testament Commentary Matthew 1-7*, p. 446. Chicago, IL: The Moody Bible Institute.

2. MacArthur, J. (1985). *The MacArthur New Testament Commentary Matthew 1-7*, p. 432. Chicago, IL: The Moody Bible Institute.

3. Smith, J. (2009). *The Good and Beautiful Life*, p. 188. Downers Grove, IL: InterVarsity Press.

4. MacArthur, J. (1985). *The MacArthur New Testament Commentary Matthew 1-7*, p. 433. Chicago, IL: The Moody Bible Institute.

5. Willard, D. (1988). *The Divine Conspiracy*, pp. 243-244. San Francisco, CA: HarperCollins Publishers.

6. Smith, J. (2009). *The Good and Beautiful Life*, p. 202. Downers Grove, IL: InterVarsity Press.

7. Smith, J. (2009). *The Good and Beautiful Life*, p. 190. Downers Grove, IL: InterVarsity Press.

8. Keller, T. (2015). *The Songs of Jesus: A Year of Daily Devotions in the Psalms*, p. 125. New York, NY: Viking.

9. MacArthur, J. (1985). *The MacArthur New Testament Commentary Matthew 1-7*, p. 434. Chicago, IL: The Moody Bible Institute.

10. Zodhiates, S., ed. (1996). *Hebrew-Greek Key Word Study Bible*, p. 1682. Chattanooga, TN: AMG Publishers.

11. Stott, J. (1978). *Christian Counter-Culture*, p. 130. Downers Grove, IL: InterVarsity Press.

12. Willard, D. (1988). *The Divine Conspiracy*, p. 241. San Francisco, CA: HarperCollins Publishers.

13. MacArthur, J. (1985). *The MacArthur New Testament Commentary Matthew 1-7*, p. 437. Chicago, IL: The Moody Bible Institute.

14. MacArthur, J. (1985). *The MacArthur New Testament Commentary Matthew 1-7*, pp. 432-443. Chicago, IL: The Moody Bible Institute.

15. Willard, D. (1988). *The Divine Conspiracy*, p. 266. San Francisco, CA: HarperCollins Publishers.

16. Kendall, R. T. (2011). *The Sermon on the Mount*, p. 350. Bloomington, MN: Chosen Books.

17. MacArthur, J. (1985). *The MacArthur New Testament Commentary Matthew 1-7*, p. 443. Chicago, IL: The Moody Bible Institute.

18. MacArthur, J. (1985). *The MacArthur New Testament Commentary Matthew 1-7*, p. 447. Chicago, IL: The Moody Bible Institute.

19. Hindson, E., Dobson, E. (1999). *The Knowing Jesus Study Bible*, p. 1365. Grand Rapids, MI: Zondervan Publishing House.

20. Kendall, R. T. (2011). *The Sermon on the Mount*, p. 372. Bloomington, MN: Chosen Books.

21. Stott, J. (1978). *Christian Counter-Culture*, p. 192. Downers Grove, IL: InterVarsity Press.

22. Cates, B. (1975). Do You Really Care? *Baptist Hymnal*, p. 316. Nashville, TN: Convention Press.

23. DeMoss, N. (2003). *Surrender*, pp. 72-73. Chicago, IL: Moody Publishers.

24. DeMoss, N. (2003). *Surrender*, p. 103. Chicago, IL: Moody Publishers.

25. DeMoss, N. (2003). *Surrender*, p. 101. Chicago, IL: Moody Publishers.

WEEK 10

1. Thomas, M.I. (2006). *The Indwelling Life of Christ*, pp. 169-170. Colorado Springs, CO: Multnomah Books.

2. MacArthur, J. (1985). *The MacArthur New Testament Commentary: Matthew 1-7*, p. 452. Chicago, IL: Moody Bible Institute.

3. Phillips, J. (2009). *Exploring the Gospel of John: An Expository Commentary*, p. 170. Grand Rapids, MI: Kregel Publications.

4. Weber, S.K. (2000). *Holman New Testament Commentary: Matthew*, p. 103. Nashville, TN: Broadman & Holman Publishers.

5. Rogers, Dr. A. (2017). How to Weather the Storms of Life. *Adrian Rogers Sermon Archive: Matthew 7:24-27*. Signal Hill, CA: Rogers Family Trust.

6. Phillips, J. (2009). *Exploring the Gospel of John: An Expository Commentary*, p. 178. Grand Rapids, MI: Kregel Publications.

7. Phillips, J. (2009). *Exploring the Gospel of John: An Expository Commentary*, p. 168. Grand Rapids, MI: Kregel Publications.

8. Weber, S.K. (2008). *Holman New Testament Commentary*, p. 104. Nashville, TN: Broadman & Holman Publishers.

9. Foster, R. (2018). *Celebration of Discipline*, p. 193. San Francisco, CA: Harper Collins Publishers.

10. Willard, D. (1988). *The Divine Conspiracy: Rediscovering our Hidden Life in Christ*, p. 343. London, England: Harper Collins Publishers.

11. Willard, D. (2014). *Living in Christ's Presence: Final Words on Heaven and the Kingdom of God*, p. 147. Downers Grove, IL: InterVarsity Press.

Made in the USA
Coppell, TX
10 December 2020